Post-Referendum Sudan

This book is a product of a joint initiative of CODESRIA, UNECA, and Africa Research and Resource Centre (ARRC) with support from IDRC, Trust Africa and Sida.

Post-Referendum Sudan
National and Regional Questions

Edited by

Samson Samuel Wassara
Al-Tayib Zain Al-Abdin Muhammed

Council for the Development of Social Science Research in Africa
DAKAR

© CODESRIA 2014
Council for the Development of Social Science Research in Africa
Avenue Cheikh Anta Diop, Angle Canal IV
BP 3304 Dakar, CP 18524, Senegal
Website: www.codesria.org

ISBN: 978-2-86978-588-5

All rights reserved. No part of this publication may be reproduced or transmitted in any form or by any means, electronic or mechanical, including photocopy, recording or any information storage or retrieval system without prior permission from CODESRIA.

Typesetting: Alpha Ousmane Dia
Cover Design: Ibrahima Fofana

Distributed in Africa by CODESRIA
Distributed elsewhere by African Books Collective, Oxford, UK
Website: www.africanbookscollective.com

The Council for the Development of Social Science Research in Africa (CODESRIA) is an independent organisation whose principal objectives are to facilitate research, promote research-based publishing and create multiple forums geared towards the exchange of views and information among African researchers. All these are aimed at reducing the fragmentation of research in the continent through the creation of thematic research networks that cut across linguistic and regional boundaries.

CODESRIA publishes *Africa Development*, the longest standing Africa based social science journal; *Afrika Zamani*, a journal of history; the *African Sociological Review*; the *African Journal of International Affairs*; *Africa Review of Books* and the *Journal of Higher Education in Africa*. The Council also co-publishes the *Africa Media Review*; *Identity, Culture and Politics: An Afro-Asian Dialogue*; *The African Anthropologist* and the *Afro-Arab Selections for Social Sciences*. The results of its research and other activities are also disseminated through its Working Paper Series, Green Book Series, Monograph Series, Book Series, Policy Briefs and the CODESRIA Bulletin. Select CODESRIA publications are also accessible online at www.codesria.org.

CODESRIA would like to express its gratitude to the Swedish International Development Cooperation Agency (SIDA), the International Development Research Centre (IDRC), the Ford Foundation, the Carnegie Corporation of New York (CCNY), the Norwegian Agency for Development Cooperation (NORAD), the Danish Agency for International Development (DANIDA), the French Ministry of Cooperation, the United Nations Development Programme (UNDP), the Netherlands Ministry of Foreign Affairs, the Rockefeller Foundation, the Open Society Foundations (OSFs), TrustAfrica, UNESCO, UN Women, the African Capacity Building Foundation (ACBF) and the Government of Senegal for supporting its research, training and publication programmes.

Contents

Editors vii
Contributors viii
Foreword ix

Introduction
Samson S. Wassara 1

PART I
Opinions on Self-determination

1. Some Questions Regarding the Independence of South Sudan
   Mahmood Mamdani 13

PART II
North-South Relations and Regional Issues

2. The Consequences of the Referendum in Southern Sudan for the Country and the Region
   Al-Tayib Zain Al-Abdin 27
3. Consequences of the Secession of Southern Sudan on the Region
   Hamed Omer Hawi 39
4. Implications of Southern Sudan's Independence for the Horn of Africa and Beyond
   Kassahun Berhanu 51
5. Consequences of a Referendum in Southern Sudan for Sudan, Horn of Africa and neighbouring Regions
   Samson S. Wassara 71

PART III
Nation-Building of the New State

6. The Nation-Building Project and Its Challenges
   Christopher Zambakari 93
7. Factors Shaping the Post-Referendum Nation-Building in Southern Sudan in Relation to the Sudan
   B.F. Bankie 121

PART IV
Economic Policy for the New State

8. South Sudan's Priority Development Programmes, Projects, and Policies
   Benaiah Yongo-Bure 135
9. Southern Sudan: Monetary and Financial Policies and the Case for a Separate Currency
   Benaiah Yongo-Bure 159
10. South Sudanese Pound Managed Under Floating Exchange Regime: Prospects and Challenges
    Andrew Ssemwanga 183

Conclusion
Al-Tayib Zain Al-Abdin 209

Postscript on New Developments
Samson S. Wassara 217

Editors

Samson S. Wassara is Associate Professor of Political Science at the University of Juba. He obtained his PhD from the University of Paris XI (Paris-Sud). Dr Wassara has held various academic positions at the University of Juba and was twice Dean, College of Social and Economic Studies. He was UNICEF's Sudan national project manager of peace building in the section of Rights, Protection and Peace Building (RPPB) during the period 2000-2006. He teaches political science, international relations and peace. His research interests include security sector, peace studies, geopolitics and hydro-politics. Dr Wassara's most recent publications are, 'The CPA and Beyond: Problems and Prospects for Peaceful Coexistence in the Nuba Mountains', in Elke Grawert, ed., 2010, *After the Comprehensive Peace Agreement in Sudan,* Woodbridge: James Currey/Boydell & Brewer Ltd; and 'Rebels, Militias and Governance in Sudan', in Wafula Okumu and Augustine Ikelegbe, eds, 2010, *Militias, Rebels and Islamist Militants: Human Insecurity and State Crises in Africa*. Pretoria: Institute for Security Studies.

Al-Tayib Zain al-Abdin has been Professor of Politics at the University of Khartoum since 1997. He obtained his PhD from Cambridge University in 1975. Professor Al-Tayib has worked as Advisor to the Vice-Chancellor of the University of Khartoum (2007-2011). He is former Secretary General of the Sudan Inter-Religious Council (2003-2007). Professor Al-Tayib taught at the Institute of African and Asian Studies, the University of Khartoum; International Islamic University in Islamabad (1991-1996, 1999-2003); Centre for the Study of Islam and Christian-Muslim Relations, Birmingham; and at the Imam Muhammad bin Saud University in Riyadh, Saudi Arabia. He also served as the Director of Islamic African Centre, Khartoum (1980-85). He is a regular writer in Sudanese newspapers and has been active in north-south cooperation societies before and after the referendum.

Contributors

Andrew Ssemwanga, Kigali Independent University, Kigali, Rwanda.

Benaiah Yongo-Bure, Katerring University, Flint, Michigan, USA.

B.F. Bankie, National Youth Council of Namibia, Secretary and member, International Sub-Committee, Windhoek, Namibia.

Christopher Zambakari, Scholar, Northeastern University, Boston, Massachusetts, USA.

Hamed Omer Hawi, University of Juba, Khartoum, at the time of writing the paper; but currently in Bahri University after independence of South Sudan, Khartoum, Sudan.

Kassahun Berhanu, Addis Ababa University, Ethiopia.

Mahmood Mamdani, Makerere Institute of Social Research (MISR), Makerere University, Kampala, Uganda.

Peter Adwok Nyaba, Minister of Higher Education and Scientific Research, Khartoum, Sudan at the time of writing the papers; but currently Minister of Higher Education, Research, Science and Technology, South Sudan, Juba.

Foreword

Peace is Better than Unity

Peter Adwok Nyaba

'Peace is better than unity', was the slogan with which the Ethiopian People's Revolutionary Democratic Front (EPRDF) came to power in Addis Ababa in May 1991. Notwithstanding the unfortunate hostilities that later emerged between Ethiopia and Eritrea, the Ethiopian leaders have been vindicated by opting for peace rather than prolong war in order to maintain the territorial integrity of the country.

Contemporary history reveals that the territorial integrity of any country or the unity of its peoples cannot be imposed by force of arms. The era of imperialism and local despots has gone forever. Sudan had been a colonial construct since 1899 when the conquering Anglo-Egyptian forces re-occupied northern Sudan and extended their rule southwards and westwards to engulf southern Sudan and Darfur respectively. It will be recalled that 'Equatoria' was until 1910 part of the 'Lado Enclave' under the Belgian crown, while Darfur was annexed to the Anglo-Egyptian Sudan in 1916 after the defeat of Sultan Ali Dinar.

Independent Sudan (1956) had the opportunity to remain one stable and prosperous country. But the ruling political elite remained oblivious to the country's multiple diversities. It insisted on defining the country along the two parameters of Arab and Islamic orientations. The policy to construct a highly centralised state based on these parameters precipitated civil wars initially in southern Sudan and then in other parts of northern Sudan, notably southern Kordofan, Blue Nile, eastern Sudan and, finally, in Darfur.

In fifty-five years of social and political engineering, the Sudanese political class failed in the state and nation-building processes. That about 99 per cent of southern Sudanese voted for secession in the referendum which led to Sudan's dismemberment epitomises this failure. The turbulent history of the Sudanese state formation may have been a factor in the South Sudanese decision to break away. However, governance, and good governance for that matter, remains the determinant factor in Sudan's stability as a state and nation. Governance rooted in the country's multiple diversities could have been the only guarantee for Sudan's unity and viability.

So when we speak about the consequences of southern Sudan's secession, it is important and imperative to focus on the future rather than on the past. Each of the emerging two states, the predecessor and the successor, carries the virus for future instability and possible dismemberment. The South Sudan has been running its affairs independently for the last six years, thanks to the Comprehensive Peace Agreement (CPA). The ruling elite have committed grievous mistakes of governance that jeopardised the opportunity for mitigating the negative consequences of war.

Following the tragic death of Dr John Garang, a paradigm shift from liberation to a power agenda occurred, triggering a power struggle between various competing factions. This manifested itself in the widespread insecurity in southern Sudan, ethnic conflicts, corruption in government and society, lack of social services, and so on. No wonder that some spectators of the Sudanese theatre passed the verdict that South Sudan would emerge as another failed state. It was only owing to the civilised and orderly manner with which southerners behaved during the referendum that some of those people changed their minds. The ruling political elite in South Sudan must change their *modus operandi* if South Sudan is not to slide back into conflicts and anarchy.

Similarly, the ruling political elite, particularly the NCP, should draw a serious and honest lesson from the secession of southern Sudan. A modern state cannot be built with the instruments of political domination, oppression and social discrimination. The voice for South Sudanese secession grew louder only during the *Inqaz* regime. This was precisely for lack of accommodation of different views, while at the same time projecting an Arab-Islamic identity on the South Sudanese. The mistakes of the 1950s and 1960s should not be repeated. The strong calls for regional self-rule coming from Blue Nile, southern Kordofan and Red Sea states should be heeded, and appropriate responses formulated immediately, lest they are transformed into calls for self-determination. The war raging in Darfur must be addressed as soon as possible; it has serious ramifications on the western part of the country.

Looking at the region, South Sudan should build good neighbourliness with the countries with which it shares common borders, including northern Sudan. This will create conditions necessary and conducive for its immediate and accelerated social and economic transformation. It is necessary because, all along, the borders have invariably divided the same ethnic communities. These communities, such as the Azande in Central African Republic, DR Congo; Kakwa and Pajulu in DR Congo and in Uganda; Madi, Acholi and Dodoth in Uganda; Taposa and their cousins the Turkana and Karimajong in Kenya and Uganda respectively; Nuer and Anywaa in Ethiopia; should become bridges for social, economic and cultural cooperation and integration.

The communities living in the north-south border areas, and who have for a long time been involved in proxy wars, should be encouraged to look at where their interests for survival lie. The Misseriya, the Rezeighat, the Kenana and all the nomadic communities who spend most of the year in some parts of South Sudan will have to change their attitude towards their neighbours in the South. In fact both governments should work together to permit free and unhindered access and to transform by peaceful means any resource-based conflict which may arise from time to time.

The independence of South Sudan is a precedent likely to trigger similar claims in other parts of Africa. One would not like people with similar historical claims to independence and freedom to suffocate in unity on account of the OAU doctrine of the inviolability of colonial borders. Nevertheless, should the ruling political elite in a particular country fail to accommodate the concerns of their disadvantaged citizens (minorities), secession becomes an attractive option. However, this option should be carefully weighed against others important factors of state viability. In this respect, the African Union should engage actively in the resolution of endemic conflicts, particularly those with ethnic and religious streak that threaten the territorial unity of member states.

Most of us assembled in this hall are academics who, by and large, are sometimes passive spectators of the social and political engineering undertaken, particularly by radical political and ideological groups that come to power. Nevertheless, within the confines of our academic profession opportunities exist for influencing the course of events. The National Council for Higher Education and Scientific Research and the Ministry of Higher Education attach importance to the peace study centres established in some of our universities: the Ahfad University for Women, University of Khartoum, University of Juba, Nyala and Alfashir universities in Darfur. Peace and conflict transformation and resolution studies should take centre stage in the coming period. I am glad that CODESRIA, UNECA and ARRF have been involved from the very beginning to provide the necessary resources and expertise for the problems of peace and conflicts in the continent.

In the Ministry of Higher Education and Scientific Research, we are developing a policy paper to be submitted to both governments, GoS and GoSS, for endorsement. The concept is for both governments to permit higher education institutions, particularly the university and the faculty, to continue working together as the vital and lively link between the two countries beyond the political and economic relationship. This will facilitate joint research activities in different spheres, research whose results should inform and guide policies. In this respect one envisages that South Sudan's secession and its consequences at the local and regional level, particularly its impact on the regional security architecture in the Horn of Africa and the Great Lakes, should constitute an important research theme. Under this wider theme peace studies can be undertaken, entailing such issues as cross-border cattle rustling, small arms and light weapons trafficking, as well as other social and cultural studies which promote understanding and harmony.

We would want to suggest to the leadership of CODESRIA to put this forum on a permanent, regular annual basis and to take on broader studies of such sensitive but unavoidable themes of Afro-Arab relationships, in the context of the simmering conflicts in the Afro-Arab borderlands of which the conflicts in Darfur, Mali and Niger are part. We cannot afford any more to bury our heads in the sand. The uprising in Arab North Africa is likely to influence events in Sudan and the rest of Africa as people cry aloud for human rights and political freedoms.

Introduction

Samson S. Wassara

The fate of Sudan, by then the largest country in Africa, was clearly decided when results of the referendum vote were announced in February 2011. Policy makers, scholars and the international community began to grapple with critical issues that might arise after the independence of southern Sudan and how different stakeholders would handle such issues during the period of uncertainty. So many national, regional and international workshops and conferences on post-referendum Sudan or South Sudan were organised by governments, regional organisations, research organisations and civil society organisations (CSOs) to treat diverse issues. Scholars and observers were influenced in such events by the uneasy partnership between the National Congress Party (NCP) and the Sudan People's Liberation Movement (SPLM) during the interim period stipulated in the Comprehensive Peace Agreement (CPA). Scholars assembled in Nairobi at the invitation of CODESRIA, the United Nations Economic Commission for Africa (UNECA) and the African Research and Resource Forum (ARRF) to reflect on the post-referendum Sudan. This book comprises most of the papers presented during the "International Workshop" on the post-referendum Sudan.

Studies undertaken by authors of chapters treat four sub-themes of post-referendum Sudan dealing with internal dynamics of the Sudan after secession and how these dynamics might affect neighbouring countries in the geopolitical regions of the Horn of Africa, East Africa, and Central Africa. Hence, this book is organised into four parts. Part I is composed of one chapter, which covers opinions of an eminent scholar on unity, self-determination, independence of South Sudan and peace. Part II contains four chapters. This part deals with the consequences of secession on relations between the Sudan and South Sudan and the impact on the Horn of Africa, the Great Lakes Region and Central Africa. Contributions in Part III examine problems of nation-building in Sudan and South Sudan. This part is composed of two chapters. Finally, the three contributions in Part IV attempt to explain the economy and monetary arrangements of South Sudan before and after secession. While Chapter 8 discusses priority in development, chapters 9 and 10 treat monetary dimensions in the post-referendum period in southern Sudan. Having outlined the key components of each part of the book, it is necessary to highlight some of the arguments coming out from some contributors.

One component of the book consists of policy issues of nation building. The second component of the book consists of chapters that treat consequences of post-referendum Sudan in different perspectives. It examines national, regional and continental dimensions of the unresolved issues that might result in the escalation of conflict in the Sudan. The third sub-theme of the book consists of economic discourses regarding the emergence of a new state in southern Sudan. Economic policy priorities and monetary policies are treated under this sub-theme. Finally, readers of the book should note differences in the use of the expression 'southern Sudan' and 'South Sudan'. The former is used to refer to southern Sudan when it was still de jure part of the Sudan in the context of the CPA. The use of South Sudan refers to the period following the declaration of independence in July 2011. The country 'Sudan' refers to the old Sudan at the time South Sudan declared independence.

Political developments in Sudan were long-term outcomes of post-cold war revolutions in the world system after socialism collapsed in the Soviet Union. A domino effect of such events swept across in Eastern Europe and also manifested itself in the Horn of Africa. The revolution in Ethiopia which led to the flight of Mengistu Haile Mariam, marked the beginning of redrawing the map of Africa and posed a challenge to the principle of maintaining colonial borders according to the Charter of the Organisation of African Unity (OAU). The revolutionary precedence set by the independence of Eritrea in early 1990s encouraged southern Sudan to press forward in the direction of independence through armed struggle and diplomacy led by the Sudan People's Liberation Army/Movement (SPLA/M). The long civil war between the government of Sudan and the SPLA came to a stalemate. It favoured a negotiated settlement that culminated in the CPA in January 2005. The key benchmarks of the agreement were the 2008 census, the April 2010 elections and the January 2011 Referendum. The latter resulted in the overwhelming vote for secession. It is the result of Sudan's referendum that is the main focus of this book.

Particularly, this book sought to examine and analyse future relations between the two countries that emerged as consequence of the referendum result in 2011 and how their neighbours would be affected by complex relationships once southern Sudan declared independence. Frameworks for analysis are drawn mostly from economic, political, social and peace analysis. Studies draw on historical, cultural, economic and geopolitical contexts. The book sheds light on potential explosive issues that, if badly managed, would escalate into violence and would destabilise the countries having common borders with Sudan. As part of regional conflict, the Sudanese conflict came to an end only when member states of the Intergovernmental Authority for Development (IGAD), and international actors combined efforts and resources to wage peace in Sudan. The studies that scholars have contributed to this book are the way forward for helping the two Sudans to cope with the results of the 2011 referendum vote. So, contributors drew attention to critical issues in the socio-economic landscape, the growing use of small arms and other negative attitudes that could spoil peaceful coexistence between Sudan and southern Sudan.

Southern Sudan voted for secession in the January 2011 referendum on self-determination. This decision had enormous consequences not only for Sudan, but also for the political and socio-economic relationships among countries of the Horn of Africa and of the central African regions. The contributions in this book examine problems that could complicate the already delicate political relations in the countries which have common borders with Sudan. This book reveals that outstanding issues such as borders, currency, citizenship that were not resolved by the CPA partners before the declaration of independence of southern Sudan will explode to a great proportion. The studies and observations in this book on post-referendum Sudan indicate that the dearth of interdependences is a threat to future cooperation and regional integration. All observations point to the fact that conflict escalation in Sudan's geopolitical regions will adversely affect neighbouring countries in many respects. Political stability in Sudan will depend on collective actions of stakeholders to ensure that peace prevails in the North and the South to guarantee human security in the region.

It is worthwhile to mention that the manner in which the CPA was implemented and the nature of relationships between the partners of the Agreement played a major role in reshaping political attitudes in southern

Sudan. The failure of the Government of National Unity (GoNU) to deliver development and services in southern Sudan led people to believe more in secession than in unity. So many projects of the CPA trailed behind schedule while others remained blue prints. Professor Kassahun Berhanu refers to this as implementation deficits. Insecurity was rampant especially in Abyei and Upper Nile State. The increased incidence of violence in oil producing states and the lack of transparency in sharing oil revenues played an important role in the drive towards separation in southern Sudan. People began to believe that they would be better-off in a separate independent state than in a united Sudan.

Reactions to these political developments in Sudan left scholars and researchers to advance interpretations of historical events in varying degrees as they unfolded. Most southern scholars believe the resounding vote for secession was justifiable and blamed economic and political elites in the North for what happened in January 2011; but others contested the thesis of secession. They argued that unity of South Sudan was not guaranteed by the choice of secession as a way forward for Africa. Issues of Arab-African cleavages in Sudan were blamed for the disintegration of the country. These polemics came out clearly in the foreword of Dr Peter Adwok Nyaba, the then Minister of Higher Education and Scientific Research of the GoNU and Chapter One by Professor Mahmood Mamdani, the Director of Makerere's Institute of Social Research. B.F. Bankie, in examining foundational factors of post-referendum South Sudan, raised similar polemical issues. Readers will make their judgements on the rationality underpinning positions of Sudanese scholars in the discourse; and those of Pan-Africanists and Pan-Arabists.

Was the choice of secession of southern Sudan a rational development for state building in the Horn of Africa and Africa in general? This question was addressed by different authors of the book. Indeed, the separation of South Sudan sent a wave of fear among African states and especially in countries that neighbour Sudan. Countries in a situation similar to that of Sudan were Côte d'Ivoire, Somalia, Democratic Republic of Congo (DRC), Angola and Chad among others. Christopher Zambakari attempted to answer the question using historiography as a method of analysis. Further, contributions of Professor A-Tayeb Zain Al-Abdin explained causes of fear, taking into consideration political developments in a number of African countries. The future of these countries depends, nevertheless, on the way political leaders and the people approach their national questions. These fears were, however, dispelled by the manner in which political leaders of Sudan and South Sudan conducted themselves before, during and after the official declaration of Sudan's referendum results in February 2011, which they all endorsed. The declaration of independence suggested the requirement of political stability in corresponding geopolitical regions related to Sudan. This was shown by the participation of Sudanese political forces, African leaders, world leaders and the international community and the speeches they delivered during the independence ceremony in Juba calling for peaceful coexistence of Sudan and South Sudan.

Many unprecedented issues surfaced when results of referendum vote indicated that people of southern Sudan rejected unity irrespective of consequences. Issues such as oil, citizenship, trespassing common borders, water resources, water points, grazing land, proliferation of small-arms and light weapons, inter-communal violence and many others emerged as thorny problems in relations between Sudan and South Sudan. These issues crosscut analyses of Sudanese researchers as most chapters of the book show. Their importance to the stability of the two states, Sudan and South Sudan, cannot be overemphasised. Violent conflicts associated with unsettled disputes could destabilise not only the two countries, but all the regions that have common borders with Sudan and South Sudan. Due importance was given to these issues in most of the contributions contained in this book. The contributing scholars in this book have critically addressed the issues and their consequences for Sudan, South Sudan and for the neighbouring regions.

Conflicts in Sudan spilled over to countries in the Horn of Africa, East Africa and Central Africa. Ethiopia, Eritrea and Uganda were more or less embroiled in the conflict generated by the war of liberation of South Sudan. Countries in the Horn of Africa and East Africa witnessed political conflicts and social impacts that were not necessarily domestic in nature. They bore brunt of each other's internal conflicts just because of proximity to the countries in domestic turbulence. Professor Al-Tayeb Zain Al-Abdin raised issues of this nature regarding the Horn of Africa and beyond. Dr Hamed Omer Hawi went further to examine the role of specific neighbouring countries in the Sudanese conflict. Reponses to these conflicts led to the regionalisation of internal conflicts. A clear example is the case of the Lord's Resistance Movement (LRA), which was no longer a Ugandan problem; but a problem of Sudan before South Sudan declared independence. The chapter provides a space in the book to explain how LRA-related conflict dynamics affected countries beyond their borders. Readers and researchers will find this book interesting to understand why stability in Sudan and South

Sudan could contribute to stability of neighbouring countries. The violent conflict in Sudan over the political status of Blue Nile and South Kordofan after the independence of South Sudan and the impact on Ethiopia justifies worries of researchers and scholars about stability internally and across the common borders. Reports indicate that about 29,000 Sudanese of Blue Nile origin crossed into Ethiopia as refugees after the Governor of Blue Nile was forcefully driven out of power. The situation could escalate further to affect the economies of the Sudan, South Sudan and Ethiopia.

Citizenship is always a problem after secession, especially in the successor state. This was an important post-referendum issue in discussions that ensued before and after January 2011 referendum results. Most of the chapters on consequences of post-referendum Sudan treated the subject at different angles. Authors of this book argued for and against the possibility of dual nationality. It came to be known that both the NCP and the SPLM had contradictory conceptions of citizenship. The NCP ruled out the idea of dual nationality and insisted that southern Sudanese living in the North will lose their Sudanese nationality. This book is coming out after South Sudan declared independence on 9 July 2011. Sudan maintained its position on the issue of citizenship after the declaration of independence of South Sudan. So, Sudanese of southern origin were dismissed from national public services in government institutions of Sudan as well as those who were working in private sector institutions. They are being repatriated to South Sudan with the assistance of International Organisation for Migration (IOM) and the government in Juba. On the contrary, there are no reports on returns of Sudanese of northern origin to Sudan from South Sudan.

The issue of borders and patterns of movement of people remained unresolved. This applies mainly to nomadic communities in the North who depend on water points and natural pastures in South Sudan. Disagreements over borders between Sudan and South Sudan remained one of the stumbling blocks in the demarcation of the boundary as stipulated in the CPA. It complicated the implementation of the Agreement in Abyei and in the transitional areas between the North and the South. The border between Sudan and South Sudan is over 2,000 kilometres, making it the longest border in Africa. Many contributors agreed that border disputes will remain a problem in relations between the two countries at the political level as well as at the grassroots level. Abyei is just a small piece of the problem that is expected to persist for years to come. The impact of environmental degradation on pastoralists in the North will continue to generate movements of animals and people into South Sudan. The question which remains difficult to answer in the book is whether or not it will be the governments or the people who will find solutions to the low-intensity conflict. This book provides an opportunity for readers to understand the gist of the problem from perspectives of both northern and southern Sudanese scholars and the possible solutions they recommended.

The post-referendum situation of Sudan entailed discussions and analysis at different levels of economic cooperation between the expected states that were to emerge after the declaration of independence of South Sudan from Sudan. This book provides a critical examination of the economy after Southern Sudan declares independence. Scholars, in their studies, raised pertinent issues of concern such as oil, the Nile water, development policies and currency. These elements constitute the core of future interactions that could lead to peace or war between Sudan and South Sudan.

This book provides a situation analysis of an oil-based economy that entails cooperation or rivalry between Sudan and South Sudan. Professor Isaac Cuir made an elaborate analysis, which suggested that oil is a double-edged sword in relations in the post-referendum Sudan. Oil was a new discovery in 1978 after the civil wars were waged over a period exceeding half a century. It can be, nevertheless, considered to be the accelerator of an ongoing conflict. The exploitation of oil was also considered to be a trigger for the signature of the CPA. Parties to this Agreement wanted to benefit from the oil wealth during the interim period. But the implementation of the wealth sharing provisions tended to generate suspicion and uneasy relations between partners of the CPA. Linkages of oil wealth to persistent disputes between the NCP and the SPLM and by extension between the North and the South cannot be underrated in the difficult process of implementation of the peace agreement. Disagreements over demarcation of boundaries between the North and the South were mostly attributed to competition for ownership of oil fields in the transitional areas. The discovery of oil in Abyei added to the rival positions held by Khartoum and Juba despite the report of the Abyei Boundary Commission (ABC) and the verdict of the International Court of Arbitration in The Hague.

Nile water is an important economic resource for the survival of communities depending on water resources. It was identified as one of the contentious issues to be tackled in the post-referendum period. The treatment of the Nile water, especially in South Sudan, is referred to in many sections of the book. The Nile is strategic for agricultural, domestic, industrial and tourist development in Sudan, South Sudan, the Horn of Africa, East and Central Africa. The utilisation of Nile water resources is regulated by the 1959 Nile Water Agreement between Egypt and Sudan, among the other nine riparian states. The narrowness of the agreement left the Nile basin a space of perennial tension despite the Nile Basin Initiative (NBI). South Sudan is becoming a new riparian state amid tension with its neighbour, Sudan and the latter with other upper riparian states. South Sudanese political leaders have not hidden their intentions to exploit the White Nile for hydropower. This book treats potential water disputes, which remained unresolved during the post-referendum period. The Nile remains one of the outstanding issues requiring Sudan and South Sudan to come to mutual understanding that would facilitate the process of establishment of an institutional water management within the legal framework of the NBI.

Another post-referendum economic issue was the currency. The question that arose during the post-referendum period was whether or not Sudan and the new state in southern Sudan would maintain the Sudanese pound so as to enhance businesses. Experience of Ethiopian-Eritrean post-secession dispute scared South Sudanese from currency union as an option for cooperation with Sudan. The withdrawal of Eritrea from the Ethiopian Birr economy and launching the Nakfa is considered by many scholars as one of the causes of tension that ensued between the two neighbours. This experience pushed South Sudanese scholars and policy makers to recommend a separate currency for the new country. Benaiah Yongo-Bure, in his contribution, examines monetary and financial policies of southern Sudan before independence. He argued for the case of separate currency in South Sudan, inter alia: 'Therefore, southern Sudan should have a separate currency and monetary policy from northern Sudan, given the different levels of development and degree of mistrust' (Yongo-Bure 2011). The issue of mistrust between northern and southern Sudan came out repeatedly in discourses concerning themes of post-referendum Sudan.

Post-referendum South Sudan was set to prepare programmes of social and economic development. Scholars engaged in discourses warned against South Sudan being classified as failed state after declaration of independence. Post-conflict South Sudan was marked by extreme poverty, lack of infrastructure and prevalence of inter-communal armed violence. This book comes out with remedial policies to prevent South Sudan from descending into a state economic and social chaos. The book provides the argument that equitable and rational transformative socio-economic programmes and policies will greatly reduce potentials for conflict. This implies policy makers should pursue policies that raise the morale of the population. People expect to see concrete projects planned to alleviate their poverty. Yongo-Bure's contribution entitled 'South Sudan's Priority Development Programmes, Projects, and Policies' addressed concerns about economic viability of post-referendum southern Sudan. South Sudanese were craving for the provision of basic services such as basic education; health, and safe water supply in the shortest period of time possible. The section of the book on the economy and economic development provides a way forward on food production such as incentives to peasants establishing marketing, transportation and storage facilities. The author advises the government of post-referendum South Sudan to consider past reports of consultant firms on South Sudan as baseline information in order to conceive economic plans for the future.

In Chapter 10 of the book, Ssemwanga postulates that a managed float exchange rate regime to ensure macroeconomic stability has been adopted and a new currency called the South Sudanese Pound (SSP) is already in circulation. South Sudan is faced with social and economic problems that include limited access to basic education, healthcare, food, water, high inflation, sovereign debt, low level of national revenue and others. Most of the problems have been exacerbated by suspending oil production during January 2012. The Government of South Sudan has come up with a number of measures to address the shortfall in oil revenue and also the over-dependence on oil revenue by establishing a Non-Oil Revenue Action Plan, as well as instituting austerity measures that relate to Government expenditure. The author bases his work on studies carried out by the IMF and the World Bank. According to his contribution, a number of studies carried out to show the effectiveness of monetary policy and fiscal policy on economic activity show mixed results. Some results indicate that monetary policy is more effective than fiscal policy, while others indicate the opposite.

PART I

Opinions on Self-Determination

1

Some Questions Regarding the Independence of South Sudan

Mahmood Mamdani

Introduction

Whatever the point of view, it would be difficult to deny that the referendum on South Sudan – unity or independence – was a historic moment. The right for self-determination marks the founding of a new political order. Nationalists may try to convince us that the outcome of the referendum, independence, is the natural destiny of the people of South Sudan. But there is nothing natural about any political outcome. Let us ask one question to begin with: who is the 'self' in what we know as self-determination? In 1956, when Sudan became independent, that self was the whole people of Sudan. Today, in 2011, when South Sudan will become independent, that 'self' is the people of South Sudan. That self, in both cases, is a political self. It is a historical self, not a metaphysical one as nationalists are prone to think. When nationalists write a history, they give the past a present existence. In doing so, they tend to make the present eternal. As the present changes, so does the past. This is why we are always rewriting the past. The outcome of self-determination in South Sudan is bound to have its strong impact on the South and the North, on the region of the Horn and the whole of the African continent. The questions of identity, statehood and Africanism will open afresh in a number of countries around the continent. The answer may not be peaceful or smooth.

The Pertinent Questions of Identity and Liberation

To return to the referendum: the referendum is a moment of self-determination. Not every people has this opportunity; not even every generation gets the opportunity. If the opportunity comes, it is once in several generations; and it comes at a great price. That price is paid in blood and in political violence. It is fitting that we begin by recalling that many have died to make possible this moment of self-determination. Let us begin by acknowledging this sacrifice, which signifies this historical moment. I do not intend this chapter to be a celebration. My objective is more analytical. Rather than tread on firm ground, I intend to pose a set of questions not so that we may answer them here and now, but as guidelines to how we may think of South Sudan in the days and months and years ahead. I will begin with four questions:

One: How should those committed to Pan-African unity understand the emergence of a new state, an independent South Sudan? What does it teach us about the political process of creating unity?

Two: As we write the history of self-determination, how will we write the history of relations between the North and the South, as the history of one people colonising another or as a history with different, even contradictory, possibilities?

Three: How did the SPLM, historically a champion of a united New Sudan, come to demand an independent state?

Four: Now that the SPLM's political project has changed, to create a new state, this raises another question: will the South establish a new political order? Or will it reproduce a version of the old political order of the old Sudan? Will independence lead to peace or will peace be just an interlude awaiting a more appropriate antidote to ongoing political violence in Sudan?

African Unity

Like the self, unity too does not develop in linear fashion, in a straight line, from lower to higher levels, as if it were unfolding according to a formula. Political unity is the outcome of political struggles, not of utopian blueprints. Anyone interested in creating unity must recognize the importance of politics and persuasion, and thus the inevitability of a non-linear complicated process.

We often say that imperialism divided the African continent. I suggest we rethink this platitude. Historically, empires have united peoples by force. France created two great political units in Africa: French Equatorial Africa and French West Africa. Britain created two great federations: the Central African Federation and the East African Federation, and it created Sudan. These great political units split up, but that division was not at the moment of colonialism, rather it occurred at the moment of independence. This was for one reason; the people in question saw these political arrangements as shackles, and struggled to break free of them. Unity can be created by different, even contradictory, means. It can be created by force, and it can be created by choice. This is why we need to distinguish between different kinds of unities: unity through bondage and unity through freedom. This is why a democratic position on African unity is not necessarily incompatible with a democratic right to separation, just as the free right to union in marriage is not incompatible with the free right to divorce. The Organization of African Unity (OAU) had two relevant provisions in its Charter: the sovereignty of all states, and the right of all peoples to self-determination. Most observers saw these as contradictory. I suggest we revise this judgement in retrospect.

We need to rethink the relation between sovereignty and self-determination. Sovereignty is the relation of the state to other states, to external powers, whereas self-determination is an internal relation of the state to its people. In a democratic context, self-determination should be seen as the pre-requisite to sovereignty. There are, in the post-colonial history of Africa, two great examples of self-determination, of the creation of a new state from a previously independent African state: Eritrea was the first, South Sudan is the second. No state in history has agreed willingly to secession of a part of its land. Secession is always forced in one way or another on a state. This is why we need to ask a question in both cases: how was secession possible? Eritrean self-determination was the outcome of two important developments, internal and external. Internally, it was the outcome of a struggle lasting nearly four decades, culminating in a military victory over the Mengistu regime, the Derg. Externally, the relevant factor was the end of the Cold War and the collapse of the Soviet Union block. The referendum that followed was notable for one reason. In spite of the close relation between Eritrean and Ethiopian armed movements, the EPLF and the EPRDF, and their joint victory over the Ethiopian empire state, the Eritrean people voted overwhelmingly to establish a separate and independent state. In South Sudan, self-determination is the result of a different combination of developments. Internally, there was no military victory; instead, there was a military stalemate between the North and the South. Thus the question: How did South Sudan win its political objective, independence, in the absence of a military victory? Until now, this remains an unanswered question.

My answer is provisional. In the case of South Sudan, the external factor was more decisive. That external factor was 9/11 and, following it, US invasion of Afghanistan and Iraq. In my view, it is only this factor, the real grip of post-9/11 fear, the fear that it will be the next target of US aggression that explains the agreement of the government in the North to include a provision for a referendum in the South in the CPA. The result of the referendum could not have been in doubt. It would have been clear to anyone with a historical understanding of the issues involved, and of the experience of the process leading to Eritrean independence, that the referendum would lead to an overwhelming popular vote for an independent state in the South. Why then did the power in the North agree to a referendum? My answer is: the agreement to hold a referendum deferred a head-on confrontation with US power.

The Meaning of Independence

Is independence the end of a colonial relationship? This is indeed how one tendency in South Sudan thinks of independence. Just as some who called for Eritrean independence spoke of Ethiopia as a colonial master. The analogy is misleading for at least one reason. Whereas the colonial power left the region, north and south will always be neighbours. You can leave your marriage partner, but you cannot leave your neighbour. Neighbours have a history, and that history overlaps geographical boundaries. Though north and south have distinct geographies, they have overlapping histories. I would like to highlight key developments in that history. The first development was that of migrations, both voluntary and forced. Let us begin with voluntary migrations. Here is one interesting example. In the period before western colonialism, even before the regional slave trade, the Shilluk migrated from the South. From amongst the Shilluk rose the royal house of the Funj which established the famous Muslim Sultanate of Sinnar. As it expanded, the Sultanate raided the South for slaves, mainly for slave soldiers. For reasons that need to be explored further, colonial historians have termed these slave raids the Arab slave trade. The Sultanate of the Funj was the first Muslim state in the history of Sudan. It brought to an end a thousand-year history of Christian states in the North. Sinnar demolished Christian states in the North and inaugurated the political history of Islam in Sudan. Given the conventional understanding that equates Islam with the North and Christianity with the South, I would like us to remember that political powers in the North, in Nubia and Beja, were Christian, and that the royal family of the first Muslim state in Sudan came from the South, not the North. In contrast, Islam came to the North in the form of refugees and merchants, not royals or soldiers. The migrations that we know of better were forced migrations, slavery. The South plundered for slaves from the seventeenth century onwards with the formation of the Sultanate of the Funj along the Nile and the Sultanate of Darfur in the West. But the slave trade became intense only in late eighteenth century when the Caribbean plantation economy was transplanted to Indian Ocean islands. The rise of a plantation slave economy had a number of consequences. Prior to it, the demand for slaves came mainly from the state; it was a demand for slave soldiers. As slave plantations were developed in the Indian Ocean islands, in Reunion and Mauritius and other places, the demand shifted from the state to the market. The scale of the demand also increased dramatically. Nonetheless, most of those enslaved in the South stayed in Darfur and Sinnar as slave soldiers. Most of those in Darfur became Fur. Most of those in Sinnar became Arab. They were culturally assimilated, mostly by consent but the kind of consent that is manufactured through relations of force. For a parallel, think of how African slaves in North America became English-speaking westerners, thereby taking on the cultural identity of their masters.

This little bit of history should disturb our simple moral world in a second way; some of the Arabs in the North are descendants of slaves from the South. The second great historical development that has shaped relations between north and south in Sudan is that of anti-colonial nationalism. The event that marks the rise of anti-colonial nationalism is the *Mahdiyya*, the great Sudanese revolt against British-Ottoman rule, known as the *Turkiyya*. Led by Mohamed Abdulla, the Mahdi, this late nineteenth century movement was, after the 1857 Indian Uprising, the greatest revolt to shake the British empire. With its firm social base in Darfur and Kordofan, the *Mahdiyya* spread first to the rest of northern Sudan, and then to the Dinka of Abyei. The Dinka said the Spirit of Deng had caught the Mahdi. Modern Sudanese nationalism begins in the 1920s with what has come to be known as the White Flag revolt. It was spearheaded by southern officers in the colonial army, and marks the turning point in colonial policy in Sudan, when British power decided to quarantine the South from the North. This is how north and south came to be artificially separated in the colonial period, with permission required to cross boundaries. This kind of separation is, however, not unusual in the history of colonialism, Karamoja too was a quarantined district in colonial Uganda. The third point is key: an even worse fate met the people of South Sudan after independence. A state-enforced national project unfolded in Sudan, at first as enforced Arabisation, later as enforced Islamisation. This, rather than the colonial period, is the real context of the armed liberation struggle in the South – for the fact is that it did not take long for both the political class and the popular classes in the South to realize that the independence of Sudan had worsened their political and social situation, rather than improved it.

SPLA: From New Sudan to Independence

The SPLA's political programme was not an independent South; it was a liberated Sudan. SPLA did not call for the creation of a new state, but for the reform of the existing state. The demand for a New Sudan was the basis of a political alliance between SPLA and the northern political opposition in Khartoum. It was the basis on which SPLA expanded the struggle from the South to border areas. When Garang signed the CPA and returned to Khartoum, over a million turned out to receive him. They represented the entire diversity of Sudan, from north to south, and from east to west. They included speakers of Arabic and of other Sudanese languages. Many drew comparisons with the return of Mugabe to Harare. Garang's return was a shock across the political spectrum, especially to the ruling class in the North.

The point of this historical survey of relations between north and south is to underline one single fact: this is not a one-dimensional history of northern oppression of the South. True, northern domination is the main story, especially after independence. But there was a subsidiary story, the story of joint north-south struggle against that domination. This has been more easily identified as a struggle against the military rulers: Aboud, Nimeiry and al-Bashir who ruled the country for about 40 years. If the SPLM had participated in the presidential elections of 2010, it would likely have won, whether led by Garang, Salva Kir or Yassir Arman. The irony is this: precisely when the SPLM was on the verge of realizing its historic goal, power in the whole of Sudan, it gave up the goal and called for an independent south. Why? Part of the answer lies in the orientation of the political leadership, especially after the death of Garang. SPLM was a movement with a strong leader; the weaker the organization, the more difference does the death of one individual make. The history of liberation movements in this region testifies to this fact. It should also remind us that it has not been unusual for strong leaders to be eliminated towards the close of an armed struggle. Remember ZANU and the killing of Tongogara on the eve of victory; the ANC and the assassination of Chris Hani, also on the eve of victory; and SPLM and the death of Garang soon after return to Khartoum. It is worth comparing SPLM with ANC. Both were successful in undermining the attempt of ruling regimes to turn the struggle into a racial or religious contest. The ANC succeeded in recruiting important individuals from the white population, such as Joe Slovo and Ronnie Kasrils. Similarly, SPLM included key cadres from the Arab population like Mansour Khalid, Yassir Arman and al-Wathiq Kemier. The difference between them is also important, whereas the line that called for unity, for a non-racial South Africa, won in the ANC, the line that called for a New Sudan was defeated in the SPLM.

In both cases, the line representing unity and that representing separation were locked in an on-going contest throughout the history of the struggle. This was indeed the difference between the ANC and the PAC in South Africa. In the case of South Sudan, the two lines were represented by SPLM and Anyanya II, the first calling for a New Sudan, the latter for an independent South Sudan. SPLM was founded as a nationalist project, an alternative to other kinds of nationalisms, to Arabism, to Islamism, but also to a separate South Sudan nationalism. The SPLM was a project to reform the state, not to create a new state. Garang's speech at Koka Dam was the most explicit statement of why the future of the South and the North lay together, why political salvation lay not in the formation of a new state but in the reform of the existing state.

Today, the line calling for independence has emerged triumphant. How did we get to this point? I have suggested that part of the answer lies in the nature of political leadership. Another part of the answer lies in on-going political developments. The key development was the experience of power-sharing. The first power-sharing agreement in Sudan was forged in 1972, as a result of the Addis Ababa Agreement. It lasted ten years; but it collapsed when it was no longer convenient for the military regime in the North. It also collapsed because the Agreement had little popular support in the North; the northern opposition was completely excluded. Why? Because the 1972 Agreement reformed the state in the South but not in the North. The CPA was built on the lessons of 1972. The key lesson was that power-sharing had been too narrow. As a result, the CPA called for a broader sharing, ranging from political power to wealth to military arrangements. Still, it remained sharing of power between elites, between two ruling groups, NCP and SPLM. It left out the opposition in both the North and the South. It was power-sharing without democratisation!

Democratisation and Violence

What would democratisation mean in the present context? Is there a link between democratisation and violence? If so, what is that link? I want to begin with two observations, one on political order, and the other on political violence. The first has to do with the link between organisation of the state and maintenance of civil peace in a post-civil war situation.

Think of Uganda in 1986. We had just come out of a civil war. The terrain was marked by multiple armed militias, the best known being UFM and FEDEMU. The Ugandan solution to this problem was known as the broad base. It was an invitation to rival militias to join the new political order, but on two conditions: first, whether monarchist or militarist, you can keep your political objectives provided you give up your arms; second, you can have a share in political power, a governmental position, provided you give up control over your militia. South Sudan, too, is attempting to create a broad base. But in South Sudan, different members of the broad base have kept not only their arms but also their command over their respective militias. Every important political leader in the SPLM has his own militia, so much so that one has to ask: what happens if a leader loses his position within the SPLM? Or loses an election? The obvious answer is, that commander leaves with his militia. Take the example of General George Athor who went into rebellion after losing last April's election to be governor of Jonglei state. He immediately led his militia into rebellion, attacking Malakal in the oil-producing state of Upper Nile. It is a sign of the times. General Athor had contested the election as an independent candidate, because the SPLM did not select him as a candidate. But one is tempted to ask: what is to prevent a general who contests as SPLM and loses the election from withdrawing with his militia? Most discussion on the question of violence in South Sudan today focuses on the spectre of north-south violence. There is hardly any discussion on violence within the South. Even when internal violence in the South is discussed, it is seen as a consequence of north-south tensions.

I suggest that we need to look at both internal and external violence, violence within state boundaries and violence between states. Let us begin with some general observations. Political violence in African states is not between states, but within states. The exception is where one state was created from within the womb of another, like Eritrea out of Ethiopia, or Pakistan out of India, or where one political class was nurtured in the womb of another, like the relationship between EPLF and TPLF, the Eritrean and Ethiopian armed movements, or the RPA in Rwanda and the NRA in Uganda. The first kind of violence abounds in post-colonial Africa: the Rift Valley in Kenya, Darfur, Ivory Coast, eastern Congo. It is common to refer to all types of internal violence as 'ethnic violence'. What is the common factor? All these cases have one thing in common. All have reformed the central state by introducing elections and a multi-party system. But elections seem to lead to violence rather than stability. Why? For a clue, I suggest we look at another similarity between these cases of internal violence. None have managed to reform the local state, the local authority or the District Authority that the British used to call a Native Authority. As a form of power, the Native Authority is of colonial origin. Colonialism spread a fiction, that Africans have a herd mentality and that they tend to stay in one place, so Africans have always lived in tribal homelands. This was their justification for why every colony was administered as a patchwork of tribal homelands. In actual fact, colonial administrations created homelands and Native Authorities. My research suggests that colonialism began with a programme of ethnic cleansing. Take the case of Buganda where all the Catholics were moved from the centre to Masaka, and Mengo was considered a Protestant homeland. Administrative counties were designated as Protestant or Catholic or, in a few cases, Muslim. The tribe or religion of the chief designated the nature of the homeland he administered. The ethnic cleansing in Buganda was religious, it was tribal elsewhere. The Native Authority made an administrative distinction between those who were born or lived in the administrative area and those who were descended from its so-called original inhabitants. The distinction, in today's political language, was between natives and *Bafuruki*. The distinction systematically privileged natives over all others. The colonial tribe is not the same as a pre-colonial ethnic group. The pre-colonial ethnic group was not an administrative but a cultural group. You could become a Muganda or a Munyankore or a Langi or a Dinka in the pre-colonial period. But you could not change your tribe officially in the colonial administration. Colonialism transformed a tribe from a cultural identity to an administrative identity that claimed to be based on descent, not just on culture. It became a blood identity. Tribe became a subset of race. Wherever the colonial notion of Native Authority has remained, the authorities define the population on the basis of descent, not residence.

Colonialism was based on two sets of discriminations: one based on race, the other on tribe. Race divided natives from non-natives in urban areas. Tribe divided natives from *Bafuruki* in the rural areas, inside each tribal homeland. The difference was that whereas natives in urban areas were discriminated against racially, natives in the tribal homelands were privileged. This administrative structure inevitably generated inter-tribal conflicts. To begin with, every administrative area was multi-ethnic. Yet, in every multi-ethnic area, official administration discriminated against ethnic minorities, especially when it came to access to land, and the appointment of chiefs, that is, participation in local governance. As the market system developed, more and more people migrated, either in search of jobs or land, and every administrative area became more and more multi-ethnic. In a situation where the population was multi-ethnic and power mono-ethnic, the result was that more and more people were disenfranchised as not being native of the area, even if they were born there. Ethnic conflict was the inevitable outcome. Africa is littered with examples of this kind of conflict. It is the dynamic that drives on-going civil wars around the continent: Darfur, Nigeria since the post-civil war constitution, eastern Congo, Ivory Coast, the Rift Valley in Kenya. Will South Sudan be an exception? Will South Sudan create a new kind of state or will it reproduce a reformed colonial state? To have some idea, we can look at the period before the CPA was signed in 2005. At the time, there were liberated areas. Since CPA was signed in 2005, the whole of southern Sudan became a liberated area. The fact is that South Sudan became independent six years ago, in 2005.

Make a comparison between liberated SPLA-held areas in Sudan with Sudan government-held areas, also in southern Sudan before 2005. Early returns are not encouraging. Structures of power in both areas are the same. Both areas are ruled by administrative chiefs that implement customary law as defined in the colonial period, as a law that systematically privileges natives over Bafuruki, men over women and old over young. From this point of view, there is no difference between how local power is organized in the North and in the South. Because the local power discriminates actively and legally between different kinds of citizens of southern Sudan, it is bound to generate tensions and conflict over time. The second type of violence, that between states, is specific to cases like Ethiopia and Eritrea, Uganda and Rwanda. Will South and North Sudan be an exception? For a start, we need to identify the sources of North-South tensions. First, there are the border-states which lie within the North or the South but have populations that historically came from both. This is the case in Blue Nile, Nuba Mountains, and southern Kordofan. The border-states were politically the most receptive to Garang's call for a New Sudan. The border-states also felt betrayed by the decision to create an independent South Sudan. At the same time, the political class in the border-states is exposed to retaliation from the northern political elite, one reason why it turned to SPLA for protection.

The second source of tension is the population of IDPs, the population of refugees from the south who lived in the north. How many of them still continue to live in the north? We do not know, but the count ranges from hundreds of thousands upwards. Are they citizens of where they live, Sudan, or of the new state from which they have historically moved, South Sudan? Like Eritreans in Ethiopia, they will be the most likely victims of a failure to think through the citizenship question. The third source of tension is in Abyei, where the Misseriya of Darfur and the Ngok Dinka have shared livelihoods and political struggles for over a thousand years. Historically, African societies had no fixed borders; the borders were porous, flexible and mobile. But the new borders are fixed and hard; you either belong or you do not. You cannot belong to both sides of the border. Will the new political arrangement with fixed borders pit the Misseriya and the Ngok Dinka against one another? Should the populations of border regions, pastoralists who criss-cross the North-South border annually in search of water in the dry season, the IDPs who have settled in their new homes, have dual citizenship?

In sum, then, there are two major sources of political violence after independence. Possible violence between north and south has three likely sources: border populations, IDPs, and peasants and pastoralists with shared livelihoods. The second possible source of violence is within the South. It arises from the persistence of the Native Authority as the form of local power that turns cultural difference into a source of political and legal discrimination. One solution for the first problem is dual nationality for border and migrant populations in the near future, which could possibly lead to a confederation in the distant future.

The solution for the second problem is to reform the Native Authority. If South Sudan is organized as a federation, how will citizenship be defined in each state in the federation, as ethnic or territorial? A territorial federation gives equal rights to all citizens who live within a state, whereas an ethnic federation distinguishes legally and politically between different kinds of residents, depending on their ethnic origin. The basic question that faces South Sudan is not very different from the one that faces most African countries. Will South Sudan learn from the African experience – on-going civil war and ethnic conflict – and rethink political citizenship and the political state in order to create a new political order? The future of South Sudan and its people rides on the answer to this basic question. The risk of violence and conflict in South Sudan may not be less than the long civil war experience between south and north.

PART II

North-South Relations and Regional Issues

2

The Consequences of the Referendum in Southern Sudan for the Country and the Region

Al-Tayib Zain Al-Abdin

Introduction

The Comprehensive Peace Agreement (CPA), which was signed between the Government of Sudan (GoS) and the rebel movement in southern Sudan (SPLM) in January 2005, ended the longest civil war in Africa. The Inter-governmental Authority on Development (IGAD) played a pivotal role in realizing that agreement in close cooperation with the big western powers. The agreement granted the people of southern Sudan the right to self-determination through an internationally-monitored referendum by the end of the six-year Interim Period. That was not an easy option for the political elite in the North, who dominated the central government since independence because their fellow northerners are the clear majority in the country, better educated and more experienced in politics and administration. The referendum may end a period of more than 150 years of a united Sudan. Nevertheless, the civil war between the government and southern rebel movements which started before independence and continued for decades, was too expensive in human lives, economic resources and political stability. Thus the government of Sudan accepted the risk of secession in order to bring peace to the whole country. On 9th January 2011, the referendum was conducted in a free and peaceful atmosphere, and as expected the result was overwhelmingly (98%) in favour of secession. The North felt grieved and disappointed while the South rejoiced at the newly-gained freedom and independence as a sovereign state. However, the government of the North has accepted the painful result of the referendum and declared that it respects the choice of the people of southern Sudan, and will be the first to recognize the new state. The separation of the two states would be effective after the end of the Interim Period on 9 July 2011. The outcome of the referendum raises a serious question: will the separation between the two parts of the country be peaceful and smooth or is it going to be friction and acrimonious. The most important factor to influence the relationship is the manner in which the two parties should settle the outstanding issues which are serious and sensitive. No doubt that the difficult experience of secession will have its repercussions on north and south, and the region neighbouring them. We shall try to cover the expected consequences on both countries and the region below. The Chapter was written immediately after the referendum but revised one year after the separation took place.

The Consequences on the Relationship Between North and South

There are a number of important issues mentioned in the Referendum Act, which should be settled by the two partners before the separation takes place, in addition to some difficult issues left over from the implementation of the CPA. Those issues are: Abyei, delimitation of borders, citizenship, currency, public service, status of the Joint Integrated Units, agreements and international covenants, debts and assets, oil concessions and production, Nile waters and land ownership. The two partners constituted, in June 2010, four joint committees to negotiate these issues under the facilitation of the African Union High Level Implementation Panel (AUHIP) led by the former president of South Africa, Thabo Mbeki. The negotiations will be supported by the IGAD, the UN and the partners of IGAD, while the Assessment and Evaluation Commission (AEC) will provide administrative support. Till February 2011, the committees made little progress in some of the easy issues, but the difficult and sensitive ones remain without agreement. They agreed to differ on citizenship, the NCP refused to give citizenship to hundreds of thousands of southerners living in the North but will let them stay for some time and protect them and their properties. However, as they are no longer citizens of northern Sudan they are not entitled to hold government posts after the end of the Interim Period, especially those working in the army, police and the security agency. The army considers the southerners who number about 30,000 in its ranks as a security risk in case of a future conflict between north and south. Those soldiers have settled with their families for many years in the North, their children have grown up in the North and most of them have never seen the South in their lives. It will be a painful experience for them to go back to the South looking for jobs and settlement in regions which they or their ancestors left a long time ago. The Government of South Sudan (GoSS) was ready to give citizenship on the choice of the northerner who lives in the South, on the basis that the southerner be treated the same in the North. The GoS feels that this is not a fair deal as the numbers, skills and economic position of the two groups are not equal. While the southerners in the North are hundreds of thousands, the northerners in the South are not more than a few thousands who work as traders or professionals residing without their families. It is not considered difficult for such professionals to resettle in the North. The government of South Sudan promised not to push them out, and allowed them to stay and work. Already, about 200,000 southerners left the North for the South during the last six months, but they suffered because living conditions were not prepared for mass returnees, and many of them were stuck in the middle of their journey because transport facilities were not available. The SPLM encouraged southerners to go back *en masse* to the South to vote in the referendum and to take part in building their new nation by whatever skills they learned in the North. It was afraid that if they stayed in the North, they might be influenced to vote for unity.

On the border issue, it is agreed that it should be open to allow thousands of pastoralist cattle keepers to cross from north to south during the dry season as they have done every year for many decades. The grazing rights for nomads are clearly stated in the CPA but it is not clear how is it going to be administered across the new international border. Furthermore, it might be prohibited or obstructed if the relationship between the governments of the two countries got worse. Nevertheless, 30 per cent of the border is not agreed upon and the two partners may have to go to some form of arbitration to solve this problem; though they agreed that demarcation should start immediately on the approved border. That was not possible because GoSS claimed later more regions as part of the South. As a matter of fact Sudan's borders with all its nine neighbouring countries have never been demarcated since independence. Both parties to the conflict were surprised to know that there was no complete map for Sudan on the first of January 1956, when the British left and Sudan got its independence. During their fifty-year rule, the British transferred a number of regions from one province to another for security or administrative reasons irrespective of the ethnic groups living in the area. On the currency issue, they have agreed to use the present one in both countries for six to nine months after the Interim Period till the South is in a position to print its own currency. As a matter of fact, each side was secretly preparing to issue its own currency before the fixed period.

On the tough issues of Abyei, oil, security and Nile water no agreement is reached till June 2012. The situation in Abyei is tense and some clashes have already taken place between the armies of the two countries, which affected the relationship of the communities living in the region, mainly the DinkaNgok and Misseriya. The Misseriya are asking for equal rights to the Dinka's, especially the right of voting in the referendum to decide the future of Abyei, since they have been living in the region for more than one hundred years. The Dinka do not accept this argument on the grounds that the Misseriya are nomads who live only for some months in the area. Although the district is not more than 10,000 sq km, it may ignite a new conflict as the two concerned communities, who were living peacefully for many decades, became politicised and do not show any sign of compromise. The Dinka, being a southern tribe, are supported by SPLM while the Arab Misseriya are supported by NCP, but the two tribes are not completely under the control of their patrons. All the foreign facilitators, including the Americans, failed to solve the deadlock between the two communities. Therefore, despite the NCP's acceptance of the referendum result which should have led to a friendly and peaceful relationship between the two emerging states, that did not happen because the pending issues between them are critical and not easy to solve. Furthermore, the NCP is not in a mood to be flexible with the SPLM which championed the vote for secession although it promised in the CPA to work for unity. The question of security is another serious problem, with both parties accused each other of supporting militia groups fighting against the other state. Being a close observer of the political scene in Sudan, I could not understand the optimistic announcement made on 9th February in New York by the UN special envoy for Sudan, Haile Menkerios, that the two sides in Sudan have agreed so far on issues including oil revenue sharing, bilateral economic relations, citizenship arrangements, open borders and non-interference in each other's affairs. Other steps under discussion include security, non-aggression and military cooperation. I wish he were right but time proved he was wrong. The whole situation shows clearly that separation within the African countries is not easy to manage, even if there is goodwill and acceptance on both sides. The experience of Ethiopia and Eritrea proves that. Given the tough and sensitive pending issues, the possibility of conflict between north and south in Sudan cannot be excluded. It is a hard lesson which should be learned by peoples in the continent. On the other hand, if the two separating states could cross peacefully the hurdles of negotiating their problems, they would play a positive role in strengthening economic cooperation between the Arab world in the north and east of Sudan with the African countries in the South and west of their homelands. The majority of the Arabs live in North Africa and they constitute the largest group in the African Union. Both Arabs and Africans have common interest in building good relations and economic cooperation, in addition to their cultural and religious heritage.

The Consequences for the North

The North cannot feel at ease after separation on the belief that it has become more homogenous in terms of ethnicity, religion and culture. To some extent this is true but the picture is not that simple. There are still many diverse and marginalised ethnic groups in northern Sudan. Some months after the secession of the South, armed conflict erupted in southern Kordofan and Blue Nile on the same basis of marginalised ethnic groups. It will be very painful for the North if the pending issues with the South are not solved in a peaceful way; it accepted reluctantly the risk of self-determination for the sake of peace. To end up with separation and war will be the worst of the two worlds. Furthermore, the North is not ready politically, militarily or economically for a new outright war. The major factor behind the southern problem, which started a few months before independence, was the failure of the successive national governments, especially military ones which ruled for four decades, to administer wisely the diversity and pluralism within a united Sudan. They were primarily concerned with the nation-building of the country in the image of a dominant Muslim-Arab culture irrespective of its serious consequences on minorities who felt marginalised because they suffered from poverty, lack of development and social services in their far-fung, neglected areas. With the present Islamic regime of *al-Inqaz* which has held power since 1989 and may continue till 2015, in accordance with the transitional constitution, the risk of failure in managing diversity exists. There is no apparent change of attitude or personalities in the structure of the semi-military regime.

The other regions which threaten the unity and peace in northern Sudan are: southern Kordofan, Blue Nile and Darfur. The states of southern Kordofan and Blue Nile were given special status in the CPA to have shares in power and wealth, some of their young men fought with the SPLM in its liberation war for a New Sudan. They thought it would be liberation for the whole country. By the fourth year of the Interim Period, they were supposed to conduct a 'popular consultation' among their inhabitants to say if the arrangements made for them in the CPA are satisfactory or not, and whether the implementation was good enough. The 'popular consultation' was not conducted on time; it will be done sometime in the future. Between 30 and 40 thousand soldiers from the two states who fought with the SPLM are left idle without work, and they will most likely not feel happy with the outcome of the 'popular consultation'. Another 30 thousand or so highly trained soldiers from the two states, are part of the SPLA in the South who would choose to side with their fellow citizens at time of conflict. The problem of Darfur, despite reduced violence in the region during the last three years, is still dragging on without final political solution between the government and the armed groups who splintered several times in the past years. The three regions are less developed than the rest of northern Sudan and have a significant African presence that pioneered the armed struggle against the Arabised centre. If the government of Khartoum does not tackle the situation in those regions wisely, they could easily turn into another south.

Economically, the government lost about 40 per cent of its annual income from the oil revenue of southern Sudan which constitutes 80 per cent of the country's foreign currency. The economic difficulties have already started to be felt by the people in the North: the domestic food prices are up at 19.8 per cent; the value of the Sudanese pound has fallen by about 30 per cent in relation to the US dollar; and, unemployment reached alarming level particularly among university graduates (about 40%). The official figure of the poverty level is at 46 per cent of the population, though academicians put it as high as 80 per cent. The World Bank report of February 2011 gives a poor picture of Sudan economy after secession: 5 per cent growth instead of 9 per cent to 10 per cent in the past few years, contraction in the oil sector, and reserves being critically low. The inflation rate in December 2010 reached 16.7 per cent; in the first half of 2012 it reached 30 per cent. The World Bank ended by saying that secession will put significant strain on economic stability in the North. Politically, polarisation between the government and the opposition parties is getting wider. All the opposition parties consider the government responsible for the secession of the South by following intransigent polices, some of them speak about the need of overthrowing the regime which came to power through a military coup. The difficult economic conditions may push people to protest in the streets of the capital, which the government cannot tolerate fearing what happened in other Arab capitals. In other words, the consequences of secession for the North are less security, economic difficulties and political problems.

The Consequences for the South

No doubt SPLM has achieved a long-awaited dream for the people of southern Sudan; at this stage SPLM is enjoying its honeymoon with most of the population in the South. However, the honeymoon might not continue for a long time because internal problems and frictions are bound to come out sooner rather than later. What might be the main problem? It is not different from the problem of the old Sudan; it is how to manage ethnic diversity in the new state and contain its ethnic conflicts, rebelling generals and extra-constitutional power struggle. The Sudan People's Liberation Army (SPLA) behaves as the liberator of the new state which should be put above every other institution. It is not yet a professional army that keeps away from interfering in politics and administration of the state. South Sudan comprises about 200 ethnic groups, almost each group has its own language, culture and geographical location. Some of those ethnic groups have historical conflicts with each other like Dinka with Nuer and Shilluk, Nilotic tribes with Equatorians, etc. Dr Samson Wassara, a distinguished southern scholar of Juba University, commented on conflicts in southern Sudan: life in the post-CPA is characterised by uneasy relationships between armed groups, IDPs, returnees and host communities. The causes of conflict are usually around: plunder of cattle, water and fish, land ownership and land use, trespassing tribal boundaries, blood feuds, family disputes over divorce and compensation, pastoralists grazing their cattle on peasants farms etc. Modern weapons and politics fuelled conflicts and increased the number of causalities. Tribal conflicts in southern Sudan in 2009 resulted in about 2,500 dead and 350 thousand displaced because of military operations in their regions.

There is a real fear among other tribes that the Dinka, being the largest tribe in the South and in control of the government and the army, will marginalise other tribes and deny them equal rights. After Addis Ababa agreement of 1972 and the establishment of the High Executive Council in the South, elections and change of governments were mainly based on tribal affiliation. The division of the region into three provinces was unconstitutionally decreed by president Nimeiry, mainly because the Equatorians showed discontent about the hegemony of the Dinka over the affairs of the whole region. The SPLM, being a liberation movement targeting nation-building, might not give due consideration to the sensitive issue of tribal diversity in the South. Since the precedent is set by the separation of the South, some tribes in the South itself (e.g., Equatorians) might also opt for self-rule because they did not get a fair deal in the administration of the Republic of South Sudan.

Other related factors may handicap the ability of the government to deal with the complex problems of building a viable modern state: the lack of basic infra-structure in the South; the complete dependence (98%) on the fluctuating oil revenue; the poorly-trained flabby civil service; the weakness of political parties and civil society groups; and the rampant illiteracy among the population (about 85%). Those problems are not confined to the new state of South Sudan, but they confront the state which does not possess enough political and administrative experience. Nevertheless, they are not insurmountable but they require time, national reconciliation and inclusiveness, stability and good governance. After a serious dispute with Sudan on transportation fees, the GoSS closed its oil fields in February 2012 causing severe economic problems to the apparatus of the government and the whole economy of the country.

The Consequences for the Region

The conflict in Sudan that lasted more than three decades has been explained in terms of ethnic and cultural diversities; a phenomenon which is to be found almost in every African country. What lesson may other African countries learn from the Sudan? We take, as an example, the Horn of Africa as the region which is more likely to be affected by what has happened in the Sudan since it is neighbouring Sudan from east and south, and having many similarities with its people. The IGAD countries, all of which are in the Horn, took the responsibility of successfully mediating in the Sudan conflict over a number of years till a final agreement is reached.

Despite the vague definition of 'ethnic group' in the African context, especially when we refer to its role in politics and conflict, it is still an important analytical concept which has to be considered. Usually scholars refer to an 'ethnic group' as the collectivity of people who share the same characteristics such as common ancestry, language and culture (including religion). The common assumption is that ethnic similarities or differences are the bases for social harmony or discord. It is expected that members of the ethnic group would have a relationship of solidarity and harmony with each other but one of cleavage and discord with those who do not share their ethnic identity. Conflicts in many African countries like: Ethiopia, Nigeria, Uganda, Liberia, Rwanda, Burundi, Angola, Zimbabwe, Democratic Republic of Congo, Cote d'Ivoire, Sierra Leone etc., are explained in terms of ethnic diversities and discord. For example, the civil wars in Ethiopia were characterised as wars between the Amharas and the Tigreans, Oromos and Eritreans; the conflict in Djibouti as between the Afars and the Issas; the civil war in Uganda as between Baganda, Langi, Acholi and Kakwa; the tribal clashes and contests in Kenya are between Kikuyu, Luo, Somali and Kalenjin. Even in homogenous Somalia, conflicts areexplained in terms of clans and sub-clans like Maraheen and Isaaq or Darod and Ogadeni. There are at least about 3,000 ethnic groups living in Africa, many of them are extended across the borders of more than one country. Africans, in full diversity, are the natural inhabitants of the African landscape.

But is it ethnicity, as such, which is the cause of conflicts? Or is it the political and economic marginalisation of some groups within society by the authority at the time? That marginalisation may well be exploited by politicised elites, who belong to those groups in order to enhance their own political career by capitalising on the misery of their people. The evidence for such behaviour is abundant among multi-party countries, where we find leaders of the marginalised ethnic groups change their support to the same ruling parties that they accused of neglecting their people or regions. The conditions of their people may continue as they were before they happily joined the government. Thus, the socioeconomic basis of ethnic hostility must be given due weight with the role of the ethnic factor. What is called ethnic conflict may just be an elite-driven conflict covered up in ethnicity. It is true that the region's ethnic groups have their own prejudices and stereotypes about each other, but these attitudes do not normally turn into conflict at the grassroots level unless they are manipulated and organised by political leaders. However, the political solution cannot be the separation of marginalised regions from the mother country as happened in the cases of Eritrea and southern Sudan, because ethnic diversity continues in the new states as it was in the old country. The difference may be that a minority ethnic group in the old country has become a majority in the new state, like the highland Tigreans of Eritrea and the Dinka of South Sudan. Once the conflict starts in the name of an ethnic group or region, fear and further animosity pervade the whole group or groups whose members are perceived as the enemy. Interestingly, neither in Ethiopia nor in Sudan or the Horn in general have we come across people-to-people violence between the so-called ethnic enemies. The conflict is mainly between 'liberation' groups and the central government which is dominated by one or more ethnic groups.

After the independence of African countries in the 1960s, liberal democracy was adopted for a short period before military regimes and one-party systems dominated the scene in most countries. The pretext for authoritarian rule was that the multi-party system did not suit the African societies divided along the bases of tribes. The autocratic rulers justified the hegemony of their power in the name of building a whole nation instead of fragmenting the country according to ethnic lines. They ended up of empowering their own ethnic communities at the expense of marginalising others, without much success in achieving their declared objective of nation-building. During the last decade of the 20th century which witnessed the collapse of the totalitarian socialist regimes in the Soviet Union and Eastern Europe, African countries started to go back to some form of democratic system of government and multi-party politics. After a long oppressive rule, it is not surprising to find out that ethnic groups emerged as the most important bases for political parties.

The Tigrean People's Liberation Front (WOYANNE) which toppled Mengistu's rule in 1991 declared that the most important issue facing the country was the 'nationalities question', and proceeded to decree that all ethnic groups, nationalities and peoples in the country could define their own territory, form their own governments, and exercise self-determination even for an independence option. The map of the country has been redrawn according to ethnic zones; but as demarcating boundaries based on ethnicity is not an easy task, the map has been redrawn more than once. However, the ruling alliance "Ethiopian People's Revolutionary Democratic Front" did its best to win the election in 2005 and 2010 by more than 90 per cent, leaving the crushed opposition to allege and cry about foul play! While in the past civil wars were waged between the central government and insurgences bearing ethnic names; in the current situation peoples of different ethnic backgrounds are confronting each other on boundaries and landownership. The Ethiopian model may not be the right approach to solve the ethnic problem in the African context. To view every problem in the country from an ethnic point of view is an unwarranted exaggeration; poverty, lack of development and services, high unemployment, class analysis and elite exploitation may go a long way to explain the country's situation. Primordial ties are ill-fitted to define a nation, there are many capable citizens who would feel that their primordial roots do not necessarily reflect their interests, needs and aspirations. The two conflicting demands of 'nation-building' and 'self-determination' have embroiled the Horn of Africa, as much of the African continent, in decades of wars and destruction. The whole notion of ethnic animosity and the domination of one ethnic group by another as the real cause of conflicts in the country, and that the solution to conflicts is the secession of the marginalised group as an independent state, is a serious and wrong conclusion.

The Ethiopian researcher, Hizkias Assefa, might have managed the right balance by advocating the address of the economic and political inequities in the system, enlarging the economic base to share resources with various ethnic groups and opening up the political system so that everyone can have access to it. The system of governance should be really democratic and respect the human rights of all citizens, allowing freedom of expression and association. A mechanism must be found to legitimise ethnic identity without making it incompatible with the formation of a larger unit of identity based on mutuality and beneficial collaboration. In this regard, a loose federal system of governance supplemented by infrastructures oriented towards regional integration may be the right answer for the dilemma of ethnic solidarity and national identity.

Conclusion

The recent developments which took place till June 2012 proved that the separation of the countries was neither smooth nor peaceful. The negotiations on the outstanding issues dragged on till May 2012 without solving most of them. A number of armed clashes took place between the two parties. The Sudan Armed Forces invaded the region of Abyei in May 2011 after one of their withdrawing units was attacked by southern soldiers, despite the fact that it was accompanied by UN officials using their marked cars. The SPLA captured the oil-producing Heglig of the North in April 2012, but it was forced to withdraw under international pressure. A conflict erupted in southern Kordofan and Blue Nile in June 2012 between the government and the northern section of SPLA, and the GoS accused the GoSS of supporting the rebellion. Tribal conflicts and rebellious generals spread violence in a number of states in the South; the south government also accused the North of helping the rebels against the legal authority. Each government believed that the other wanted to overthrow its regime, which belief made the relationship between the two countries tense and acrimonious was and therefore not conducive to solving the outstanding issues. As a matter of fact, GoSS claimed other five regions in the North which were not disputed in the Joint Technical Boundary Committee which delimited the border between the two countries; although the president of southern Sudan affirmed the delimitation as a senior member of the presidency.

The government of the South produced its own self-made map, in which it included all the disputed regions in the North and a few others in Uganda. The AUHIP rejected the map as a reference for the negotiations on the border. After the attack on Heglig in April 2012, the Peace and Security Council of the African Union and the Security Council of the United Nations passed similar resolutions demanding: the immediate cessation of hostilities; the withdrawal of all armed forces to their side of the border; cessation of helping rebel groups against the other state; and, resumption of negotiations between the two parties under the auspices of AUHIP to reach a settlement on all outstanding issues within three months. The SC resolution threatened to take appropriate measures against the party/parties which obstruct a negotiated settlement under article 41 of the UN Charter. Furthermore, it may impose a settlement on both parties on the bases of detailed proposals on all outstanding issues required from the AUHIP.

The economic situation in the two countries became seriously bad after the North lost its share in the oil revenue of the South, and the South closed its oil fields because no agreement has been reached with the North to transport the oil for export. The World Bank analysis of the economic and social impact of the shutdown of oil in the South gives a bleak picture of the economic situation and its repercussions in South Sudan. Besides the threats of the SC, the two countries have areas of vital common interest which they should care about: oil, Nile waters, cross-border trade and cattle-grazing, and shared systems of administration and social services inherited from the British during the colonial era. They have the potentials and conditions which allow them to co-exit in peace and cooperation. The international community should exert strong pressure, in a fair way, on both belligerent countries to reach a satisfactory settlement on all their differences. However, the experience of South Sudan like that of Eritrea showed that separation of a united country in Africa proved to be serious and of grave consequences to both separating states.

References

Concordis International, 2010, 'More than a Line: Sudan's North-South Border', September.
Constitution of the Federal Democratic Republic of Ethiopia, 1994, Addis Ababa, December.
Hizkias Assefa, 1996, *Ethnic Conflict in the Horn of Africa: Myth and Reality.*
Mahgoub M. Salih, 2011, 'The Outstanding Issues and the Future of North-South Relations', Unpublished article (Arabic), March.
Marcelo Giugale, 2012, 'Analysis of the Likely Economic and Social Impact of the Shutdown of Oil in South Sudan', March.
PSCAU, 'COMMUNIQUE', 319th Ministerial Meeting, 24 April 2012.
The Comprehensive Peace Agreement between the Government of the Republic of the Sudan and SPLM/A, Nairobi, 9 January 2005.
The Referendum Results, January 2011.
UN Security Council, 2012, 'Resolution 2046 (2o12) on Sudan & South Sudan', New York, 5 May.

3

Consequences of the Secession of Southern Sudan on the Region

Hamed Omer Hawi

Introduction

On 15 January 2011, the people of southern Sudan voted by an overwhelming majority of 98.6 per cent in favour of secession from the united Sudan. The referendum on self-determination was a condition in the Comprehensive Peace Agreement (CPA), which was signed between the Sudan People's Liberation Movement/Army (SPLM/A), the major rebel group in southern Sudan, and the ruling National Congress Party (NCP), at Naivasha, Kenya, in January 2005. The CPA was not as inclusive as it should be; it excluded the major political powers in northern Sudan and significant parties in the South. It gave the two warring parties full domination over the country, SPLM in the South and NCP in the North; they were in a position to determine the future of the Sudan after asix-year interim periodwithout a popular mandate.

The promise to make unity attractive as stipulated in the CPA became unattainable in the neglected conditions of democratic transformation, government of real national unity and genuine partnership between the two parties during the interim period. Under such environment, it is not possible to provide political solutionsfor the problems of the whole country or neither its two regions, north and south. It is more likely to complicate and aggravate the situation which will lead to a tense and incriminatory relationship between the two emerging states and their internal politics. The dire situation will have its negative impact on neighbouring countries and the region at large, because secession is bound to influence ethnic communities in the region. Forecasting the future at this stage may not be easy, but policies of the two governments and some news reports in each country indicate alarming consequences.

Is Secession a Viable Solution?

According to Braizat (2011), secession of the South raises the question about the effectiveness of the policies pursued by successive Sudanese governments in the field of social integration; policies which, according to the result of the referendum (January 2011), led the southern Sudanese to opt for secession by an overwhelming majority. Sudanese governments failed to base unity of the country on common citizenship in which everyone enjoyed equality regardless of his ethnic, linguistic or cultural affiliations. To Al afif (2010), northern Sudan, identifying itself with Arabism and Islam as encompassing the whole country, excluded and resisted any reference to Sudan as part of Africa. Naturally southern Sudanese refused such tendency.

It is a sad experience that the Sudanese people failed to achieve unity, to build a state of justice, equality and devolution of powers to marginalised regions in the peripheries. They failed to foster an inclusive political system and to manage the complex diversity of the country in an equitable manner. No wonder, secession became an obvious outcome of the poor political behaviour of the ruling elite since independence in 1956 till the referendum in January 2011. The problem of the Sudan is not only in the South, it is the problem of all remote regions versus the centre which monopolises power and wealth, and creates its own elite that dominates political and economic institutions excluding the rest in the far regions. That explains the conflicts and rebellions in Darfur, southern Kordofan, Blue Nile and eastern Sudan. A viable and sustainable solution to the problems of Sudan cannot be found in a prolonged negotiation ending in peace agreements with some factions leaving others; it can only be achieved through a radical change in the structure and policies of the centre towards inclusive participation, plural democracy and social justice.

It is unfortunate that the South, fed up with a prolonged war and failed promises, decided to seize the available chance to sign a separate peace agreement with the government, retreating to its regional territory, trying to tackle its own problems regardless of what happens to its former allies in the North. Southern Sudanese may not be blamed or denied their rights for a separate state, but the problem of Sudan is not yet solved, nor that of the South. If the method of self-determination is implemented in other cases, the old Sudan will end up in five or more states. The South itself will not be immune to conflicts and divisions, because of its multiple ethnic groups and historical internal conflicts. It would have been better if the whole country adopted a complementary and collaborative approach to overcome the challenges of nation-building, development, democratic transformation and integration; otherwise each regional state would confront the serious challenges alone.

Secession may be a rational choice if we look only to the many grievances and bloodshed committed under the name of maintaining unity in the country. It appeared that the ruling elite have sacrificed unity for the sake of peace, because it is said 'peace is better than unity'. However, subsequent events proved the assumption is not true; since secession took place in July 2011, peace evaded us in the relationship between the two countries and within each state of the old Sudan. That is because neither southern Sudan nor northern Sudan is a homogeneous society; both are multi diversified in terms of ethnicity, culture and religion. Therefore, secession cannot be the answer to their diversity. If self-determination is to be applied as the only solution, the two states will end up in many ethnic conflicts and several secessions.

Consequences of Secession on the Relationship Between the Two States

Concerning the relationship between north and south, there are serious suspended issues that need to be addressed in order to achieve a normal and peaceful relationship. Those issues are: borders, Abyei, popular consultation in southern Kordofan and Blue Nile, debts and assets, citizenship, oil, Nile water among others

Borders

Sudan's long north-south border remains neither settled nor demarcated despite the efforts of the joint technical committee which worked on the subject for a number of years. The committee agreed on about 80 per cent of the 2,000-km-long border. There is an intensive human and animal mobility across the border which requires a quick and flexible solution.

Abyei

The contested region of Abyei, proved to be the most difficult issue since the drafting of the CPA in Naivasha. A large number of northern nomads settle and travel through the region annually to graze their cattle in the

South during the dry season and return in the rainy season. According to Douglas Johnson, a historian on Sudan and member of the Abyei Boundary Commission, 'Abyei has so far proved to be the most difficult part of the Comprehensive Peace Agreement (CPA) to implement, more difficult than the determination of the rest of the North-South boundary or the division of oil revenues' (Johnson 2006, www.riftvalley.net/publications).

Southern Kordofan and Blue Nile States

Both regions are part of the North but many of their young people supported SPLM/A and fought with its army against the Sudan government. They were given a special status in the CPA including the right for popular consultation at the end of the Interim Period, to decide if the CPA has addressed their grievances and the agreement has been implemented in a satisfactory way. The belt of the ten bordering states extending from Blue Nile to Upper Nile, southern Kordofan down to Western Bahr al-Ghazal to south Darfur is an integrated region in terms of language, culture, economic transaction and social mobility. Those states contain the majority of Sudan's natural resources (oil, agriculture, cattle, forestry…), and constitute one-third of Sudan total area and about 40 per cent of the whole population. Demarcation of a border in this region would sharply divide and cut off a fruitful relation among the peoples of this integrated belt which has existed for centuries, resulting in hardships for both communities across the border.

Citizenship

As a result of separation, hundreds of thousands of southerners living in the North and thousands of northerners residing in the South will suffer, because they do not have the right to choose the citizenship of the state in which they have settled down with their families for many years. About half of those people were born in the 'wrong side' of the border; they grew up and married in this part of the country, never conceiving that they would be foreigners in their chosen home. Issue of citizenship is not only legal, it carries significant economic and humanitarian dimensions that are yet to be solved.

Oil and Water

Oil reserves lie mainly in the South; however all its infrastructure and services are in the North (pipeline, chemical treatment, refineries, storage and the sea port). The two parties have to come to an agreement on how to use the facilities in the North and at what price. The Nile water running from south to north has to be shared between the two states in accordance with the 1959 agreement between Sudan and Egypt. Although the South is not in need of the Nile water at this time, it still has the right to know its share and to decide what to do with it. The bargain on oil and water is bound to be affected by a deal on other issues as well.

It is ironical that those issues, which have been difficult to solve, could have been strong elements to support the unity of the whole Sudan, because they demonstrate how interdependent the two sides of the country are. Aldabello (2010), an author from the integrated region, described the natural richness of the area in details, which would have been beneficial for both countries. It contains most of the current oil production, and known for its abundant rainfall, fertile soil and the diversity of its natural wealth. John Garang called the area a region of *Tamazuj* (intermix) rather than *Tamas* (adjacent), the commonly used name; and he thought the whole Sudan should be a country of *Tamazuj*. Time might prove to the governments of the two countries that they need each other more than they ever thought. However, the two present governments are not likely to attempt a stronger linkage between the two states because of bitter experiences, mutual mistrust, ideological differences and national aspirations. The common understanding which existed between the two delegations during the long process of Naivasha negotiations became something of the past; the scene has completely changed to the worse. Each government will take its course in a different direction. Islam and Arabism is expected to be strengthened in the North, while secularism and Africanism will be entrenched in the South. According to a public opinion survey conducted by Faris Braizat, 80 per cent of the Sudanese in the North support the removal of all restrictions on the travel of Arab citizens to the Sudan, and to allow free exchange of commodities with the Arab world, which indicates strong support for the policy of Pan-Arabism (Braisat 2011).

On the other hand, South Sudan is drawing closer to the East African countries in economy, politics and culture. East African states have benefited from the secession by opening their markets to the needs of the South: commodities, labour, investment and construction. The South found cheap skilled labour and a reachable market for its huge oil production. Nevertheless, it has real problems to deal with: ethnic diversity and conflicts, widespread poverty, high illiteracy rate, poor infrastructure, lack of basic social services and a flabby, inexperienced civil service, and rampant corruption. At the same time, expectations of the new-earned independence are high among the population, especially the youth. The North is bound to be a loser by the secession of the South because it lost 20 per cent of its population, 25 per cent of its land and about 40 per cent of its annual revenue. It marks a political failure to manage diversity in the country which still exists in the North. The North has to cope with the serious consequences of the secession: war in southern Kordofan and Blue Nile, increased tension in Darfur and maybe eastern Sudan; it further increased opposition in urban centres of the North and the hard-hit economy.

However, the difficult experience of secession might be in way usefulfor both countriesto reconsider their positions for the future; the new situation provides the two states with an opportunity to develop normal relations between two close neighbours without the bitterness, animosity and the huge cost of the long civil war. The troubled relationship of the past prevented any positive engagement or fruitful cooperation. Thus, after secession, the two states may be wise enough to engage peacefully with each other, seeking cooperation and friendly relations on the bases of common interests and mutual benefits.

Consequences of Secession on the Stability of the Region

Africa's founding fathers agreed on the borders left by colonial powers purposely to avoid the possible conflicts among rival tribes and the contest for natural resources across the borders in neighbouring independent states. The East African region in particular was described by International Crisis Group as having the following characteristics: history of regional meddling, proxy wars, cross-border entanglements, border disputes, resource competition and competing ideologies; besides a host of common ethnic groups which illustrate the interconnectedness of this region and the central position Sudan occupies in it (Crisis Group Report 2010).

The secession of southern Sudan is likely to affect the East African region as well as many African countries with similar diversity, ethnic structure and minority problems. However, some African leaders may choose to look at it from a positive angle, as president al-Bashir tried to do. He said at the occasion of announcing the result of the referendum: 'Secession of southern Sudan should not be viewed by African states as an inspiration for separation in other African countries; it should be looked at as an example of a peaceful settlement for a long conflict.In other words, instead of looking at the empty part of the cup, we try to see the full half.' The consequences of the secession of southern Sudan on the stability of the region depend mainly on the following factors:

(i) The nature of relationship that the two emerging states of Sudan will establish between them; positive relationship will have a positive impact on the region and the vice versa. Thus, it is important for neighbouring countries to support the establishment of good relations between the two sides of Sudan; they have potential capabilities of doing so, if they wish.

(ii) Since Sudan lies in the fort lines between Eastern, Central and North Africa regions (politically, socially and culturally); the internal policies adopted by each side can either foster good relations between the different regions of Africa or sensitise and provoke a negative impact. The success of each side in building a viable political system which serves the well-being of its people will help the whole region to interact positively.

(iii) The type of relations established by neighbouring countries with each part of the Sudan will have its good or bad impact. If it is a balanced, cooperative and non-interventionist relation, it will help both parts.

In the past, the problem of southern Sudan has created tensions between northern Sudan and neighboring countries, namely: Uganda, Eritria, Kenya and Ethiopia. All of them, at one time or another, helped southern rebel movements against the government of Khartoum. The realisation of secession will relieve the region from mutual hatreds and reciprocal destabilisation attempts caused by uneasy relations between north and south. Uganda, through its good relations with the new state of South Sudan, may succeed in solving the rebellion of the Lord's Resistance Army (LRA) in its northern border. Tensions between Sudan and other neighbouring countries may gradually be normalised and the whole region moves forward to build connecting roads, engages in the exchange of commodities and seeks different kinds of fruitful cooperation. However, this positive scenario requires a significant amount of goodwill on the part of neighbouring countries, particularly Uganda and Kenya that may feel threatened by good relationship between Sudan and South Sudan.

Positions of Neighbouring Countries

The neighbouring countries to Sudan were, directly or indirectly, affected by the civil war on its territory. Each state has its security concerns, economic interests, ideological preferences and external links that shape its policies towards Sudan. Most of them were in favour of an independent southern Sudan; they saw an economic opportunity in the oil wealth of the new state that can be utilised for their benefit. If we look at the positions of the closest neighbours to Sudan we will find the following:

Kenya

Kenya has supported SPLM since it was ousted from Ethiopia in 1991; and SPLM soon established its headquarters in Nairobi. Kenya became the logistical entrance for SPLM to all areas of southern Sudan. Since Kenya hosted the peace negotiations at Naivasha for three years, which produced the CPA that allowed the right for self-determination to the South, it is natural that it would expect to be rewarded for its services. It will set its eyes on big infrastructure projects, an emerging commodity market and an opening for investment and creation of jobs. Kenya Commercial Bank has already opened eight branches in South Sudan since 2006; hundreds of Kenyans have been working in construction, transport and the private commercial sector. Kenyan officials and South Sudanese started discussions on a multi-billion-dollar pipeline (1,400 km) from Juba to the coastal port of Lamu. Khartoum has registered repeated complaints protesting Kenya's direct involvement on issues dealing with its national sovereignty. In September 2008, a shipment of weapons including T-71 and T-72 tanks, anti-aircraft guns, RPG-7V grenade launchers, BM-21, 122 mm rocket launchers, thousands of rounds of ammunition, and spare parts was hijacked on the way by Somali pirates. It was ostensibly an acquisition of Kenya's defence ministry but it was purchased by the government of southern Sudan to be transported later to South Sudan. Kenyan officials acknowledged their government's role in facilitating weapons transfers to southern Sudan (Crisis Group Report, March 2010).

Uganda

Uganda has social and cultural ties with southern Sudan; the Acholi tribe has for many years lived across the border in both countries. Uganda has supported the rebel groups of southern Sudan since their first inception in 1955. After Naivasha agreement, while the official policy of Uganda was to respect the CPA which gives preference to unity, some senior officials in Kampala privately encouraged secession. Ugandan government announced in public forums that unity of the Sudan has not been made attractive to the southerners by their northern counterparts. A Ugandan minister said: Kampala may pay lip-service to orderly resolution of the CPA but will no doubt support independence of the South regardless of the recognition of Khartoum or even of African Union (Crisis Group, March 2010). Today, Ugandans are believed to be the largest group of foreign nationals working in South Sudan. Ugandan exports to the South showed three-fold increase in just two years (2006-2008) making South Sudan the number one recipient of Ugandan goods worldwide (Crisis Group,

May 2010). However, security considerations remain Kampala's primary strategic interest. Uganda continues to seek a strong security partner and stable buffer zone on its northern border, which it claims would help to prevent the re-emergence of insurgent groups. Besides, Uganda is afraid of an imagined Arab and Islamic expansion in the region.

Ethiopia

The Ethiopian government played the most crucial role in supporting SPLM/A during its early days of war in the 1990s. However, after the fall of Mengistu, things changed and relations with Khartoum were restored and economic relations were rapidly growing. Today, Ethiopia maintains significant ties with South Sudan while keeping good relations with Khartoum. Ethiopia has an interest to balance its relations with the two sides of Sudan, thus it took a neutral position towards independence of the South. Regional security remains a primary concern for Ethiopia, given the instability in Somalia, confrontation with Eritrea and its own domestic fragility. Addis Ababa can neither afford a renewed war in Sudan nor an additional enemy in Khartoum. It has its share of separatist groups, such as the Oromo and Ogden communities. This is why Ethiopia will not encourage a new dispute in the region. As a matter of fact, it aspires to win new friends to its side. In spite of that, Ethiopia supported the right of self-determination and showed its respect for the independence of the South. The religious and cultural ties with the South have been balanced by significant mutual economic benefits and water links with the North. But at one time, Ethiopia was accused of transporting armaments to Juba in 2008 (Lewis 2009).

In general, concerning the positions of the neighbouring countries towards separation of the South, it is only Ethiopia which remained neutral in the conflict with good relations with both sides. However, the shift of oil to the South and the future size of trade might outweigh in favour of stronger links with the new state. Meanwhile, the economic relationship between Juba and Addis Ababa has expanded considerably in the areas of investment, trade and communication. There are regular flights between the two cities, and the state-owned Commercial Bank of Ethiopia has begun business in South Sudan.

Eritrea

The Eritrean government faces a dilemma: on the one hand it supported the SPLM/A and Sudan's opposition groups; on the other hand it opted lately for stable relations with the government of Khartoum. In the early days of the Inter-governmental Authority on Development (IGAD) peace talks, it defended the principles of secular Sudan and the right of self-determination for southern Sudan. At that time it worked for regime change in Khartoum rather than for secession. Afewerki also supported the opposition of eastern and western Sudan (Beja Congress and Sudan Liberation Army of Darfur). In the meantime, finding himself isolated in the region, Afewerki made a rapprochement with Khartoum. He openly proposed the postponement of the referendum which Khartoum asked for; but to some observers, Eritrea's position on South Sudan independence is likewise unreliable. Afewerki's policy may be driven by self-preservation rather than principles. Being isolated in the region and beyond, he is ready to seek allies anywhere. He managed in the last few years to expand private business with South Sudan, which is likely to flourish because of Eritrea's rigid economic system.

The two Sudans' Future Trends: East African Community and the Arab World

The role played by East African Community (EAC) on the secession of southern Sudan has weakened the position of northern Sudan in the regional forum. Before referendum took place, senior members in EAC welcomed, in advance, the membership of South Sudan if it became an independent state. The government of Sudan viewed this stand as an encouragement for secession. On the other side, the community was divided on the membership of the Sudan; Uganda and Tanzania were openly against it and eventually it was referred to the next summit meeting. It is not likely that Sudan will get the membership of the EAC in the near future. A number of those countries took a position on the division of Nile Waters Agreement opposite to that of Egypt and Sudan, the South is likely to side with them. In the future, most likely the North will strengthen its economic and cultural relations with North Africa and the Arab world while South Sudan will build its relations with East and southern Africa. To some people in the North, although the IGAD played a positive role in reaching the peace agreement in Sudan, the price was very high for Sudan.

Sudan has always kept good relations with Arab countries, especially Egypt, Saudi Arabia and the Gulf states. In 2004, presidents Al-Bashir and Mubarak of Egypt signed the 'four freedoms agreement', guaranteeing freedom of movement, residence, work, and ownership of property in the two countries. Estimates put the number of Sudanese residing in Egypt today as high as three million. Because of its historical relationship and its strategic Nile link, Egypt has always supported the unity of Sudan. Despite American pressure, it has never accepted the right of self-determination for southern Sudan. On the other side of the Red Sea, hundreds of thousands of Sudanese are living and working in Saudi Arabia and other Gulf states earning considerable money to help their families back at home. The radical political changes towards democracy in North Africa and some other Arab countries will make economic and political collaboration with Sudan even stronger because of the popular Islamic dimension in all these countries. Sudanese relations with West Africa will remain unaffected and will continue to serve as a bridge between the North and other African countries, because of the significant Muslim presence in the region.

Conclusion

The real problem of the Sudan which led to the separation of the South and conflicts in other regions is the failure of the central authority, for many years, to manage diversity of the country on fair and equitable bases, besides external interventions. The government could not read the plain words on the wall that something drastic is going to happen unless the centre changes its attitude towards the marginalised regions. However, the CPA is designed to suit the hostile partners who wanted to grab power in the North and in the South. Other political powers in both regions were left with no role to play in the political drama going on in their midst. The southerners, who voted overwhelmingly in favour of secession, did not vote against the northerners but against the policies of the ruling elite which betrayed its national mission. It is not hopeless that sometime in the future the Sudanese people in the North and South will reconsider some form of unity or close relationship to bring them together. Both countries wanted peace, freedom, equality, stability and social welfare; if they do not achieve that by separation under their present semi-military governments, they may in the futureturn towards a form of unity again.

The survey conducted by Braizat (2011) concerning the views of northerners towards secession found out that 62 per cent of them were in favour of a future union; particularly the educated class which has always been against secession. There is also an inverse relationship in the survey between age and support for secession: the older a person is, the less likely he or she would support separation. The survey also showed that those who were economically poor and those who were less satisfied with government policies opposed secession; but the economically well off, and satisfied with government policies did not oppose secession (Braizat 2011:18).

Neighbouring countries might have done better for all of Africa if they supported the central idea of Dr John Garang, the charismatic leader of the SPLM, of a united new Sudan which shares power and wealth equally among its entire people irrespective of their race, culture or religion. The people of the North do sympathize with the southerners who suffered in the past, but they do not agree that their grievances should lead them to separation, realizing the agendas of colonial powers who worked for their own interests. Independence means that one should be one's own master instead of serving the policies of big powers anywhere. The big lesson for the North is that unity of the country cannot be achieved by repression or military means; it comes easily by justice, equality, freedom and good management of diversity.

References

Al afeif, El Bagir, 2010, *Crisis of Identity in Northern Sudan: Dilema of Black People with White Culture* (Arabic), translated by El Khatim Adlan Centre, Khartoum.

Aldabello, Sulaiman Mohammed, *Abyei: from Koka Dam to the Hague* (Arabic), Vol.1 Khartoum Institute for Press and Publication.

Braizat, Faris, 2011, *Sudanese Public Opinion after Secession*, Arab Centre for Research and Policy Studies, Doha.

Crisis Group Africa Report, May 2010, *Sudan: Regional Perspectives on the Prospect of Southern Independence*.

Crisis Group, February 2010, interviews with Kenyan officials.

Crisis Group, February 2010, interviews with senior officials in Juba, New York.

Deng, Francis, 1999, *Conflicting Visions: the struggle of identity in Sudan*, Vol.1, translated by Hassan Awad, Cairo: Centre for Sudanese Studies.

Johnson, H. D., 2003, *The Root Causes of Sudan's Civil Wars*, Bloomington.

Kulabako, F., 2010, 'Uganda-South Sudan trade expo on next month', *Daily Monitor*, Kampala, January.

Lewis, M., 2009, 'Skirting the Law: Post-CPA Arms Flows to Sudan', Sudan Working Paper No. 18, September.

Munzoul, A. M. Assal, 2011, *Nationality and Citizenship Questions in Sudan after the Southern Sudan Referendum Vote*, CHR Michelson Institute.

Raafat, Iglal, 2011, *Effects of Establishing Independent South Sudan on Sudan and Neighbouring Countries*, Doha: Arab Centre for Research and Policy Studies.

Sudan Issue Brief No.15, December 2009, 'Human Security Baseline Assessment'.

4

Implications of Southern Sudan's Independence for the Horn of Africa and Beyond

Kassahun Berhanu

Background

The Horn of Africa sub-region, of which Sudan is a constituent part, is famed as a place where aspiration of centrifugal forces to independent statehood is rampant as is the case in several other parts of the continent. The countries of the Horn are knit together by common socio-cultural and economic features that are underpinned by episodes of conflict and cooperation (Mukwaya 2006:35-56). While, on the one hand, they pose as hotbeds of intra and interstate conflicts, on the other hand theymanifest attempts at forging stability and cooperation. The Horn of Africa is still noted for the taking shape and escalation of violent conflicts marked by rebel activities, military coups, ethnic and ideology-based insurgencies, human rights violations, human and arms trafficking, interstate rivalry and state collapse, and currently terrorism. This has induced many scholars to label the region as an extension of the Middle East hot spot.

Sudan is the largest country in Africa comprising different major tribes and hundreds of smaller groups that are spread in 25 states, the totality of which make up the polity. During most of Sudan's early history, the different peoples have intermingled by co-existing under an environment of collision and collusion mediated by a host of historical, socio-economic and political forces and factors. During the post-colonial era that commenced in 1956, the peoples of Sudan experienced major tribulations and cleavages that adversely impacted on efforts towards realizing political stability and national cohesion. The major historical drivers of contradictions among and between different sections of Sudanese society include a number of factors like identity (Arabism versus Africanism), religion (Islam versus Christianity), divergence on the form and essence of the state (secularism versus theocracy), governance failure, uneven regional development, and skewed distribution of societal resources (wealth and positional goods). The post-independence history of Sudan is replete with prolonged bloody civil wars of which the first civil war (1955-1972), the second civil war (1983-2005), including the ongoing Darfur crisis, are the major ones; prompting a number of peace-building initiatives spearheaded by third parties of various persuasions at varying times (Johnson 2006:93). Of these initiatives, the most significant ones are the 1972 Addis Ababa Accord and the 2005 Comprehensive Peace Agreement (CPA), widely regarded as groundbreaking in terms of putting an end to the first and second civil wars of the post-colonial era respectively. The CPA is the more acclaimed of the two not only for its role in closing one of the few enduring civil wars (1983-2005) in the continent but also its relevance to the issue under consideration.

This chapter seeks to examine the likelihood of southern Sudan's accession to independent statehood, resulting from the outcomes of the recent referendum as stipulated by the Comprehensive Peace Agreement, and the multifaceted implications thereof for the Horn of Africa sub-region.

Antecedents Revisited

Studies conducted so far dealing with Sudanese civil wars and aimed at providing a clear picture of their underlying causes, processes and dynamics, actors, peace-building initiatives, the CPA, and issues surrounding probable developments in the post-referendum years are limited in scope and coverage. This is notwithstanding that several scholars have attempted to shed light on the aforementioned concerns by focusing on one or a few aspects of them. Whereas some argue that the problem of the north-south conflict is embedded in the policy of British colonial rule that propelled socio-economic disparity and uneven development, instilling a sense of distinctiveness between the two (al-Rahim 1973:11), others are of the view that the root causes of the unfolding and escalation of the conflicts could be attributed to racial, religious, and cultural differences resulting in stereotype, discrimination and marginalisation. A careful look at the pre-independence political history of the Sudan, however, attests to the validity of the two views that in combination reinforced each other, thereby laying the basis for north-south dichotomy and divergence, entailing the predicaments that Sudanese societies were forced to endure. Hence the unfolding of the two civil wars is a consequence of the interplay of several of the aforementioned factors rather than an outcome of single, isolated triggers. Nevertheless, other factors such as ethnicity, religion and ideology served as fallbacks to enforce claims and counterclaims of the major protagonists that invoked them. It is worth noting also that the super-imposed merger of north and South Sudan as one independent country in the mid-1950s appears to have compounded the already existing problems rather than addressing them. These problems wereexacerbated by the ill-devised policies and attendant practices of successive civilian and military regimes that controlled the reins of power in post-independence yearswhich brought about the mishaps that wreaked havoc on the major fabrics of societal life (Hamid 1989). The kindling point that plunged the Sudan into the first civil war was the imposition of the Arabic language and Islam throughout Sudan during the Aboud military regime (1958-1964) that sought to enforce them through state repression directed mainly against southerners. The latter responded by recourse to armed resistance through the agency of their insurgent movements (Anyanya I and II) that spearheaded the struggle for secession of the South (Kebede 1999:14).

The first civil war came to a halt following the signing of the Addis Ababa Accord in 1972. Based on the agreement reached between the Numeiry regime and the Anyanya, the Accord stipulated that southern Sudan was to benefit from arrangements of wealth and power-sharing and most notably from the right to enjoy regional autonomy. Accordingly, the South was made a self-governing unit with its own legislative, executive and judiciary institutions using English as the working language of the region and the Anyanya army was integrated into the national defense force serving in the South (Wama 1997:9). However, the central element of the Accord aimed as stalling the quest for secession by limiting the terms of settlement to autonomy within an overall framework of preserving national unity soon came to naught. In the hope of curtailing possibilities for any unified southern opposition, the Numeiry regime amended the national constitution in 1980 by dividing southern Sudan into three provinces in contravention to the intent and spirit of the Accord. To make matters worse, the regime declared the imposition of Sharia law to be applied in the country in 1983. Moreover, the discovery of oil near Benitu in southern Sudan prompted the government to resort to scheming aimed at subsuming Benitu within North Sudan. The cumulative effect of all these led to the de facto abrogation of the 1972 Agreement and the resumption of another round of conflict between the government and the SPLM/A, formed in 1983 in Ethiopia, under the leadership of Colonel John Garang Mabior setting the stage for the commencement of the second civil war that lasted for over two decades.

In the subsequent years following the ouster of Numeiry, military and civilian regimes alternated in power until the overthrow of Sadiq al-Mahdi's civilian coalition by a joint military coup led by Omar Hassan al-Bashir and Hassan-al-Turabi's National Islamic Front (NIF). This came to pass amidst a raging civil war and haphazard efforts that were underway to resolve the problem. The NIF-led military regime intensified its war efforts in the hope of pulverising the SPLM/A, which proved futile but entailed misery and devastation thereby deepening the already looming crisis (Mersha 2004:52). The human cost of the conflict was so immense that about two million people mainly from southern Sudan died; 5.5 million people, mainly southerners, were displaced and more than half a million people fled seeking refuge in neighbouring localities in Ethiopia, Uganda, the Democratic Republic of Congo and Central African Republic (Edward 2007:227-28). As the conflict persisted and assumed regional and international dimensions, several state and non-state external actors across a wider spectrum got directly and indirectly involved, thereby making the conflict bloodier and more intricate and also changing its dynamics (Hardallu 2001:261). These impacted on the balance of power between the NCP and SPLM/A and the course of peacemaking initiatives. After a series of protracted efforts, the Bashir regime and the SPLM/A came to the negotiation table and finally signed a historic peace accord known as the Comprehensive Peace Agreement (CPA) in Naivasha, Kenya, in 2005.

The CPA as Groundbreaking

The CPA is the composite of six agreements, namely: the Machakos protocol, the protocol on security arrangements, and the protocols on the resolution of conflicts in the three areas of Abyei, Nuba Mountains, and the Blue Nile signed in Kenya between 2002 and 2004 by the GoS and the SPLM/A. It is hailed as a serious and historic instrument embodying several sections dealing with power and wealth-sharing arrangements that are deemed crucial in addressing the underlying causes and escalation of recurrent conflicts (Healy 2008:36). With some justification and despite its alleged shortcomings, the CPA is viewed as an important milestone in shaping recent political developments in the Sudan in the sense of setting the stage for transformation towards a better future anchored in equality, democracy and justice. To this end, it made it incumbent on the signatories to commit themselves to the implementation of the terms and conditions enshrined in the agreement by displaying unfailing commitment that translates into practice. As one of the building blocks of the CPA, the Machakos protocol represents the basis for the other edifices in that it comprises a broad framework setting forth the principles of governance during the interim period and thereafter. Indeed, the Machakos protocol is about transforming the political landscape and state-society relations by extricating the country from the ills of war, deprivation, authoritarianism, human rights violations through entrenching an overall environment marked by democracy and equitable sharing (Large 2010).

The CPA provides for the establishment of an autonomous Government of southern Sudan (GoSS) and associated local governments including their participation in the Government of National Unity (GoNU). GoSS is also entitled to exercise powers and functions other than those reserved for GoNU (national security, nationality, immigration, foreign policy, currency, national natural resources, etc). As per the pertinent provisions of the CPA, in the run up to the national elections, seats in the national legislature shall be allocated to NCP (52%), SPLM (28%), non-signatory northern political forces (14%), and non-signatory southern political forces (6%). Moreover, the CPA stipulated the establishment of commissions such as National Constitutional Review Commission charged with the task of promulgating an interim national constitution for the transitional period, and the southern Sudan Referendum Commission that monitors the January 2011 referendum on self-determination of the people of southern Sudan, among others.

Wealth-sharing provisions relating to land ownership and natural resources and oil and non-oil revenues are also included. Although issues of land and natural resources are not thoroughly addressed, the CPA provides for the establishment of a National Land Commission, and a southern Sudan Land Commission to arbitrate contentions over such resources without contravening the jurisdiction of the courts (UNMIS 2010:19). With regard to oil revenues, guiding principles for the management and sharing of oil resources are issued by providing for the establishment of a National Petroleum Commission charged with the task of formulating policies and monitoring their implementation. As per the provision, at least 2 per cent of the net oil revenue is assigned to oil producing regions and the rest produced in southern Sudan is apportioned equally between GoNU and GoSS, whereas oil produced in the North belongs exclusively to GoNU. Terms of sharing between GoNU and GoSS of non-oil revenues originating from federal sources in the South such as customs and immigration, airport taxes etc. are also specified in the protocol on wealth-sharing.

The protocol on the three areas of Abyei, Nuba Mountains, and the Blue Nile also constitutes an essential component of the CPA. Abyei is a contested area situated between Bahr el-Ghazal in the south and southern Kordofan in the North. Due to historical factors dating back to colonial rule in the first decade of the twentieth century, Abyei is tied up with both North and South Sudan in geographic, ethnic, and political terms. In the light of this, the area is provided with special administrative status under a local executive council whose members are to be elected by its residents. As stated in the CPA, the onus of determining its boundaries rests on the Abyei Boundary Commission (ABC) to come up with 'final and binding' decision. The CPA states that at the end of the interim period in 2011, the residents of Abyei are entitled to cast their votes either to remain in the North or form part of southern Sudan in the referendum due to be held simultaneously with that of southern Sudan. However, the populations of Nuba Mountains and Blue Nile State are given the right to engage in 'popular consultation' through which they can reflect their views on the terms of the CPA applicable to them. The protocol on security arrangements provided for the establishment of a Ceasefire Political Commission (CPC) composed of senior military representatives from both sides to supervise the implementation of permanent ceasefire arrangements and determine the implementation modalities. As per this protocol, the troops of both contracting parties shall be redeployed along the line of the north-south border of 1 January 1956. Joint Integrated Units (JIUs) are also to be constituted drawn from the Sudan Armed Forces (SAF) and SPLA to act as symbols of national unity and expected to pose as a new national army provided that the referendum affirms unity against southern separation. The two parties are also duty bound to discharge the tasks of disarming, demobilising or reintegrating other armed forces aligned with either of them, thereby affirming the SAF and SPLA as the only legally recognized armed forces operating in the country.

Progress in Implementation

Since the commencement of the implementation of the CPA in 2005, several obligations and commitments specified thereof have been enforced in stages, albeit surrounded by political controversies and misgivings between the parties regarding a number of issues. Regarding the power-sharing aspect of the agreement, the promulgation of the Interim National Constitution on 9 July 2005 as a supreme law of the land became an entry point for subsequent undertakings marking the end of the pre-interim period. Accordingly, the GoNU was instituted with al-Bashir as president, John Garang as first vice-president, and Ali Osman Taha as vice president. A month later, the national legislature comprising the council of states and the national assembly was formed on 31 August 2005. As per the CPA power-sharing formula, the council of states was composed of two representatives of each of the 25 states and two representing Abyei, whereas the national assembly was composed of a total of 450 members apportioned as follows: NCP (234 members), SPLM (126 members), other northern political forces (55 members), other southern political forces (27 members), and nationally recognized celebrities (8 members). GoNU formed the National Elections Commission on 17 November 2008 to expedite preparations for the subsequent national elections. With the aim of consolidating the country's democratic transition and installing a responsible national government to oversee the January 2011 referendum, national elections were carried out. In January 2010, voter registration and candidate nominations were completed in which 16.4 million voters were registered and 72 political parties contested by fielding 12 candidates for the office of the president, 2 for the office of president of GoSS, 189 for state governors, and 4,136 for national assembly membership. The election was held from 11-15 April 2010, and after a week the commission disclosed the results, in which NCP candidate Omar al-Bashir was declared as elected securing 68.24 per cent of the votes cast and the SPLM candidate, Salva Kiir, maintained his incumbency as president of GoSS wining 93 per cent of the votes cast in the contest.

The GoNU established the National Population Census Council (NPCC), which conducted a national census between April and May 2008 with a view to preparing the ground for the April 2010 elections and the 2011 referendum on self-determination of Southern Sudan and Abyei. Its report dubbed 'Sudan Census Priority Results' was officially released showing that northern Sudan accounts for 78.9 per cent while southern Sudan constitutes 21.1 per cent of the total population of the country. However, SPLM/A rejected the results as being 'flawed and incredible', and warned GoNU against using it as a basis for adjusting the power-sharing and wealth-sharing arrangements (DRDC 2010). As provided for in the Machakos protocol, the Southern Sudan Referendum Act was issued in 2009 establishing the Southern Sudan Referendum Commission on 23 August 2010 to organize and conduct the referendum by preparing a referendum register, formulating rules and regulations, setting referendum duration, sorting and counting votes, laying the criteria for affirmation of results, and taking disciplinary measures on voters, among others. The Referendum Act states that a simple majority (50% +1 of the votes cast) decides the outcome of the referendum on the proviso that 60 per cent or more of the registered voters turn out for the referendum in order to qualify it as valid. It was decided that failure to meet these conditions shall lead to a repeat vote within 60 days. Accordingly, voter registration commenced on 14 November 2010 lasting until 8 December 2010 in the course of which a total of four million Southern Sudanese were registered to cast their votes starting on 9 January 2011 *(Daily Monitor* 2010:4).

A great deal of *progress* has been made with respect to implementing the wealth-sharing protocol. Oil revenue-sharing has been undertaken since 2005 through the National Petroleum Commission. According to IMF reports, oil revenue covers 98 per cent and 60-70 per cent of the GoSS and GoNU budgets respectively (ISS 2009:no.6). The ministry of finance and economic planning of the GoSS reported that it received $669.92 million from the national government as its share of oil revenue for the first quarter of 2010.

Deficits in Implementation

Despite the aforementioned progress and positive developments, a number of shortcomings and drawbacks could be discerned in the overall balance sheet of the implementation process. For example, implementation of some important provisions such as conducting population census and undertaking national elections, among others, was allegedly behind schedule. As stated in the Machakos protocol, conducting the national population census should have been accomplished within two years following the commencement of the interim period (before 9 July 2007) as a precondition that forms the basis for conducting national elections and the January 2011 referendum. Funding and other capacity constraints were mentioned as causes for the delay (Brosche 2007:1-24). It could be claimed that, regardless of the validity of the justification, delays in implementation at times not only exacerbated the existing mistrust between the parties but also entailed political crisis that could have had far-reaching consequences. A case in point is SPLM/A's temporary suspension of its participation in GoNU in October 2007 on account of several defaults in border demarcation, redeployment, and transparency of oil revenues. This notwithstanding, however, SPLM/A resumed its participation a month later and thus salvaged the CPA from floundering. Nonetheless, the CPA's resilience was undermined on several occasions as a result of tacit manoeuvrings of the NCP driven by reluctance in enforcing several aspects of the agreement out of fear of being at the losing side. Different reports and controversies surrounding accusations and counter-accusations indicate that CPA's implementation was bedevilled by unevenness across the various provisions based on the selective preferences of the two parties.

According to some sources, implementation of the CPA provisions that are applicable to the three transitional areas, namely, Abyei, the Nuba Mountains, and the Blue Nile states did not show much progress. Whereas the latter two are granted only the right to popular consultation through which their legislatures can reassess their political arrangements and raise their concerns for renegotiation, Abyei was accorded special treatment (see the Abyei Annex and Protocol) in the CPA as compared to the other two. Abyei featured high in the series of negotiations that took place between the government of Sudan and the SPLM/A leading to the signing of the CPA. The negotiations took note of the importance of Abyei and formulated a special protocol, which was annexed to the main document designated as the Abyei Annex.

The two principals to the CPA agreed on a number of issues like setting up a special administration for Abyei under the Presidency of GoNU, the sharing of oil revenues originating from the locality, continued and unhindered access to traditional grazing areas by both Ngok Dinka and the Misseriya, and allowing the residents of Abyei to vote whether they wish to become part of the South or remain in the North at the end of the six-year interim period. The signatories, however, differed on the issue of defining the area that constitutes the Abyei Special Administration. It was in this connection that agreement was reached to establish the Abyei Boundary Commission (ABC) with a mandate '…to define and demarcate the nine Ngok Dinka Chiefdoms transferred to Kordofan in 1905'.

The final text of the Abyei Annex adopted by the two parties determined the composition of the 15-member ABC, which shall include five persons each representing the delegations of NCP and SPLM/A, and five impartial experts nominated by the US (1), the UK (1), and IGAD (3). As stipulated in the Annex, the ABC was charged with the task of collecting testimonies from the representatives of the people of Abyei and the surrounding areas, listening to the presentations of the two delegations, and collecting pertinent material on the Sudan from the British Archives and other pertinent sources. This was aimed at enabling the Commission to 'arrive at a decision that shall be based on scientific analyses and research'. Accordingly, in April 2005, the experts proposed the Rules of Procedure that were unanimously adopted by the delegations of the two Principals as final and binding on the parties. It was clearly stated in the Rules of Procedure that in the absence of consensus based on mutually agreed position of the two sides, the experts were charged with the task of pronouncing a final and binding decision to the Presidency of GoNU (Johnson 2011:3).

In the absence of consensus on the part of the delegations of the two principals (NCP and SPLM) and after careful consideration of the propositions made by the two delegations and a thorough examination of available evidence collected from the aforementioned primary and secondary sources, the team of experts made a decision that the nine Ngok Dinka chiefdoms were located in and around the contested Abyei Area (including Abyei town) at the time of the transfer of the locality from Bahr-el-Ghazal in the South to Kordofan in the North by the colonial administration in 1905. The team of experts nominated by the governments of the US, UK and IGAD officially and formally communicated their decision to this effect to the Presidency of GoNU on 14 July 2005. This was immediately rejected by President Bashir and the leadership of the NCP on the grounds that the experts exceeded their mandate. Disagreement over this issue lingered until 2008 leading to an armed confrontation between SAF and SPLA in and around Abyei town. After some bloodletting and dislocation, the two sides agreed to take the matter to the Permanent Court of Arbitration (PCA) in the Hague, which in July 2009 ruled on the case by defining another territorial boundary of Abyei to an area focused on the permanent settlements of the Ngok Dinka. The ruling gave control of the oil fields in the north-east corner of the region to the North. On the other hand, the focus of the PCA decision on the area of the Ngok permanent settlements excluded much of the area settled by the Misseriya during the war on the basis of which demarcation of the new boundary was envisaged to take place in 2009, which did not materialise due to the resistance of 'local elements of SAF and the Misseriya'. It is argued that 'Abyei has so far proved to be the most difficult part of the Comprehensive Peace Agreement (CPA) to implement, more difficult, even than the determination of the rest of the north-south boundary or the division of oil revenues'.

The implementation of the CPA has so far encountered several obstacles such as the lack of will on the part of the NCP, the lack of capacity on the part of the SPLM/A, and the lack of continued engagement and perseverance on the part of the international community whose attention is deflected by what they view as more urgent and pressing concerns. The NCP also appeared to have anticipated that the South would vote for secession anyway and thus saw no need to labour on CPA's implementation. On the other hand, the SPLM/A also seemed to have been less committed to implementing the macro aspects of the CPA by working towards ensuring that the outcome of the referendum results in the crowning of its desired goal of separation (ICG 2006:3). In a nutshell, the CPA has made remarkable progress despite several shortfalls that tended to threaten its potency at different times. Now that the outcome of the recent referendum has amply demonstrated the indomitable will of the people of Southern Sudan to realize the highly cherished goal of accession to independent statehood, it is worthwhile to attend to possible developments that accompany the birth of a new independent polity in the Horn of Africa, namely Southern Sudan.

Implications of South Sudan's Independence for the Sub-region

Following the signing of the CPA in January 2005, the separation versus unity prospect in the post-interim period has been the centrepiece of political speculations, projections and manoeuvrings of different sets of potential and actual stakeholders in the Sudan itself and beyond. This is notably more of an issue of concern prevalent in the line of thinking and tactics and strategies of the two major protagonists, namely the NCP and the SPLM/A. On top of a history of oppression and bloody confrontation that underlie the old relations of the two major actors, there has been a pronounced incongruence between the NCP's rhetoric favouring the CPA's implementation on the one hand and its practices marked by half-hearted commitment on the other. This contradictory approach culminated in the entrenchment of mutual mistrust exhibited at different times. In the subsequent years following the tragic death of John Garang in particular, the mutual and reciprocal antagonism and suspicion began to deepen and gain ground over time thereby strengthening the position of hardliners in the ranks of both groups.

Way back prior to the January referendum, several pointers indicated that secession had become virtually inevitable and that the priority objective of democratic transformation of a united Sudan became a questionable scenario. For instance, the SPLM/A candidate for the office of president, Yasir Arman withdrew from the contest in the June 2010 national elections alleging that the exercise was not free, fair, and democratic signalling SPLM/A's possible disengagement from national politics. Moreover, the SPLM/A appeared to be highly suspicious of the possibility of transforming Sudanese national politics due to NCP's intransigence as regards resolving the underlying causes that triggered the crisis in Darfur. Another signpost eclipsing prospects for a united Sudan related to SPLM/A's interpretation of the then forthcoming referendum as the 'final walk to freedom' or 'freedom through referendum' as signified by the release of a new Southern Sudanese national anthem that exhorted southerners to seriously think of opting out. This was compounded by the 31 October 2009 speech of GoSS President, Salva Kiir Mayardit, urging Southern Sudanese to vote for independence by saying, 'you have the opportunity to choose between being free in our own nation or second class citizens in a unified country' (Said 2010:1). In short, the possibility for making 'unity attractive' seems to have been relegated to the backyard when the fateful day of conducting the referendum came on the scene, resulting in the overwhelming vote cast by southerners in favour of separation. Save for some isolated incidents in the Abyei area, the referendum was carried out in a manner free of tensions and violent confrontation. As stated by President Bashir, the NCP was committed to duly acknowledging and accepting the outcome.

Now that the secession of Southern Sudan appears to be a foregone issue, shedding light on possible developments that impact on the state of affairs both in the Sudan and the Horn of Africa would be worthwhile. Among others, these include: citizenship and identity; security in general and human security in particular; access to and management of resources (oil and Nile waters); borders and movement of peoples; livestock and goods; and, infrastructural development and regional integration.

Citizenship and Identity

In view of the outcomes of the recent referendum, negotiations associated with citizenship that were already underway between NCP and SPLM/A under the auspices of the AU along with other post-referendum issues such as border demarcation, national assets and debt, a new oil deal and sharing of the Nile water resources should continue in earnest (AU 2010:4). It has been noted that many southerners living in the North have already started moving back to the South for fear of facing probable persecution in case of subsequent developments following the outcomes of the referendum. In the negotiations on citizenship, the two parties to the CPA agreed that 'citizenship status of the people would not change' and 'their rights remain intact anywhere in the country' until new nationality laws are promulgated by both the North and the South following the expiry of the CPA in July 2011 (ICG 2010:7). Given the recent developments signified by indications of the inevitability of the separation of South Sudan, determination of the citizenship status of southerners in the North and northerners in the South in the times ahead remains a daunting task.

On the other hand, inter-ethnic rivalry could threaten the peace dividend brought about by the CPA and make the new polity of South Sudan fragile unless divisions and rivalries within the South itself are overcome through recourse to a variety of confidence-building measures. It is known that South Sudan is not a homogeneous entity given the existence of dozens of ethno-cultural formations (the major ones being the Dinka, the Nuer, and the Shilluk) whose inter-ethnic relations have been marred by a plethora of competitions and rivalries over various issues during both the distant and recent past. The future, therefore, is replete with several challenges that necessitating that the SPLM/A employs foresight and builds capacity so as tolay conducive ground to handle identity and citizenship-related concerns within the South and beyond its new borders where ethno-cultural affinities and boundary contiguities overlap. In this regard, potential sources of mutual suspicion and antagonism should be properly addressed by entrenching an environment of trust and confidence across the board.

It should be noted that several ethnic groups led by their respective political entrepreneurs perceive that the leadership of the SPLM/A has been dominated by members of the Dinka ethnic group who allegedly control the security, the civil service and public resources under GoSS in a disproportionate manner (Wambugu 2010:17). Unless such perceptions and corresponding realities on the ground related to these are properly addressed in good time, a sense of insecurity and apprehension among other ethnic groups in the South can prevail thereby laying the basis for internal split and factionalism in the ranks of the SPLM/A triggering alignments and counter-alignments along ethnic lines with far-reaching consequences, giving rise to internal fragmentation and eventual civil war. Moreover, the problem can affect the relations between the new polity and its neighbours, where the existence of similar ethnic groups with diverse citizenship overlaps across their common borders warrants that they engage in unequivocal agreements to avert possible misunderstandings and rivalries that could unfold subsequently. The likely separation of South Sudan, therefore, necessitates recourse to negotiation between Sudanese across the broadspectrum involving all political actors on the one hand and neighbouring countries sharing borders with it on the other, to determine certain issues of paramount importance associated with citizenship and identity.

Security

The African Union has on various occasions urged both the North and the South to desist from extending support to opposition groups or insurgent movements seeking to operate against each by hosting them in territories under their jurisdictions. However, both parties have repeatedly got involved in mutual recriminations alleging that renegade factions and outside belligerents are threatening their security, or that of other states in the sub-region following the signing of the CPA. For ages, the people of Southern Sudan have been victims of injustice perpetrated first by Arab slave traders, followed by oppressive colonial rule and, subsequently, successive post-colonial regimes. It is clear that the common experiences of southerners in the past have nurtured a growing sense of southern nationalism consolidated by successive liberation movements, notably Anyanya I and Anyanya II, and finally SPLM/A. This evoked the perception that common southern identity is a product of shared experience of injustice and various other forms of alienation. Nevertheless, in the absence of foresight and proactive measures aimed at forging a durable sense of common belonging based on mutual respect, equitable sharing and equality, it is likely that the fledgling nation could encounter internal fragmentation. As envisaged in the CPA, both parties appear to have reneged on their pledges in terms of facilitating repatriation and resettlement of Southern Sudanese refugees and disarmament of militia groups, which are detrimental to efforts aimed at promoting durable peace both in the Sudan and beyond. There were even certain instances where instability in Southern Sudan spilled over into the Gambella region of Ethiopia, Darfur, northern Uganda, and the Central African Republic due to the porous nature of common borders and unchecked proliferation of arms (Omeje 2010). The spread of cattle-rustling into the Gambella region has fueled inter-tribal fighting and caused unanticipated security problems in the area, which forced both the Ethiopian and the South Sudan governments to conduct monthly security consultations to thwart security threats along their common border.

There are also some indications that the NCP is taking some measures as part of its drive to recast North Sudan as an Islamic state following the outcome of the referendum leading to the separation of the South. In the course of the CPA peace process the NCP managed to retain Sharia as a source of legislation in the North, thereby hampering the possible transformation of the state to secular status. Besides, it is to be recalled that in the course of the negotiations on citizenship issues, the NCP warned that any person voting in the referendum would be a southerner who would lose his/her citizenship rights in the North, which implies that it was planning to create an Islamic state following separation of the South after the referendum. Apprehensions resulting from these and similar other trends and tendencies, therefore, prompt the concerns among neighbouring countries that would be alarmed by possible threats from the ascendancy of militant Islam in the context of already precarious situations in the Horn. This would be to the detriment of putting in place a regional security architecture based on mutual interests and common objectives. The separation of South Sudan has a significant impact on the sub-region and beyond as it is likely to be a source of inspiration for thriving centrifugal forces striving to effect changes in the status quo in some countries in a manner that could have adverse implications for the realization of African unity at large. Leaders of some African countries like Libya and Chad, among others, cautioned that what is likely to happen in the Sudan could be contagious by bringing about a domino effect in the continent, posing grave danger to peace and security (Temin 2010:1). In this respect, one is forced to think of Somaliland (in Somalia), the Ogaden (in Ethiopia), and Darfur (in the Sudan) whose political entrepreneurs aspire for secession and could as a result gain impetus,thereby leading to turbulence of a wider scale in the sub-region. Hence there is concern that such developments would lay the ground for the transformation of latent intra-state conflicts into more intensified civil wars between the political regimes and ethno-nationalist insurgent movements. If this scenario became a reality, the already dismal human security situation of populations in the affected countries would be exacerbated.

Access to and Management of Resources

It is likely that independence would result in enhancement of Southern Sudan's oil production and regional infrastructural development endeavours. It is worth noting that since 2006, despite uncertainties surrounding subsequent matters during the remaining phases of implementing the CPA, GoSS has been negotiating possible involvement of Chinese and Japanese firms in its oil sector to construct a 1,400 km oil pipeline worth $ 1.5 billion that would link Juba to Lamu port on the Indian Ocean coast of Kenya. This appears to have been prompted by its desire to reduce the degree of its dependence on northern Sudan ports. So far, both parties to the CPA share oil revenues originating from production fields in the South as per the CPA wealth-sharing formula. The separation of South Sudan, however, would alter the existing arrangement which requires renegotiation between the two principals on the matter. In this regard, the challenge would be how to manage the oil economy including revenue sharing and rental tax on the pipeline and transportation of oil for export in view of South Sudan being landlocked.

In addition to the aforementioned, the inevitable separation of Southern Sudan undoubtedly impacts on the access to and management of water resources such as the Nile, which is one of the bones of contention between the upper and lower riparian countries both in the Horn and beyond. It is envisaged that the emergence of South Sudan as a new independent polity entails increased complication of the regional hydro-political setting of the Nile Basin, which is already enmeshed in sharp disagreement between the lower and upper riparian countries. It is common knowledge that whereas the upstream sources contribute 100 per cent of the waters of the Nile, the lower ones (Egypt and Sudan) insist to continue as sole users by preserving the status quo based on the 1929 and 1959 Treaties that exclude the former. This state of affairs has engendered not only unregulated competition among the countries of the Basin but also inter-state rivalry to the extent of affecting the peace and security of the region. In their bid to address problems and misgivings surrounding the use of the waters of the Nile, the countries of the Basin embarked on the task of developing a Common Framework Agreement (CFA) under the auspices of the Nile Basin Initiative (NBI). The CFA, which is hoped to set the stage for the establishment of the Nile Basin Commission in 2012 that oversees the joint utilisation and management of the Nile waters, is vigorously rejected by Egypt and Sudan on the ground that it adversely impacts on their established use rights. In this connection, it should be noted that South Sudan is rich in water resources given its location as a transit zone of the White Nile and the Blue Nile. Hence its likely accession to independence has considerable impact on the existing regional hydro-political milieu.

First and foremost, the first step in the aftermath of the independence of South Sudan could be revitalizing the Jonglei Canal Project that was disrupted in 1983 when the second civil war commenced. This by itself poses a threat to the vital interests of both Egypt and North Sudan, given that the share of the Nile waters that they previously received could be diminished as a result. Second, South Sudan will ally with the seven upstream countries against North Sudan & Egypt concerning the division of the Nile water among all the states shoring the Nile. In view of this, what matters is its future policy to determine what implications its new position would be regarding the on-going controversy on the use of the waters of the Nile. Two scenarios could be envisioned in this regard. The first is that South Sudan might insist on the maintenance of the status quo by invoking the 1959 Agreement on the 'full utilization of the waters of the Nile' agreed between Egypt and Sudan to share 55.5 billion cubic meters and 18.5 billion cubic meters respectively. This implies that South Sudan would claim its share of the 18.5 billion cubic meters of the water allocated to the old Sudan. The second scenario is that South Sudan may disown the 1959 Agreement and thus articulate its desire for renegotiation aimed at forging a new arrangement in tandem with the position of the majority of the upstream countries as a result of which it would qualify for candidacy to the CFA, which could be a matter of serious concern for North Sudan and Egypt. It is likely that the latter two may suspect, albeit with some justification, that for historical or transitional political reasons South Sudan could join the other states opposed to the perpetuation of the status quo.

Borders, Movement of People and Goods and Regional Integration

Following the de facto abrogation of the Addis Ababa Accord by nullifying Southern autonomy and the introduction of Sharia law in the early 1980s, the Numeiry regime was accused of manoeuvring to redrawthe 1956 north-south border to bring the territories and the oil rich areas of the South into the fold of the North. Following the signing of the CPA, concern associated with unresolved border issues was one of the points of contention that led SPLM/A's temporary suspension of its participation in the GoNU in October 2007. Regarding the claims and counterclaims surrounding Abyei, the Permanent Court of Arbitration has ruled on the case in July 2009 despite which border demarcation on the ground remains stalled due to NCP's foot-dragging (AI 2011:2). Unsettled concerns relating to border demarcation between old the Sudan and some of its neighbours like Ethiopia, among others, could persist under the new dispensation requiring the South to grapple with the matter following its entrenchment as a new polity.

The independence of South Sudan is also viewed to impact on regional integration, infrastructure development, bilateral and multilateral trade and economic cooperation in the sub-region in various ways. The prevailing assumption is that for historical and cultural reasons, Southern Sudan may move much closer to its neighbours in East Africa and the Horn to boost its position in sub-regional and international trade without forfeiting its ties to the North. Bilateral economic relations between Ethiopia and South Sudan are already picking up as a result of the CPA that provided favourable conditions fortheresumption of trade along their common border after 2005. The Gambella trading post in Ethiopia, which is connected with Sudan via the Baro-Akobo river-route, augmented trade among borderland communities and became a source of income for both countries accruing from customs duties on import and export goods thereby facilitating conditions for free movement of people and enabling relatives separated during the civil war to reconnect and live together (Bayissa 2010:233).

There are indications that neighbouring states are considering the emergence of an independent South Sudan as a window of opportunity in view of the latter's potential endowments in untapped natural resources and as a destination hub for their exports. This is already demonstrated by considerable influx of businesses and people from Kenya, Uganda, and Ethiopia anticipating job and investment opportunities. The evidence is that business operators from these countries are heavily engaged in South Sudan's private sector including service provision, construction, air transport, insurance, infrastructure development, and NGO undertakings. It is also reported that neighbouring states are supportive of Southern Sudan's independence in anticipation that it would boost regional trade by opening the door to formal treaties and accession to the East African Community (EAC) and the Common Market for Eastern and Southern Africa (COMESA). In terms of infrastructural development, there are a number of projects that are already underway like a new sea port along Kenya's Indian Ocean coast, a railway that connects Juba to Kenya, Uganda and Ethiopia, and extension of the Trans-African Highway Network linking South Sudan to Mombasa.

Conclusion

The CPA proved to be a major and relatively effective instrument in addressing several of the root causes of the conflict in Sudan. In several respects, it signalled a major departure from other similar initiatives attempted hitherto. This is despite contentions and controversies surrounding the relations between the two signatories as regards a number of issues, notably the north-south border demarcation, transparency regarding oil revenue, and claims and counterclaims on Abyei. In view of the imminent separation of the South that is already determined by the outcomes of the January 2011 referendum, several developments affecting potential and actual stakeholders within Sudan and the countries in the core and greater Horn of Africa are envisaged to unfold subsequently. In spite of the excitement and euphoria that would normally accompany the birth of a reconfigured South Sudan, opting for separation in and by itself is not a sufficient condition to beget substance in terms of putting to rest the mishaps experienced in the past for good. Hence a daunting task awaits the leaders of both North and South Sudan and other stakeholders in the region and the international community in several respects. A repeat of past follies that rocked basic fabrics of socio-economic and political life across the board could be avoided by paving the way for durable peace and stability provided that all the concerned actors at various levels synchronise their efforts to this end. The major onus of facilitating smooth transition under a new dispensation primarily falls on the leaders and other actors in North and South Sudan, who are expected to show unwavering commitments aimed at putting things right by working closely with and involving their populations under their respective areas of jurisdiction. The focus of engagements in the aftermath of the inevitable separation should, therefore, be on paramount concerns like good governance, democracy and equitable sharing. Concurrently, it is incumbent on the two sides to spearhead efforts towards addressing a plethora of unresolved issues like the north-south border demarcation, including Abyei, and other post-referendum concerns in a manner that could result in win-win outcomes to the benefit of all sides. Neighbouring countries that share borders with both North and South Sudan, regional economic communities (IGAD and EAC), and the AU, among others, could contribute to the transformation process in encouraging and assisting the two parties to resolve their differences and address their entrenched inadequacies of various sorts that militate against the realization of peaceful transition. State actors in the region can also help in this regard provided that they extricate themselves from their limitations marked by short-sighted approaches and furtherance of parochial self-serving interests in their dealings on matters related to internal governance in their countries and regional and sub-regional issues. Major players in the international system are better placed to alleviate pressing shortfalls and put an end to the predicaments of the sub-region through working in tandem with all relevant actors.

References

African Union (AU), 2010, 'Post-referendum Issues', in Peace and Security Council Report, November
Al-Rahim, A., 1973, 'Arabism, Africanism, and Self-Identification in the Sudan', in D. Wai, ed., *The Southern Sudan: The Problem of National Integration*, London: Frank Cass.
Alier, A., 1973, 'The Southern Sudan Question', in D. Wai, ed., *The Southern Sudan: the Problem of National Integration*, London: Frank Cass.
Amnesty International (AI), 2011, 'Sudan's 2011 Referendum: Human Rights Concerns', available at www.amnestyusa.org/sudan.
Bayissa, R., 2010, *War and Peace in the Sudan and Its Impact on Ethiopia: The Case of Gambella* 1955-2008, Addis Ababa: Addis AbabaUniversity Press.
Brosche, J., 2007, 'CPA: New Sudan, Old Sudan or Two Sudans?' *Journal of African Policy Studies,* 13(1).
The Daily Monitor, 'Southern Sudan Referendum', Monday, 6 December 2010.
Darfur Relief and Documentation Centre (DRDC), 2010, 'The Fifth Population and Housing Census in Sudan -An Incomplete Exercise', Geneva.
Edward, J.K., & Idris, A., 2007, 'The Consequences of Sudan's Civil Wars for the Civilian Population', in J. Laband, ed., *Daily Lives of Civilians in Wartime Africa: From Slavery Days to Rwandan Genocide*, London: Greenwood Press.

Hamid, B.M., (1989), 'Devolution and National Integration in the Southern Sudan', in Abd Rahim Muddathir, Raphael Badal, Adlan Hardallo and Peter Woodward,eds, *Sudan since Independence*, Brookfield: Gower.

Hardallu, A., 2001, 'Sudan–Schism within the Ruling Party: What Role for Civil Society in Conflict Resolution?', in *Networking with the View to Promoting Peace towards Sustainable Peace-Civil society Dialogue Forum for the Horn of Africa*, Nairobi: Heinrich Boll Foundation.

Healy, S., 2008, *Lost Opportunities in the Horn of Africa: How Conflicts Connect and Peace Agreements Unravel*, London: Chatham House.

Institute of Security Studies (ISS), 2009, 'Post-2011 Scenarios in Sudan: What Role for the EU?', No. 6, November.

International Crisis Group (ICG), 2006, 'The Long Road Ahead', (unpublished).

International Crisis Group, 2010, 'Negotiating Sudan's North-South Future', Africa Briefing, No. 76.

Johnson, D., 2006, 'Peace, Genocide and Crimes against Humanity in Sudan', in P. Kaarsholm, ed., *Violence, Political Culture and Development in Africa*, Athens: Ohio University Press.

Johnson, D., 2011, 'The Road Back from Abyei' (unpublished commentary), January.

Kebede, G., 1999, 'Sudan: the North-South Conflict in Historical Perspective', in Girma Kebede,ed., *Sudan's Predicament. Civil war, Displacement and Ecological Degradation*, Singapore: Ashgate.

Large, D., 2010, 'Southern Sudan before the Referendum', London School of Oriental and African Studies, available at kms1.isn.ethz.ch/.../ARI1672010_Large_Southern_Sudan_Referendum.pdf, accessed on 3/ 2/2011.

Mersha, B., 2004, 'Sub-Regional Approach to Conflict Resolution in Africa: The Case of IGAD's Mediation Role in the Sudan', MA thesis, Addis Ababa University.

Mukwaya, K., 2006, 'The Politics of International Terrorism in the Security Complexes in the Greater Horn of Africa: An Overview from Uganda under Movementocracy', *African Journal of International Affairs*.

Omeje, K., 2010, 'Dangers of Splitting a Fragile RentierState: Getting It Right in Southern Sudan', Occasional Paper, ACCORD.

Said, A.M., 2010, 'Don't Forget Sudan', available at http://weekly. ahram.org.eg/ Accessed on 20/1/2011.

Temin, J., 2010, 'Secession and Precedent in Sudan and Africa', Peace Brief, WashingtonDC: United States Institute of Peace.

United Nations Mission in Sudan (UNMIS), 2010, 'The CPA Monitor', Monthly Report on the Implementation of the CPA, Vol.6.

Wama, L.B.,1997, 'Prolonged Wars in Sudan', A Research Paper presented to the Research Department, Air Command and Staff College.

Wambugu, N., 2010, 'The Next Struggle', *BBC Focus on Africa*, April-June 2010.

5

Consequences of Referendum in Southern Sudan for Sudan, Horn of Africa and Neighbouring Regions

Samson S. Wassara

Introduction

Voting in the referendum has resulted in an overwhelming choice of secession for southern Sudan, a fact that was recognized by the Government of the Sudan (GoS) and the international community on 7 February 2011. This historical event has paved the way for the declaration of the 54th State in Africa in the nearest future. This situation calls for internal and external adjustments and adaptations of relationships in the Sudan and in the geo-political regions.

Political, social and economic gains or losses for the North or the South are subject to further negotiations to avert renewed violence in the region. Sharing of oil revenues, water resources and other issues such as citizenship and nationality remain tricky in the post-referendum period. Further, fears of beneficiaries from losing peace dividends of the CPA could become problematic in the run up to the declaration of a new sovereign state in southern Sudan. All these factors are a challenge to partners and friends of the peace agreement. Issues related to population movements (IDPs and nomads) and the common border between the North and the South are yet to be settled.

In the Sudan, armed conflict alone had been the main cause of the dislocation of the population. Attitudes of policy makers and ordinary people in the North and the South split after the Comprehensive Peace Agreement (CPA) signed on 9 January 2005, especially during the period leading towards the end of the interim period. The Government of National Unity (GoNU) and political forces in the North were alarmed by trends of events in the South that were in favour of voting for secession. The CPA stipulates that people in southern Sudan will vote in a referendum to determine the political future of the Sudan. This benchmark in the implementation of the CPA is enshrined the Interim National Constitution (INC) (GoNU 2005:134). The two documents contain details of transitional arrangements leading to the end of the interim period in 2011. However, the parties to the agreement, the National Congress Party (NCP) and the Sudan People's Liberation Movement/Army (SPLM/A) have to come to terms with the secession of southern Sudan and subsequent declaration of independence in July 2011.

Events in the Sudan have not only changed the political landscape of the country, but have serious repercussions in the Horn of Africa, the Great Lakes region and Central Africa. Secession of the South from the Sudan is the second after that of Eritrea from Ethiopia since the establishment of the Organisation of African Unity (OAU) in 1963. This new development in the Sudan is more dramatic to Africa compared to the case of Eritrea. The number of countries and sub-regions that have complex relationships with the South is cause of concern. Recognition of the referendum results at national, regional and international levels is one thing, but supporting the successor states to enhance harmony in the region is another challenge.

The question is how will the successor states cope with the challenges of peaceful coexistence? To what extent are the neighbours and African Union (AU) member States prepared to contribute to the stability of the Sudan, which is the key to Africa development? And how would African countries and organisations curtail secession tendencies in other African countries in similar situations like the Sudan? The purpose of this chapter is to put ideas on the table for expanded discussions of secession in the continent of Africa.

Physical Linkages and Prospects for Political Stability

The ideal situation for peace in Sudan depends on a mutually agreed secession, which took place on 7 February 2011. The first phase of averting renewed war was attained in the Sudan. The referendum resulted in secession. There are, nevertheless, many important issues remaining to be dealt with to forge interdependence between the South and the North and within southern Sudan as well. It is incumbent on CPA partners to identify determinants that would strengthen mutual dependence at the end of the interim period on 9 July 2011 and even far beyond. The post-referendum political environment is associated with vulnerabilities, which could easily drag the North and the South into lose-win confrontations.

Interdependence between the South and the North is a crucial factor in maintaining peace and stability in the Horn of Africa and other regions. Scholars describe the concept of interdependence as situations in which actors and events in different parts of a system affect each other (Nye Jr. 2000:179-184). There must be determinants to stimulate mutual dependence to offset the negative sensitivities accumulated during the period of armed conflict in the Sudan. The north-south surface transportation connections are weak because of prolonged neglect of southern Sudan in national plans. There were no all-weather roads linking the North and the South since independence. The railway line that linked the South and the North became dysfunctional in 1980s and remains so in the interim period of the CPA.

Roads linking northern and southern parts of the Sudan are in terrible shape. Road and railway bridges were blown out as war strategy. River transportation was partially functional, but always paralysed by the civil war. Only air transport connected some principal towns. This was expensive for movement of goods and services. The present condition of roads hampers return processes, resettlement of people, rehabilitation of essential services and future economic development. The CPA provided many opportunities to construct major road networks between the North and the South and to repair the Babanusa-Wau rail link. However, sections of roads of Kosti-Renk-Melut and Kharasana-Pariang-Bentiu were built to connect the North to oil producing areas in southern Sudan. Transport facilitates internal trade, domestic interactions, business interests and knowledge of the other. All states lying south of the Sudd swamps are weakly connected with the North. Consequently, many communities in southern Sudan are encapsulated into their homelands in the ten states without wider contact with one another.

Communications networks play a similar role like the roads networks. Many mobile phone operators have, nevertheless, invested in the South. All major urban centres and cities in the ten states of southern Sudan are connected by northern-based mobile operators. The presence of these operators has contributed to improved transactions of public and private businesses. This is an exemplary service which, if reinforced by surface transport networks, would consolidate interdependence between the South and the North. The emerging states from the old political system are expected to promote transportation and communications in order to boost internal and external businesses and to lay sound foundations for future cooperation. In short, opportunities for nurturing interdependence constitute a challenge in future relationships between the North and the South when secession of southern Sudan materialises.

Remaining Conflicts and Emerging Identities in the North

The most pressing issue concerns the status of southern Kordofan (Nuba Mountains), Blue Nile and Abyei. According to the CPA, the populations in the first two areas have the right to exercise 'popular consultation' on whether or not they are satisfied with the implementation of the CPA. Positive outcome of the consultation will result in the confirmation of the present arrangement after the expiry date of the interim arrangement. The issue at stake is whether these regions are not going to constitute a 'new south' of the northern Sudan as far as emerging political conflicts are concerned. These regions were involved in Sudan's civil war that ended in 2005. The hangover of the liberation mentality may continue to cloud relationships between these regions and the centre. The successor state in southern Sudan, in concert with the government in the North, will need cooperation in order to de-escalate whatever new conflict may arise in the future.

Of like concern as the problem relating the two regions above is the uncertainty surrounding the political environment in Abyei in the post-referendum period. Partners of the CPA have the tradition of disagreement over the territory. Disagreements between the CPA partners over Abyei could ignite another cycle of violence. This area saw the worst violence in May 2008, which led to the destruction of Abyei Town, displacement of the population including returnees and the temporary evacuation of UNMIS and NGOs (Wassara 2009:13). The Abyei area was left without authority for some time. Although the CPA partners sought a judicial solution, the ruling of the International Court of Arbitration in The Hague of 2009 remains a blue print. No border demarcation has taken place since the verdict of the Court was announced. The Abyei case is volatile in the relationships between the North and the South. While the referendum operations ran smoothly in southern Sudan, Abyei witnessed prolonged violent confrontations between armed groups in which lives were lost, people injured and properties destroyed.

Further, the Darfur conflict remains uncertain because the Darfur Peace Agreement (DPA), which promised a referendum on Darfur by the middle of

2010, is no longer functioning (Art. 56 of the DPA). The civil war continued despite the participation of some Darfur factions in the Government. However, if armed conflict intensified in Darfur it would likely spill-over the north-south border. Darfur rebels might seek sanctuary in forests of Western Bahr el Ghazal in South Sudan, a scenario that might draw the latter into the conflict between the Khartoum regime and the Darfur insurgency. A similar situation developed when the Sudan Armed Forces (SAF) started bombardment of frontier villages of Western Bahr el Ghazal before the referendum under the pretext of pursuing Darfur rebels into southern Sudan (CIGI 2011:7). Therefore, continued civil war in Darfur is a threat to stable relationships between the state in the North and the emerging sovereign state in the South.

Finally, eastern Sudan is a conflict region where the National Democratic Alliance (NDA) and SPLM/A were present before the CPA was signed in 2005. Conflict actors in the region were given a separate treatment in the search for peace in the Sudan. The GoS and rebel groups in eastern Sudan entered into a separate agreement under the name of eastern Sudan Peace Agreement (ESPA) on 14 October 2006. Under the terms of the agreement, a regional government was established that included three states: Gedarif, Kassala and Red Sea. The ESPA endorsed the June 2000 Tripoli Agreement between the GoS and the Free Lions, which gave political rights to the Rashaida people believed to be latecomers to the region from the Arabian Peninsula. Ethnic groups of the region, namely the Beja, Ben Amer and Rashaida have constructed a new political identity, which is problematic to the authorities in Khartoum (Abdel Ghaffar and Manger 2009:101-103).

Hence, regional identities are emerging in increasing numbers in northern Sudan. There are four distinct regions (Blue Nile, Darfur, eastern Sudan and the Nuba Mountains) where identity politics could cause problems for the post-referendum government in the North (Ottmann and Wolff 2007:19-27). The secession of southern Sudan could influence political activists in the northern part of Sudan to claim greater autonomy, a situation that could further weaken the central government in Khartoum. In case the North does not adjust to the new situation, it is feared that some of these regions may even consider secession as a solution to disputes between them andthe centre. The greatest concern is that political forces in these regions were partners of SPLM/A during the years of armed struggle against the regime in Khartoum. They may be tempted to involve southern Sudan to support their political causes. Should the new State support such a cause, that act will be detrimental to consolidation of peace in both north and south, and in neighbouring countries.

Human Security in the South: Problems of Arms and Violence

Many factors contributed to the resurgence of violence and insecurity in southern Sudan in the post-CPA period. The most obvious factor is the breakdown of law and order that destroyed traditional mechanisms of conflict resolution at the community level. The rise of civilian defence forces supplanted the power and authority of tribal chiefs, community leaders and faith-based institutions. The GoSS as well as the State and County administrations were unable to control local warlords. Post-CPA security institutions were unable to protect citizens and their property from armed groups within or outside communities. The incidence of cattle rustling rose dramatically in pastoralist communities. Unemployed youth who have lost traditional coping mechanisms organised into militia-like criminal groups that engaged in banditry. Hence, the interim period of the CPA witnessed violent clashes between tribal communities in a number of states of southern Sudan. Some causes of such clashes were political; but most of them were attributed to cattle rustling and other forms of banditry.

The availability of small arms among the civilian population might not be the cause of insecurity in southern Sudan, but it has certainly exacerbated the violence. In the light of the poor security situation, and as result of the inefficiency of law enforcement institutions, people feel the need to turn to small arms and light weapons (SALW) to defend themselves and their property. In the past, pastoralist communities in southern Sudan used traditional weapons to defend their livestock from predators and rival groups, causing minimal causalities compared to the present day.

Young has compiled an exhaustive list of 60 different militia groups allied with the SAF or SPLA (Young 2006:42-48). Many war-time militias splintered due to disagreements over their integration into the SPLA or SAF. The huge number of militia groups complicated the implementation of the CPA in southern Sudan because the unabsorbed groups used to create insecurity and continuously switched sides between the SAF and the SPLA. Many militia groups and demobilised SPLA soldiers that were dissatisfied with the post-CPA security arrangements have melted into their communities with their weapons. The failure to handle the integration of militia groups into the SPLA is a source of outbreaks of armed violence in Upper Nile and Unity states. These groups engage in other forms of inter-communal violence such as banditry and cattle rustling.

The proximity of southern Sudan to conflicts in the Horn of Africa and the Great Lakes Region has adversely influenced its social, political and security environment. Most of the conflicts have their roots in economic underdevelopment, environmental hazards, repressive political systems, and competition over natural resources. Patterns and trends of conflict differ in nature across the region. The Horn has experienced both inter- and intra-state conflicts. The end of the superpower rivalry left a power vacuum that regional powers sought to fill. Such political interference and competition for influence created a fertile ground for dissident movements with cross-border connections.

Stockpiles of weapons are in abundance in the conflict-affected countries neighbouring southern Sudan. Studies (Lewis 2009:47-49) show that there is an abundance of SALW in Uganda, the Democratic Republic of the Congo (DRC) and Chad that find their way into southern Sudan. Many communities take advantage of the wide availability of small arms to establish community military formations with the aim of forcefully acquiring property from neighbouring communities. The result is a cycle of communal violence and militarisation.

Cross-border ethnic relationships play an important role in the flow of weapons in the region. Present state boundaries cut across several ethnic groups. The control of trans-border peripheries has been a nightmare for the GoS, but is becoming even more problematic for the GoSS after its establishment in 2005. Many ethnic groups straddle the borders between southern Sudan and Ethiopia, Kenya and Uganda; for example, the Acholi, Anuak, Nuer and Toposa. Regional conflicts involving states in the Horn of Africa have led political systems to the exploit such communities for their political and strategic interests in the region (De Waal 2007:9-15).

Civilian disarmament in southern Sudan is a complex undertaking that requires a sharp understanding of inter-communal relationships and cross-border dynamics. Southern Sudan is a segmented tribal society where traditional authority was terribly eroded during the civil war. The civil war contributed to community ownership of an excessive number of small arms and light weapons. There was a definite pattern of community militarisation and livestock-related violence in southern Sudan. The movement of cattle from Dinka and Nuer villages to the lowlands along the White Nile and its main tributaries results in recurring dry-season violence between communities over grazing land and fishing rights; and other pastoralists such as the Murle, Toposa and Boya engage in cattle rustling. These communities have acquired modern assault weapons that have increased fatalities in communal violence.

Challenges for New States in Old Sudan

The major challenge, which governments of the North and the South have to overcome include things like: citizenship, disarmament of civilians, professionalisation of security sector institutions, making of laws, and diversification of economic activities. The government in the South will have to negotiate access to sea ports, a necessity for landlocked states.

Citizenship and Identity

Citizenship and identity are ambiguous concepts with reference the Sudanese society. In the Sudan, the law emphasises the concept of nationality. The Nationality Law of 1957 (amended in 1974) is based on ancestry and descent, although naturalisation is a lesser important basis for qualifying to be identified as Sudanese. Ancestry or descent is not a necessary and sufficient condition for being a citizen of the Sudan. The basic requirement is belonging to a community in the Sudan. However, the law discriminates against some ethnic groups in northern Sudan as well as in southern Sudan (Assal 2011:4-7). Border peoples of the country undergo stringent procedures to obtain nationality certificates in order to identify themselves as Sudanese citizens. Besides biological parents, the law requires witnesses and elders of the communities to justify that an applicant is born to parents who live or lived in the Sudan. These are the complications that the new State in southern Sudan has to deal with immediately before the declaration of independence is made.

The referendum vote for secession is homework for policy makers in North Sudan and South Sudan. According to the 1961 Convention on the Reduction of Statelessness to which Sudan is not a signatory and the 1999 International Law Commission (ILC) clauses on Nationality of Natural Persons in succession of States, the Predecessor State should ensure that the situation of statelessness is prevented in the Successor State. Inhabitants of the latter, including aliens, have the right to choose a nationality in either of the two states (Brownlie 1990:661-665). Several proposals were advanced about citizenship and nationality in the run up to the 2001 referendum vote in the Sudan and afterwards. Dual nationality/citizenship was considered as an option for the Sudanese born in the two States before 2005. This option was rejected outright by the NCP.

CPA partners hold different positions on this issue. According to a recent study (Assal 2011:10), the NCP leaders maintain that southerners living in the North will have to return to their new home and those who choose to remain behind will be treated as foreigners. The SPLM position on the issue of nationality is that there should be no discrimination in the Predecessor State and the Successor State. Southerners who choose to stay in the North should be granted citizenship and northerners in the South likewise. As the Government of Sudan has accepted the results of secession, it is logical for the NCP to abide by the international rule and practice that the Predecessor State cannot withdraw nationality from an inhabitant unless that person has acquired a domicile and nationality of the Successor State.

The issue of nationality and citizenship is yet to be resolved within the remaining interim period. There is already a precedent set during the independence of the country. The Sudan was a Condominium under the British and the Egyptian rule. At Sudan's independence, residents of foreign origins (Egyptians, Syrians, Cypriots, Greeks, Turks, Armenians, etc) were given the opportunity to acquire Sudanese citizenship or remain citizens of their countries of origin, but fulfil conditions of residence as defined by Sudanese laws. Therefore, this section is concluding by borrowing the idea of Brownlie that 'sovereignty denotes responsibility for people' and it will be a crime to treat the southern Sudanese population in the North as stateless after secession.

Water Resources and Waterways

South Sudan is emerging as a new riparian state in the Nile basin after the result of the January 2011 referendum is secession. The new State may become the 11th member of the Nile Basin Initiative (NBI) if it adheres to the 2002 Constitutive Act of the water organisation. This political development has serious implications for the existing arrangements and problems related to the sharing of water resources between the lower riparian states, Egypt and the Sudan, and the other upper riparian states. The history of the Nile water sharing agreements was much influenced by theory of absolute territorial integrity (Godana 1985:38). The theory states that the upper riparian states should not undertake projects to harness sections of a river system on their territories if such works affect adversely water interests of other basin states. This theory favours downstream states such as Egypt and the Sudan. Experts maintain that there is a form of hydro-hegemony enjoyed by Egypt and the Sudan by virtue of previous agreements. The signatories of the 1959 Nile Water Agreement control water resources and coerce the upper riparian States into accepting an unjust allocation of water quantities (Mirumachi and Allan 2007:2-5).

Most of the existing Nile water agreements excluded the upper riparian states. The agreements of 1929 and 1959 included only Egypt and the Sudan. These two countries allocated for themselves nearly all water quantities of the Nile River system. The demographic explosion and corresponding food, power and water shortages coupled with water sharing in the two agreements have been sources of tension in the Nile basin. Egypt took advantage of endemic conflicts in upstream countries to benefit from the share of water when the upper riparian states were engulfed by armed conflicts since the signature of the 1959 Nile Water Agreement (Okoth 2007:85-88).

Causes of water scarcity in the lower riparian states (Egypt and Sudan) are attributed to climatic conditions such as evaporation in the great swamp (the Sudd) in southern Sudan. It is estimated that 14 billion cubic metres of water are lost in evaporation in the Sudd swamp alone (Wassara 1994:112). The 1959 Agreement contains clauses defining construction works for water drainage in the White Nile River system located in southern Sudan. The remaining major planned water projects were in southern Sudan but stalled due to the civil wars in the region. The 400-kilometre Jonglei Canal project was planned to drain 4.7 billion cubic metres of water from the Sudd swamp in southern Sudan. The project, started in 1978, was halted six years later by the civil war. Northern Sudanese and Egyptian interests in controlling access to Nile water and its resources still persist and the independence of southern Sudan is a matter of concern for its northern neighbours.

Opportunities for the development of hydro-economy in Egypt and North Sudan lie in southern Sudan. It is where all the rivers descending from the Nile-Congo water divide converge to create the largest wetland in the Nile basin known as the Sudd. The Sobat River, which descends from the Ethiopian highlands, also meets the White Nile at the northern end of the Sudd near Malakal. At the same time, another wetland, the Machar Marshes in eastern Upper Nile, retains considerable quantities of water descending from the Ethiopian highland. Both the Sudd and the Machar wetlands are targets of water drainage projects conceived in the early twentieth century, refined in subsequent plans by the Anglo-Egyptian condominium administration and reformulated by Egypt and the Sudan to be the core of the 1959 Agreement on full utilisation of the Nile waters.

Southern Sudan is emerging as a sovereign state in a water-related contested area of regional interests; but is not a signatory to any existing treaty. This political development is a threat to Egypt's hydro-hegemony over the Nile Basin. If South Sudan refuses to recognise the 1959 Nile Water

Agreement, the Egyptian government will be compelled to renegotiate the water agreement and the other upper riparian States may take advantage of this situation to mount pressure on Egypt and the Sudan to endorse the new agreement framework developed by the Nile Basin Initiative (NBI) member States (Kagwanja 2007: 325-329). As the emergence of a new State in southern Sudan is imminent, the sharing of the Nile water is likely to be an intriguing factor in its foreign policy. The question to consider is to what extent could South Sudan exploit the situation to its advantage?

The positive side of the Nile is that the river has served southern Sudan for more than a century as an access to the outside world. Southern Sudan is a landlocked region, which is thousands of kilometres away from seaports. The Nile waterways made it possible for different types of trade to flourish in the South. Given the poor state of surface transport infrastructure in southern Sudan, the NileRiver is an important transportation outlet for the South. Although journeys on the Nile River waterways are painfully slow, there are very few competitively cheap, alternative transport systems at work now. The waterway facilitated domestic trade and enabled the supply of commodities to local markets, delivery of humanitarian and relief goods during the war and, currently, the massive return of Internally Displaced Persons (IDPs) from the north to southern Sudan. The strategic importance of the Nile is not only for sharing water resources, but as a permanent link between peoples of the South and the North.

Oil as a Binding or Breaking Factor

Sudan is the third largest oil producer in sub-Saharan Africa. According to the BP Statistical Review of World Energy, the country pumps about 490,000 barrels per day. Most of the oil produced in the Sudan is found in the South (Krumova 2011). Oil production in southern Sudan adds to its strategic importance. Multinational companies such as the American Chevron and the French Total were initially involved in the exploitation of Sudanese oil; however, sanctions of the Western World against the Sudan redirected oil investments towards Asia (China, India and Malaysia).

The oil producing region is linked to Port Sudan by a pipeline running over 1,000 kilometres through which oil is transported and then exported to China and other world oil markets. The multinational companies that have maintained a presence in southern Sudan since prior to the signing of the CPA are the China National Petroleum Corporation (CNPC), the Malaysian Petroliam Nasional Berhad (PETRONAS) and the Indian Oil and Natural Gas Corporation (ONGC). These companies signed their contracts with the

Khartoum regime to which they pay allegiance. More than one-third (35 %) of oil revenues go to the drilling companies, while the rest is shared between the North, the South and the oil producing states according to an agreed formula of revenue sharing in the CPA.

Oil could be a factor of cooperation and collaboration between governments in the North and the South after secession. Krumova, the optimist, wrote under a bold headline that 'Oil Ties North and South Sudan despite Expected Separation'. The analyst argues that separation of southern Sudan will alter the CPA revenue-sharing formula to the advantage of the South.

The North holds, nevertheless, the key to oil production that would enable it to raise its stakes during negotiations with the South on revisions of the CPA formula for sharing oil revenues. It controls the oil infrastructure such as the pipeline, storage and export reservoirs on the Red Sea coast. In addition, it has the technical expertise to extract the oil. The South does not possess this advantage. It will take the South many years to find an alternative for oil production and exportation. Both governments rely much on oil revenues. Accordingly, 98 per cent of the GoSS budget relied on oil revenues; 50 per cent of the domestic revenue of the North came from oil and 93 per cent of exports came from oil in 2009 (Krumova 2011). This situation is likely to enhance cooperation and collaboration if economies of the North and the South are to avert crises.

In a situation where this optimistic outlook is affected by vulnerability factors, foundations of the economic performance will be profoundly shaken in the post-independent South Sudan. The question is what factors would provoke non-cooperation or non-collaboration of the sovereign states that will emerge at the end of the interim period? The most important factor will be the southern demand for transparency as far as documents of contracts and transactions between the GoS and the Asian oil multinationals are concerned. Another factor will be the request for majority revenue sharing reverting to southern Sudan. The referendum took place and the GoS accepted the result that tilted in favour of secession. Disputes remain, nevertheless, over which oil fields are subject to wealth sharing, how new oil sharing structures work and who determines the status of the existing contracts. These questions are yet to be addressed adequately before the end of the interim period.

Both the North and the South will be losers if resource-related conflicts escalate to provoke a renewed war. As the economies of the North and the South are profoundly influenced by oil revenues as mentioned above, the oil production will be adversely affected. One adverse effect of a war is that there would be no sufficient finances for the belligerents to uphold war economies. Further, the war situation would be much more complex than the one experienced before the signature of the CPA. The SPLA has entrenched itself in the southern states where they were absent, especially in the oil fields. The Sudan Armed Forces (SAF) would have the daunting task of driving out the SPLA from oilfields, a situation that would interrupt oil production for a considerable period of time. The end result would be serious deterioration or near-collapse of economic performances in both the North and the South.

The North-south Border and Pastoralist Communities

A seceding southern Sudan will have a common border with the North, which will be the longest border in Africa (about 2,000 km). The issue of the border is sensitive because of natural resources such as water; pasture and oil are located in borderlands. This could be settled between the North and the South through negotiations. Most of the boundaries between African countries have not been marked on the ground despite the fact that these countries attained independence about half a century ago. Grassroots communities rarely recognize political boundaries. Pastoralists in both north and south have vague notions about international and local borders. Their borders end where there is water and rich grazing areas. The movement of armed nomadic tribes of the North across the north-south border into southern Sudan does invite predatory activities. The reason why the north-south border is sensitive at the communal level is because of the availability of natural resources such as water sources and grazing land.

Although ethnic clashes were frequent between border communities in the North and the South, they had developed mechanisms for resolving emerging conflicts over grazing lands and water sources. The politicisation and militarisation of communities, which was a civil war strategy, affected adversely the good relationships that existed between communities on both sides of the common border. So long as communities are militarised and communal relations are politicised, it is certain that inter-communal violence could invite military confrontations in border regions between the North and the South after secession. In this respect, the states that will emerge in the North and the South need to re-consider the concept of soft border, which allows seasonal movements of nomads across common borders. These movements could be made safe by replicating war-time peace markets that enhanced border trade. The idea peace markets in borderlands were already embraced by border communities during the civil war, especially in Northern Bahr el Ghazal.

Regional Dimensions and Prospects for Integration

The secession of southern Sudan will impact on neighbouring states in the Horn of Africa, East Africa, Central Africa and regional organisations. The independence of southern Sudan may alter inter-state diplomacy and relations not only in the immediate neighbourhood, but in the whole of Africa. Secession will affect power configuration, security and economic environment in the regions mentioned above. States bordering southern Sudan and proximate regional organisations are likely to position themselves to interact with what some policy experts (Hemmer 2010) refer as 'the new kid on the block'. The rise of southern Sudan as an independent country has repercussions of various degrees at different levels in its geopolitical regions.

In the Horn and Neighbouring States

Southern Sudan, emerging soon as a sovereign state, is a landlocked political entity. It is located more than 1,000 kilometres away from the main ports of Port Sudan on the Red Sea coast and Mombasa on the Kenyan coast of the Indian Ocean. The new state will be an important political player in the region. Southern Sudan shares common borders with Ethiopia in the East, Kenya, Uganda, in the South and South-east; Democratic Republic of the Congo (DRC) and Central African Republic (CAR) in the South and South-west. Sudan's conflict was easily felt in the countries of the region.

Cross-border entanglements and regional rivalries with almost all immediate neighbours paralleled the internal conflicts, shifting according to regional dynamics and opportunistic political interests. For example, southern Sudanese refugees, mainly the Nuer and the Dinka, shifted the population balance in favour of the Nuer reducing the influence of the Annuaks in Gambela state. The involvement of Mengistu regime in supporting the SPLA militarily had its backlash when the Derg regime was overthrown in 1991. The Ethiopian Revolutionary Democratic Front (ERDF) regime in Ethiopia left an opening for its backer, the Sudan government, to deal a fatal blow to the SPLA (Sima 2010:197-203). Local conflicts between the Nuers and the Annuaks in Ethiopia spill over into southern Sudan and vice versa. So, many examples could illustrate similar situation along common borders with the other neighbours of southern Sudan. This situation led an African scholar (Mesfin 2009) to consider the Horn of Africa as a security complex.

Neighbours of southern Sudan had influence on events during the war without getting directly embroiled in military actions. In the process of peace each neighbour pursued its political and economic interests in southern Sudan. Hemmel (2010:2-4) outlined relations between southern Sudan and its neighbours in the advent of its independence. Most of the issues related to north-south relations are already explored in the sections above. Sudan and its neighbours, which have history of fuelling each other's conflicts, have mended their relations.

The CPA made it possible for Ethiopia, Kenya and Uganda to make serious inroads into southern Sudan through diplomatic relations and businesses including air connections and road links. All these countries have established Consulates in Juba, the Capital of southern Sudan. The other neighbours are French-speaking countries, namely the Democratic Republic of Congo (DRC) and Central African Republic (CAR). Although these countries share common borders; have same people on both sides of the border and experience similar conflicts, their engagements with southern Sudan remain relatively weak. They share two main problems: the atrocities of Uganda's Lord's Resistance Army (LRA) and flow of illicit weapons across common borders (Marks 2007:25-30; Lewis 2009: 47-49). These problems should have strengthened mutual resolves to deal with regionalisation of rebel movements. Instead, Uganda deals with these countries with its military presence on their territories and in southern Sudan. In short relations between southern Sudan and French-speaking neighbours are anchored in the security sector.

In Regional Organisations

Shared utilization of water resources could serve as a basis of regional integration for southern Sudan. It is worth mentioning that a water-related organisation known as the Nile Basin Initiative (NBI) was launched in 1999 and is in progress. Southern Sudan is likely to be a member when the country declares independence because the country was technically part of the Sudan which participated as a member of the organisation. The country has a large river basin through which flows the Nile River from Uganda; the Bahr el Ghazal and its tributaries descend from the Nile-Congo water divide plateau in the west; and the Sobat and its tributaries descend from the Ethiopian highlands. These river systems create the world's largest wetland known as the Sudd. Major water projects were planned in southern Sudan but never developed due to the civil wars in the region. The 400-kilometre Jonglei canal project was planned to drain 4.7 billion cubic metres of water from the Sudd swamp in southern Sudan for use in northern Sudan and Egypt. The project, started in 1978, was halted six years later by the civil war. Northern Sudanese and Egyptian interest in controlling access to Nile waters persists and the possible independence of southern Sudan concerns its northern neighbours. Water security issues are currently negotiated by the Nile Basin countries within a temporary framework dubbed the Nile Basin Initiative and are likely to grow in importance. The emergence of southern Sudan as a sovereign state implies readjustment of functional relations with the Sudan and with the other riparian states to ensure uncontested participation.

IGAD brokered the CPA and shares the responsibility of monitoring developments in Sudan. This sub-regional organisation is not simply empowered to negotiate conflicts among member states, but is a developmental authority covering the Horn of Africa and East Africa. Mediation of conflicts in the region is just one function for which a secretariat was established in Kenya. There are a host of developmental relations that IGAD has to manage from its headquarters in Djibouti. As secession is the outcome of the vote in the referendum 2011, this organisation will have to deal with old and new challenges when southern Sudan declares independence in July 2011. Its role as a developmental organisation was challenged by natural and man-made factors. For instance, environmental degradation attributed mainly to droughts is one of the natural factors. It affects hydrology and vegetation of the region which affect human and pastoral security. These are the issues southern Sudan will be sharing with member states of the organisation. Concerning post-conflict problems in the Sudan, IGAD is represented in the Sudan by a Special Envoy in the Assessment and Evaluation Commission (AEC), a CPA monitoring structure.

The African Union (AU) is the continental organisation in which IGAD is one of the sub-regional organisations. The organisation has a conflict mediation function, which is vested in its Peace and Security Council proposed at the Lusaka Summit in 2001. It has fifteen members responsible for monitoring and intervening in conflicts, with an African force at its disposal. African Union military intervention is limited to Darfur in northern Sudan where it has deployed peacekeepers from African countries. The AU will be an active participant in events leading to the independence of southern Sudan because it mandated IGAD to negotiate the conflict in Sudan and Somalia. It also mandated Thabo Mbeki in 2009 to follow up CPA implementation and democratic transformation in Sudan. This is seen by specialists in conflict management as a duplication of efforts that requires proper coordination with IGAD responsibilities.

Southern Sudan is expected to join the African Union and the relevant regional organisations. These are the IGAD and East African Community

(EAC). The AU, the IGAD and the East African Community are expected to assist the new state in southern Sudan to pursue positive diplomacy with all neighbours including the Sudan. African and world representatives witnessed the declaration of results of the referendum as the last benchmark of the CPA on 7 February in Khartoum. Despite this ceremonial declaration, however, violent crisis scenarios are still haunting the North and the South. It is the moral and political responsibility of African regional and continental organisations to build confidence between the North and the South and between the South and its neighbours. This goal could only be achieved through dialogue. The AU and IGAD have the daunting task of dealing with intriguing factors that may complicate and sour inter-state relations between the Sudan and southern Sudan that may have implications for the Horn of Africa.

Conclusion

People fear the flare up of violent conflict between the North and the South after the declaration of independence in southern Sudan. If violence breaks out between the North and the South under any circumstance, it could spread out rapidly, aggravate the conflict in the Blue Nile, south Kordofan, Abyei and Darfur and may draw some neighbouring countries into its circuit. The government in Khartoum is already sending warning signals to GoSS requesting the expulsion of Darfurian and other opposition figures from Juba. These signals could be seen as a warning about future relations between the two parts of the Sudan in the process of separation.

There are, nevertheless, a set of priorities that actors in the two independent republics emerging from the old Sudan should consider in different areas of governance. They include the pillars such as international and regional relations, governance, security and justice systems, the economy and the social interactions. For example, the maintenance of political stability in northern and southern Sudan is essential for healthy trends of interstate relations in the Horn of Africa, East Africa and in Central Africa. This will depend on positive diplomatic actions of countries of the regions to promote sustainable peace through continuous dialogue among neighbours.

Another important observation is that southern Sudan and its neighbours are countries where civil wars have contributed to the proliferation of small arms. The DRC, as a neighbour, is still struggling to establish law and order in the country. In southern Sudan, the transformation of the SPLA, professionalisation of police and other organised forces and demilitarising the state and communities are the way forward towards consolidating political stability. This action would be strengthened by promulgation of laws and the professionalisation of the justice system in southern Sudan. The two political entities emerging from the Sudan need more cooperation and involvement of their neighbours in dealing with regionalisation of rebellions and laying foundations for internal political stability and enforcing law and order.

The economy of southern Sudan is another pillar, which looks fragile because of dependence on oil to a larger extent. The percentage of oil dependence in the two parts of the Sudan becoming separate states has already been shown in the preceding sections of this Chapter. The GoSS, in collaboration with actors in the private sector and communities, should enhance the diversification of the economy. This will depend on economic policies and strategies of the government. Efforts are yet to be seen in expanding tax bases for raising non-oil revenues for public expenditure. Southern Sudan is depending heavily (98%) on oil revenues for running its economy. The improvement of the economy depends of the strength of research in development processes in southern Sudan. Commissioning research will be badly needed to rationalise the formulation of policy framework of the government in the new state.

Finally, the different groups in society must be seen as active participants in all policy priority areas in southern Sudan. The politicians and policy makers have to encourage open dialogue between sectors of the population and the government. This includes the active participation of civil society organisations and independent media. These actors are important in the conception of policies, strategies and actions in the framework of common vision of the new state. However, there is tendency in southern Sudan to seek military solutions to local differences. The multiplication of armed violence after elections and the referendum, especially in Upper Nile, tend to paint a gloomy picture of the anticipated Republic of South Sudan.

References

Ahmed, Abdel Ghaffar M. and Leif Manger, eds., 2009, *Peace in Eastern Sudan: Some Important Aspects for Consideration*, Bergen: BRIC.
Assal, Munzoul A. M., 2011, *Nationality and Citizenship Questions in Sudan after the Southern Sudan Referendum Vote*, Bergen: CMI.
Brownlie, Ian, 1990, *Principles of Public International Law*, 4th edition, Oxford: Clarendon Press.
De Waal, Alex, 2007, 'Sudan: International Dimensions to the State and its Crisis', Occasional Paper No.3, London: Crisis States Research Centre.

Godana, Bonaya Adhi, 1985, *Africa's Shared Water Resources: Legal and Institutional Aspects of the Nile, Niger and Senegal River Systems*, London: Frances Pinter.

GoNU, 2005, *Interim National Constitution of the Republic of the Sudan* 2005, Khartoum: Ministry of Justice.

Hemmer, Jort, 2010, 'Southern Sudan: the new kid on the block?' CRU *Policy Brief*, The Hague: Clingendael Conflict Research Unit (Netherlands institute of International Relations), Maart 14.

Kagwanja, Peter, 2007, 'Calming the Waters: East African Community and Conflict over the Nile Resources', *Journal of Eastern African Studies*, Vol.1, No. 3.

Krumova, Kremena, 2011, 'Oil Ties North and South Sudan Despite Expected Separation', *Epoch Times*, January 16.

Lewis, Mike, 2009, *Skirting the Law: Sudan's Post-CPA Arms Flow*, Geneva: Small Arms Survey, Graduate Institute of International Studies.

Marks, Joshua, 2007, *Border in Name Only: Arms Trafficking and Armed Groups at the DRC-Sudan Border*, Geneva: Small Arms Survey, Graduate Institute of International Studies.

Mesfin, Berouk, 2010, *The Horn of Africa as a Security Complex: Towards a Theoretical Framework*, Pretoria: PSA (Institute for Security Studies), October.

Mirumachi, Naho and Allan, J.A.,2007, *Revisiting Transboundary Water Governance: Power, Conflict, Cooperation and Political Economy*, London: King's College.

Nye Jr., Joseph S., 2000, *Understanding International Conflicts: An Introduction to Theory and History*, 3rd edition, New York: Longmans, Inc.

Ottmann, Martin and Wolff, Stefan, 2007. *Content and Context: Autonomy and conflict settlement in Sudan*, Nottingham: CCMCR University of Nottingham.

Okoth, P. Godfred, 2007, 'This Nile River Question and the Riparian States: Contextualizing Uganda's Foreign Policy', *African Sociological Review*, Vol.11, No. 1

Sima, Regassa Bayima, 2010, 'Changes in Gambela, Ethiopia', in Elke Grawert, ed., *After the Comprehensive Peace Agreement in Sudan*, Woodbridge: James Currey/Boydell & Brewer Ltd.

The Centre for International Governance Innovation (CIGI), 2011, *Security Sector Reform: Southern Sudan*, No.4. Waterloo, Ontario: CIGI, January.

Wassara, Samson S., 2009. *The Comprehensive Peace Agreement in the Sudan: Institutional Developments and Political Trends in Focus Areas*, Bergen: CMI.

Wassara, Samson Samuel, 1994, *Le régime juridique international du basin du Nil: comparaison avec d'autres basins fluviaux*. Thèse de doctorat. Faculté de Droit, Université de Paris XI.

Young, John, 2006, *South Sudan Defence Forces in the Wake of the Juba Declaration*. Geneva: Small Arms Survey, Graduate Institute of International Studies.

PART III

Nation-Building of the New State

6

The Nation-Building Project and Its Challenges[1]

Christopher Zambakari

Introduction

On 9 January 2005, the signing of the Comprehensive Peace Agreement (CPA) brought an end to the brutal civil war that engulfed Sudan before its independence in 1956. The CPA established the Interim Constitution of Southern Sudan enacted in 2005, which formed the semi-autonomous Government of Southern Sudan (GOSS) in the southern part of the Republic of Sudan. This will effectively be transformed into the Government of the Republic of South Sudan on 9 July 2011. The root causes of the war included disputes over resources, the role of religion in the state, self-determination, the distribution of power, and the institutional legacy of colonialism. The ensuing conflict devastated a significant part of Africa's largest country and deprived Southern, Western, and Eastern Sudan of stability, growth, and development. Consistent with the mandate of the CPA, in January 2011, South Sudan effectively voted to secede from North Sudan. The new nation in the South is set to be inaugurated on 9 July 2011. More than two million people have died and four million have been uprooted due to the civil war. The signing of the Comprehensive Peace Agreement in 2005 was the beginning of a long march to peace. Since the Referendum on self-determination has been successfully held, it is necessary to think about the project of nation-building that lies ahead. This essay is divided into three sections: Sudanese colonial state, political violence, and political reform. In the first section, the chapter focuses on the institutional legacy of Indirect Rule in South Sudan. In the second section, attention turns to issues driving political violence and grievances of the marginalised areas. The dilemma will be illustrated by looking at the surge in political violence in the Disputed Regions[2] as reflective of the dilemma that faces both North and South Sudan in a post-referendum era. In the last section of the essay, I will argue that the way out of the current predicament in the Disputed Areas, which lies in building a more inclusive political community in the North and South that respects unity in diversity, is contained in the conceptual framework known as the New Sudan, as articulated by the Sudan People's Liberation Movement/Army (SPLM/A). I will further argue that a successful nation-building project will depend on how the Government of South Sudan (GoSS) and the Government of Sudan (GoS) manage to build a more inclusive state, which addresses the citizenship question.

Sudan: An Overview

Sudan, known as 'bilad-al Sudan', or land of dark people, is the largest country on the African continent, 2,505,810 sq km, and approximately one-third of the size of the United States of America, or about a million square miles-- equal in size to the United States east of the Mississippi River. According to some estimates, the country has 500 different ethnic groups, speaking 130 languages (Garang 2005). Sudan has a rich cultural heritage as a cradle of African civilization. Historians call it the corridor between Egypt and Central Africa. It shares a border with nine States: Egypt to the North, the Libyan Arab Jamahiriya to the North-west, Chad and the Central African Republic to the west, the Democratic Republic of the Congo to the south-west, Uganda to the south, Kenya to the south-east, and Eritrea and Ethiopia to the east. The land has an ancient history, dating back to 2,600 BC. The country was subdivided into kingdoms and Sultanates that occasionally fought for supremacy at various periods. After the British occupied Egypt in 1882, they took over Sudan from 1898 and ruled it in conjunction with Egypt until 1955. Khartoum, the capital city,[3] is located at the confluence of two rivers: the Blue Nile, carrying with it the rich residue from Lake Tana, passing through the highlands of Ethiopia; and the White Nile that is a source of life for inhabitants along its path, flowing from Lake Victoria along the Kenya, Uganda and Tanzania borders.

Sudan is rich in mineral wealth with an abundance of crude oil, natural gas, gold and chrome, and agricultural products such as long staples of cotton, sugar, gum Arabic, wheat, maize, sorghum, and various tropical fruits. In addition, it also has large cattle ranches throughout the country and exports surplus of cattle, sheep and camels to the Arabian Gulf countries. In 1956, Sudan became the first country, administered by Great Britain, to become independent after World War Two. 'The Sudan's Civil War, also the first in postcolonial Africa, began, with the Torit Mutiny, a few months before independence was attained on January 1st 1956" (Johnson 2003:1). Since its independence, Sudan has been ruled by a series of unstable parliamentary governments and military regimes. The current Republic came into existence in 1916, during the early part of the Condominium Rule. This arrangement of the joint British and Egyptian government ruled Eastern Sudan from 1899 to 1955. Capturing the transition in Sudan from one political rule to the next is quite fascinating, yet challenging. Much has been written in the past about the cultures of various ethnic groups, land and history of the country, so time will not be spent on those subjects. On 9 January 2011, South Sudan exercised its right to self-determination as enshrined in the provisions of the CPA and voted overwhelmingly for secession from North Sudan (SSRC 2011; UNSC 2010).

The challenges facing the new state in the south are enormous. Among the pending issues that have yet to be resolved are the fate of Abyei, Southern Kordofan and Blue Nile. Second, concern remains for many Sudanese living in the Disputed Border Regions as well as Southerners in North Sudan and northerners based in South Sudan (UNSC 2010). The situation is explosive in the Disputed Border Regions. This urgency prompted UN experts to warn that if the problem in Abyei is not brought under control it 'could derail the implementation of the peace agreement that ended the country's civil war' (UN News Centre Home 2011). Third, Sudan's long north-south border remains undemarcated, with progress slow on fixing the boundaries. Current negotiations are based on colonial-era maps that reflect the border as it stood at Sudan's independence in 1956; but with the frontier crossing oil and mineral rich areas, the issue is contentious. Fourth, debt/legal treaties have not been settled. Sudan's crippling debt, estimated at US$36.8 billion, of which US$30.8 billion was in arrears at the end of 2010 (The World Bank 2011), remains a major concern in the North as well as in the South. Southerners say Khartoum spent the cash it received from international lending institutions on arms during the 1983-2005 civil wars, and thus, the South should not shoulder the liability of repayment because it never benefited from the loans. Fifth, building a southern identity is work in progress—without a common northern enemy, many fear political fractures within the South. Sixth, there is a failure to integrate militia after a process of militarisation, disarmament, and reintegration of former combatants. Leaders in the South must work to bring together often disparate groups, including opposition forces and those outside the mainstream SPLM movement to form a true inclusive political community.

Citizens without a Home: The Plight of IDPs and Refugees

The violence in Sudan has already cost the lives of millions, and there is no sign that violence has ended. Instead, in the period shortly after the referendum, hundreds of people have been killed in clashes in the South and in the Disputed Regions. Sudan Tribune, USA Today and IRIN reported that in March 2011, more than 100 people were killed in two separate clashes involving the Sudan People's Liberation Army (SPLA) and 'armed elements identified as loyal to renegade groups operating in the two states of Greater Upper Nile' (IRIN 2011b; Sudan Tribune, 2011; USA Today 2011). The months of January and February were no less violent since the Geneva-based organisation, Small Arms Survey, reported that more than 200 people were killed when Lt. Gen. George Athor, a dissident Sudan People's Liberation Army (SPLA) commander, took up arms after losing in the governorship election in Jonglei State (Small Arms Survey, 2011). The problem is exacerbated by two other matters, which complicate the situation in South Sudan further: Internally Displaced Persons (IDPs) and Refugees returning from neighbouring countries or from outside of Africa altogether. A look at UN statistic reveals the magnitude of the problem.

Table 1: Numbers of IDPs and Refugees in Sudan

Number at a Glance (DCHA and OFDA, 2011)		Source
IDPs[4] in Sudan	In Darfur: 1.9 million In S. Sudan: 612,452 In N. Sudan: 1.7 million[5] In E. Sudan: 68,000 **Total: 4.28 million**	UN-November 2010 OCHA[6]-November 2010 UNHCR[7]-December 2009 OCHA-October 2010
Sudanese Refugees	From Darfur: 275,000 From Southern Sudan: 138,270 **Total: 413,270**[8]	UNHCR-January 2010 UNHCR-February 2009
North-South & Three Areas Returnees October 30, 2010 to February 8, 2011	IDPs: 2 million Refugees: 330, 000 **Total : 255, 623**	UNHCR-November 2010 OCHA/RCSO[9]-February 8, 2010

Source: OCHA 2010, OCHA/RCSO, UN 2010, and UNHCR 2009-2010

The South Sudan Relief and Rehabilitation Commission (SSRRC) reported that 21,000 people are stranded in deplorable living conditions in IDP camps around Khartoum. These people sold property and businesses off when it was announced by the Government of South Sudan (GoSS) that they should return to the South. In the case of Abyei, the region that connects South Sudan to North Sudan, violence has already cost hundreds of lives. The UN staff in Abyei suggest that more than half the population has left the town, with the number of displaced ranging from 20,000 to 25,000 (DCHA and OFDA 2011; IRIN 2011a, 2011b).

Last, the number of South Sudanese living in the North ranges from 1.5 million to 2 million and a large number will not return to the South due to the difficult living conditions in the South and current instability in the region. These are the realities as they stand: proliferation of ethnic violence, a Disputed Border Region pending consultation, millions of IDPs stranded throughout the country and over half a million refugees yet to find a permanent home. In addition to the numerous challenges facing the South, the most pressing issue that it will have to resolve should it decide to solve the issues fueling the ensuing violence, is the question of citizenship.

In order to conceptualise the violence occurring in Sudan, one must first and foremost understand the issues that led to the violence and continue to sustain the cycle of violence over time. The main issue that links Côte d'Ivoire, Nigeria, Liberia, Sierra Leone, Ethiopia, Somalia, Burundi, Rwanda (Mamdani 2001c), Democratic Republic of Congo (Mamdani 2001b, 2011; Nzongola-Ntalaja 2004, 2006), Uganda, Kenya, and South Africa, to the event that has led to the breakup of Africa's biggest country, Sudan, is that of citizenship and nativity (Beshir 1968, 1975; Deng 1997, 2010; Harir 1994; Idris 2001, 2005; Mamdani 2009) – a question of who belongs and who does not belong (CODESRIA 2003). Who is a native and indigenous to the homeland, and who is foreign, alien or non-native in a tribal homeland? These questions centre on the legitimacy to have a native authority to advocate for one's right. They revolve around the issue of belonging and the rights and entitlements that accompany civil citizenship. Every post-colonial African conflict has revolved around the question of citizenship.

Today, Sudan is the defining example of the failure to reform the colonial system and build an inclusive polity. To illustrate the point and the difficulty in building a more equitable society that engages in a peaceful nation-building that is democratic, transparent, and inclusive of the diversity within the country, I will present the case of an Ethnic Administrative Division in South Sudan: the one-county-one-tribe policy (Zambakari 2011:42-43). In doing so, I hope to bring the study of South Sudan into the mainstream study of post-colonial Africa, along with the challenges that most African countries face and the dilemma of unity in diversity.

Problems of the Sudan: North and South

The twentieth century was a period in human history replete with never-before seen violence. One cannot help but ask: What is the reason behind the proliferation of violence in the post-colonial Sudan? Is it that violence is embedded in Sudanese cultures? If the kind of violence taking place after independence from the late 1950s is not revolutionary, counter-revolutionary or even anti-colonial, how does one make sense of this new kind of violence? Let us first explore the grievances that led to the signing of the Comprehensive Peace Agreement to frame the largest problem and turn to the specifics by looking at the politics of county creation in Southern Sudan and how that is laying the groundwork for future conflicts.

On 9 January 2005, the Sudan People's Liberation Movement/Army (SPLM/A) and the Government of Sudan (GoS) signed a peace agreement called the Comprehensive Peace Agreement (CPA), which ended the conflict in Southern Sudan that had been going on since 1983.[10] The CPA was the outcome of the so-called Machakos peace process, which began in July 2002 (Brosché 2007:2). It was composed of six partial agreements that have been signed by the two parties. The Agreement included important stipulations for South Sudan to achieve the goal of self-determination for the people through a referendum organised in 2011. The signatories to the CPA came to the realization that South Sudan had been continuously dominated by North Sudan (Nyaba 2010). Resources were not allocated equally between the regions. Power was highly centralised in the hands of a few in Khartoum. To cite one case, the process of Sudanisation of civil service, which took place shortly after the Juba Conference of 1947, resulted in only six out of 800 posts going to Southerners (Bassiouni 2010). The history of South Sudan, along with other marginalised areas, is one of political, social, and economic oppression (Brosché 2009; Deng 2006; Harir 1994; Wai 1973). Thus, the CPA set out to correct the imbalances through power-sharing, decentralisation of authority, equal allocation of revenue from oil between the North and the South. More important, the CPA included the provision for a referendum on the self-determination of the South to be held at the end of the interim period.

The interim period has seen development in South Sudan as a result of the wealth sharing provision which allocated 50 per cent of the revenue from oil to the Government of South Sudan. The area of reform of national and local institutions of governance, however, has been contradictory as the London School of Economics' report showed (LSE 2010). According to the CPA too much centralisation of power in Khartoum was part of the problem of Sudan; so decentralisation became a de facto solution. In Southern Sudan the government experimented with decentralisation only to return to a highly centralised system. At the local level, the government policy was to enact a legislation called the Local Government Act in 2009 which was seen as a way to delegate power to the local institutions. However, this policy too is tainted by something familiar in Sudanese history, the mode of rule adopted by British strategists to govern Sudan. This was an administrative mechanism characterised by a duality in law which translated into parallel structures, one governing those in the urban areas, and another system governing the peasants in rural areas. It was a policy which enabled British colonial administrators to divide up the majority of peasants into hundreds of smaller minorities and effectively deny them the political rights to mobilise or act as a majority. The next section looks at the consequences of this way of organising the mass in the countryside.

Ethnic Administrative Division – One-County-One-Tribe

Today, the South consists of ten states: Central Equatoria, Eastern Equatoria, Jonglei, Lakes, Northern Bahr el Ghazal, Unity, Upper Nile, Warrap, Western Bahr el Ghazal and Western Equatoria. According to a report by the London School of Economics on the dynamics of conflict in Sudan, the case study that illustrates the tendency for a proliferation of states, counties, and homelands is best seen with the Eastern Equatoria State (EES), which had two main districts: Torit and Kapoeta. Kapoeta is home to the Toposa and Didinga. Kapoeta was the first to subdivide into three counties: North (Didinga), South (Buya), and Eastern (Toposa/Nyangatom). Torit subdivided into three more counties: Magwi (Acholi and Madi), Ikotos (Dongotona and Lango) and Lafon/Lopa (Lopit and Pari) (2010).

Today, Eastern Equatoria has eight counties, and this number is increasing. The division is not arbitrary or accidental but reflects the reality on the ground, local and national politics above and real grievances at the local level. The capital of a county is located in the dominant tribe's homeland, which gives the tribe both political representation and access to resources. The most important resource is land. Government representatives are recruited from home areas. This method of ruling and organising the mass of peasantry is not unique to Sudan. It is, in fact, one that is fairly common in Africa.

The creation of Ethnic Federalism, a constellation of tribes with corresponding local governments can be seen in the case of Nigeria, which has a provision in its constitution, called the Federal Character,[11] in addition to the Ethiopian constitution,[12] which mandates that each tribe has a homeland or 'one-county-one-tribe rule (Haile 1997; Zambakari 2011:42-43). Uganda has an institution devoted to the management of the mass of peasantry in the rural area called the Ministry of Local Government. Sudan has copied this mode of governance, and through the Local Government Act 2009, created a hybrid system incorporating a Customary Law and Council into Local Governance. This is an institutional legacy from the British mode of rule in Africa, Indirect Rule, which functioned on a dual system: one governing the urban city dwellers and another for the peasants in the countryside. Even when done with the intent of satisfying certain disenfranchised groups, this policy produces enormous violence and instability within a country. It pre-empts the creation of a true inclusive state and focuses on a mode of governance which produces many smaller 'nation-states' within the larger state.

The division is built on certain assumptions. It is argued by proponents of this continuous subdivision that the political map must follow the cultural map of a region at the national level and at the county level. African countries that adhere to this policy also rely on ethnic quotas to fill positions in government, in federal institutions, in universities and in the armed forces. This raises a series of questions about the qualification for those positions and the unintended consequences of the policy itself. How does the state identify who can and cannot apply for jobs in state institutions? What are the criteria used in recruiting for these positions and how does the state achieve its objectives without turning citizenship into an ethnically-defined membership in a native homeland? The real problem is that cultural and political boundaries should coincide and that the state should be a nation-state – that the natural boundaries of a state are those of a common cultural community (Mamdani 2005).

Mamdani has made this observation in a number of places with regard to other African countries, and the crisis that ensues as various groups seek to have representation by having a tribal homeland. Mamdani writes, "For no matter how much we redraw boundaries, the political crisis will remain incomprehensible until we address the institutional – political – legacy of colonial rule" (Mamdani 1998, 2001b, 2005, 2011). As the paper for this Chapter was being written, the Lopit and the Pari had filed for new counties, claiming that they could no longer coexist. This is not confined to Eastern Equatoria alone.

Today, there are demands in Western Equatoria, Bahr el Ghazal, Central Equatoria, and Juba (the capital of South Sudan) to create counties based on ethnicities, and each ethnicity should be entitled to its homeland.

With a country as diverse as Sudan, one must ask: where does this process of continuous political fragmentation end? There is one problem which is a direct outcome of this particular mode of organising a population: political violence. What happens when IDPs and refugees return to South Sudan? Where will they live? Should they be confined to already demarcated states with respective counties, or should they also fight to have their own counties? How about immigrants? What happens to immigrants who do not have a county? If the right to land and political representation follows an ethnic system whereby everyone has a homeland what happens to immigrants who have neither a homeland in Sudan, nor representation in the form of a Native Authority?

The answer lies in a particular form of the state that has emerged in Africa after independence. The reality of the post-colonial state in Africa can be summarised as follows: in an increasingly integrated global economy, people move to wherever they have the chance for a better life. A dynamic economy moves people, mostly labour migrants, outside their 'tribally defined homeland' and forces them to cross over different boundaries. However, the colonial state penalizes especially those that are most dynamic, those who respond to favourable economic conditions across political boundaries, those who go in search of employment and better living conditions outside their countries. It brands them as aliens, non-indigenous, foreigners (Mamdani 1989, 2001b, 2005; Nzongola-Ntalaja 2004). The cases of the Banyarwanda in Uganda and in Eastern Congo, the Ghanaians in Nigeria, and the Burkinabe in Ivory Coast are illustrative of these tendencies in the post-colonial period. In each of the mentioned cases, violence has been the outcome, as those defined as natives and indigenous confront those branded as non-natives and non-indigenous.

In the next section, I will discuss the colonial state in Africa and the relevance of its study as it applies to South Sudan. In doing so, I hope to show that the development in Sudan is not unique to Sudan but a problem that affects all African countries. Last, I will look at the reform of that state and draw relevant lessons from a country where a successful reform has been undertaken, war brought to an end, setting an example that inspired the signing of the CPA. The same lesson has applied where mass violence has been stopped, such as in Mozambique. The Mozambican National Resistance (RENAMO) was involved in some of the most heinous crimes in Mozambique, cutting off hands, maiming, burning villages, deliberately targeting civilians, kidnapping children and forcing them into carrying out brutalities against their own parents and friends. The US State Department estimates that one million Mozambicans perished during the civil war (The US Department of State 2010).

In Mozambique, like in South Africa, violence was brought to an end through political reform. Today RENAMO sits in Parliament and not in prison. The peace agreement signed in 2005 between the Sudan People's Liberation Army/Movement (SPLA/M) and the National Congress Party (NCP) was also modelled on similar understanding, whereby there was no military victory but a stalemate between the adversaries. Both parties agreed with the signing of the Comprehensive Peace Agreement (CPA) that no one was to be held accountable for the atrocities committed in Sudan during the civil war.

The key in every case has been political reform of the state, prioritising political reform over criminalising opponents. At the core of the political reform is the recognition that we must not see all public violence as criminal. It was only when the South Africans decriminalised political adversaries, expanding the realm of political membership, that there was an opening for dialogue, which resulted in the transformation ushered in by a post-apartheid South Africa. That same political imagination was at work in the dialogue which delivered the CPA in Sudan, and the violence came to an end.

The African example of how to resolve the citizenship question, manage diversity within unity, and reform the colonial state can be seen with South Africa's transition from apartheid to a democratic system. This, more than the lessons of the European Nation-State, is relevant for containing non-revolutionary violence based on political exclusion in South Sudan.

Making Sense of Non-Revolutionary Violence in Africa

Those who study violence distinguish between two dominant forms: violence which makes sense, and violence which does not make sense. In an attempt to come to terms with the consequences of a bloody century, which are still being manifested in the twenty first century, scholars group revolutionary violence, anti-colonial struggles during the decolonisation phase, as meaningful and humane. This kind of violence is said to be progressive.

The second kind of violence is said to be reactionary and regressive; thus, it is counter-productive. This latter kind is meaningless violence which seems to defy reason and therefore lies outside the scope of understanding. It is devoid of meaning. The former is a legacy from the European Enlightenment, which viewed politically organised violence as a necessary component of progress. The latter is linked to the process of state formation in Africa. It is an outcome of the mode of rule used to colonise Africa in the nineteenth century.

Columbia's leading scholar on African Politics, Mahmood Mamdani, has called the latter type of violence that is said to be devoid of meaning, non-revolutionary violence (Mamdani 2001a). Progressive violence or 'good violence' is also associated with the legacy of Karl Marx, who famously professed that 'revolution is the midwife of history' (Mamdani 2007:7). This tradition finds its genesis in the French Revolution. Since the French Revolution, violence has been understood as essential to progress. On the other hand, the Marxist paradigm failed to account for non-revolutionary violence – violence which does not remain class specific but transcends both class and ethnicity. Its failure was in its inability to understand the kind of violence that pits the impoverished and disempowered against each other. With non-revolutionary violence, the lines of battle are not drawn by wealth and poverty, but by differences not economic in nature (Mamdani 2001a:1).

In Africa, we see a significant reduction in interstate conflict but a proliferation of ethnic conflicts within states. This development can be seen in Sudan. Whereas the CPA brought the war between the North and South to an end, the South has been plagued by mass inter-ethnic violence. The Northern and Western regions, Nuba Mountains, Abyei, and Southern Kordofan, all have been engulfed in a series of violence which cannot be characterised as revolutionary or counter-revolutionary. This kind of violence is non-revolutionary. The outcome of non-revolutionary violence easily leads to ethnic and racial cleansing.

Political Violence and Ethnic Cleansing

Most violence in Africa is related to access to resources and participation in the political process. The most important of resources is access to land. A good place to start is to study how land was treated under colonial rule. For the British, the lesson they learned in India led them to remove land from the market and hand it over to the Native Authority, who effectively governed its allocation to those designated as natives and deprived those considered non-natives. According to leading British colonial administrator, Lord Lugard:

> The Native Authority is thus de facto and de jure ruler over his own people. He exercises the power of allocation of lands, and with the aid of the native courts, of adjudication in land disputes and expropriation for offences against the community (1929:203).

In this sense, a non-native could rent but not own land. Land belonged to the collective membership and was accessed as a customary right. Given that the rich, whether native or non-native could purchase land anywhere, what then was the reality of the poor peasant? If 'you could not afford to buy land in the first place, you could still claim land "customarily", in your "home" area, from your "customary" chief, as a "customary" right, under "customary" law' (Mamdani 1998:2). The outcome was a strong sense of ethnic belonging. All this led to a heightened sense and drive to belong to a tribe, whose land would be accessed exclusively as a customary right from the Native Authority by those considered natives of the land.

From the 1930s through the 1940s, the British colonial policy in the South gained momentum. Besides the conscious effort to shape the identity of the subjects in both the North and South, a far more brutal outcome of the British Southern Policy was reflected in the forceful displacement of people from one region, where they were considered non-indigenous, to another, where they were considered indigenous. It involved the purification of all the ethnic groups considered foreign to the region. Contacts between the two regions were restricted. Historically, Sudan was also home to immigrants from East and West Africa, who moved wherever the living conditions were suitable for settling, and those making their way to Mecca.

Tribes such as Banda, Dongo, Kreish, Feruge, Nyangulgule and Togoyo, who adopted Islam and Arab cultures and maintained constant contacts with Arab tribes in Central and Western Sudan (Darfur and Khordofan), were forcefully removed from their regions and resettled in other areas away from the influence of their Northern Arab neighbours (Beshir 1968:51). The policy adopted and implemented throughout Southern Sudan resembled a similar project in apartheid South Africa with the administration of a Pass System. Characteristic of this project was the re-tribalisation of the population, fragmented into distinct ethnic groups and restriction of movement outside the tribal homeland. This was a political project, which led in ethnic cleansing and racial purification so as to create a homogenous group throughout Sudan. Mohamed Beshir captured the outcome of the Southern Policy as it was being implemented throughout Southern Sudan:

> In pursuance of this policy, all natives of Darfur and Khordofan were prevented from entering Bahr al Ghazal. No natives of the latter were allowed to go to Khordofan or Darfur. The traditional contact between the Dinka and Arabs which took place annually at the common grazing grounds of Bahr al Arab was reduced to the minimum. The Dinka settled in the North were asked to return

so that 'a more complete separation could be enforced'. A Pass System, similar to that applied in South Africa, was applied, in order to control the contact between North and South. In a meeting held at Kafia Kingi on 14 February 1940, between District Commissioner, Western District, Bahr al Ghazal, and his counterpart in Darfur, it was agreed that only those Northerners who had passes signed by the District Commissioner would be allowed to enter Raga District (Beshir 1968:51).

The British colonial project shaped and changed the very nature of the organisation of resistance in Sudan through the mechanism of law. This project defined individuals and grouped them into categories. The policy laid by the British in the early twentieth century in Sudan also explains the cycle of violence in Darfur in the West of the country and the deadlock over the Disputed Regions, with Abyei being the most contested area. So explosive is the dispute over Abyei that it is instructive to compare it to yet another explosive unresolved dispute, the dispute between India and Pakistan over Kashmir. Abyei has already proved to be a destabilising force for North and South Sudan. Without reaching a region-wide consensus, which will settle the underlining issues over political participation, access to pasture and land, Abyei may end up turning into Sudan's 'Kashmir'.

The problem in Abyei between the Ngok Dinka and the Misseriya, the conflict between the Camel Nomads of the North in Darfur and the agriculturalists in Southern Darfur, is that the demand for tribal homeland in Southern Sudan revolves around the same issues: political representation, access to pasture for cattle, and claims to a tribal homeland which will advocate on behalf of the tribe. Without resolving the underlying issues, the violence will not subside. Instead, the frequency and intensity of the new waves of violence will be far more deadly, given that the region is heavily armed, and the central governments do not have a monopoly over arms.

The regions have not been thoroughly demilitarised. Militias have not been completely disarmed and reintegrated into the armed forces or back into society. The central governments in Khartoum and Juba have not acquired total monopoly over arms or the control and traffic of weapons into the region.

Land has always been an asset in Africa. It is the source of livelihood for the mass of peasantry. With British Indirect Rule, access to land and participation and representation in local governance was assigned to native authorities who administered land and settled local disputes. Violence in the post-colonial period cannot be understood as revolutionary, counter-revolutionary or anti-colonial. It must be understood as a result of a particular mode of organising the colonised. It is the outcome of the process of state formation (Beshir 1968; Harir 1994; Idris 2005; Mamdani 1996).

Furthermore, the kind of violence which is ethnic in character, whereby the battle lines are not drawn on the basis of wealth or poverty, cannot be solved by a top-down approach, foreign aid, development assistance or military intervention. This is because, to use the word of Frantz Fanon, post-colonial violence is what pits the 'Wretched of the Earth' (Fanon 1963) against each other, the poor against the poor, and the disempowered against the disenfranchised.

Wealth and poverty are not the determining factors, but non-economic factors are the driving force fueling and sustaining what Mamdani has called 'non-revolution violence' (Mamdani 2001a). The base of this violence was laid in the colonial period. Its legacy and institutions were inherited at independence by nationalists. Rather than reform the institutions inherited at independence, African states have struggled over the past five decades to fix what colonialism left behind. Some countries have demonstrated the will to move forward after the tragedy of colonial administration. In the last section, I want to return to the conceptual framework of the New Sudan, pioneered by the late Dr John Garang, as an alternative nation-building project.

I will argue that this alternative offers the best solution to the problems of the Sudan, in the North, in the South and in the Disputed Border Regions. I will contextualise the discussion by drawing on the experience of South Africa, where violence was brought to an end without resorting to criminal justice. In this light, the CPA can be seen first and foremost as a political settlement, which brought an intractable conflict to an end without anyone standing trial.

The Political Challenge in South Sudan

The period between 2009 and 2011 has seen a rise in violence throughout South Sudan and the Border States (Zambakari 2011:43-45). Conflicts continue in Eastern and Western Sudan. Table 2 summarizes incidents recorded over a three-year period in South Sudan and the number of people killed in those incidents. Lise Grande, Deputy Special Representative of the Secretary-General of the UN and Resident and Humanitarian Coordinator in South Sudan, reported that '60,000 people have been affected by recent violence; more than 350,000 people have been displaced during 2011 by rebel militia and inter-communal fighting' (UNOCHA 2012). The military invasion and occupation of South Kordofan and Blue Nile States by the Sudan Armed Forces (SAF) has 'forced 75,000 people to seek refuge in South Sudan's Unity and Upper Nile since June' (UNOCHA 2012). As of December 2011, 4636 people have been killed in South Sudan.[13] The following four States have the largest number of people killed: Jonglei, Unity, Lakes and Upper Nile. Jonglei accounts for 42.6 per cent of the total killed, Unity 16 per cent, Lakes 10 per cent and Upper Nile 8 per cent. This prompted the Government of South Sudan to declare Jonglei 'a disaster zone' (UNOCHA 2012). Together, these four states account for 77 per cent of the overall total while the remaining six states account for 22.89 per cent (Zambakari 2012a). The year 2011 was particularly deadly in the sheer number of people killed and those displaced.

Table 2: Number of People Killed in South Sudan between 2009 and 2011

	Top Four States						
	Jonglei	Unity	Lakes	Upper Nile	Subtotal	6 other States	Total
Incidents #	333	109	106	55	603	246	849
Total Killed	1976	754	468	377	3575	1061	4636
%	42.62	16.26	10.09	8.13	77.11	22.89	100

Source: Data from ongoing Doctoral Research: College of Professional Studies, Northeastern University, Boston, MA.

The immediate task for the Government of South Sudan (GoSS) is to address this escalation of ethnic violence and proliferation of armed groups. The increasing number of Internally Displaced Persons (IDPs)[14] from the Border States and within South Sudan, the relationship between peasant communities and pastoralists with shared livelihoods needs to be effectively managed or else violence is the natural outcome of mismanagement.

In the long term, the political challenge will be how to build a more equitable society that engages in peaceful nation-building, is democratic, law-abiding, transparent, and inclusive of the diversity within the country. This challenge was noted by John Garang at the Koka Dam Conference in 1986 (Garang 1992) The solution to the national crisis in Sudan was summarised in the concept of the New Sudan. The New Sudan was a conceptual framework for a country that was inclusive of all its multiple ethnic groups, pluralistic and embracing all nationalities, races, creeds, religions and genders. While the

CPA resolved the armed confrontation between the SPLA and the NCP, it has come short in resolving the fundamental problem of the Sudan.

New Sudan and the Way Forward

The most important formulation of the problem of the Sudan was articulated by the late Dr John Garang, Chairman and Commander-in-Chief of the Sudan People's Liberation Movement/Army (SPLM/A). Garang's understanding of the fundamental problem of the Old Sudan informed and shaped how the CPA was drafted, and later the ideology of the rebel movements in Darfur, Ingassana, and in the Disputed Border States. At the Koka Dam Conference in Ethiopia in 1986, the leading opposition parties in Sudan, along with the SPLM/A, met to discuss the future of Sudan. The meeting had a significant and symbolic meaning in that it brought together all political forces in Sudan except two parties: Democratic Unionist Party (DUP), the Khatmiya-based political organisation, and the Muslim Brothers (Garang 1992:113). At this Conference, Garang acknowledged the problem facing South Sudan specifically when he pointed out that the 'Southern Problem' was less southern in nature but more Sudanese in character (Garang 1992:240). It was a problem epitomised by a certain organisation and centralization of power at the centre which left the peripheries poor, underdeveloped, and under-represented.

According to this problem formulation, 'marginalization in all its forms, discrimination, injustice and subordination, constituted the root causes of the conflict that could not be addressed in a piecemeal fashion by dishing out handouts and concessions to the disgruntled and rebellious groups whenever a conflict erupted in a particular region' (Deng 2010:18-19). The exclusion of the majority from playing an active role in the governance of the country is another issue that is highlighted by scholars who focus on the state as the root cause of the crisis.

To illustrate the stable exclusion of the vast majority in Sudan from governance, a comprehensive study of the period after independence (1956-2000) showed that northern and central Sudan have controlled 60-80 per cent of ministerial positions[15] though they represented only 5 per cent of the total population estimated to be around 32 million when the study was conducted (Alex 2005:464-465). Most economic indicators, including federal and states' actual expenditure as a percentage of GDP,[16] regional revenues and expenditures per capita as per cent of value for North between 1996 and 2000, infant mortality rate and life expectancy by region, and literacy and primary school enrolment, show a consistent pattern in the period after independence, indicating that peripheries suffered an acute crisis of marginalisation and economic strangulation (Alex 2005:464-478). North and Central Sudan have better indicators while all marginal regions are worse off economically and acutely disenfranchised as a result of government policy. Power is highly centralized in the hands of a minority in Khartoum (LSE 2010:38).

According to Garang, the Old Sudan inherited at independence was 'the dwarf of the Arab World' and the 'sick child of Africa' (Garang 1992:126). The solution to the fundamental problem was 'to involve an all-inclusive Sudanese state which will uphold the New Sudan. A new political Sudanese dispensation in which all Sudanese are equally stakeholders irrespective of their religion, irrespective of their race, tribe or gender' (Garang 2005). The New Sudan was in fact the raison d'être for the SPLM since its inception (Nyaba 2010:142).

The crisis demanded a radical restructuring of power at the centre (Garang 1992:125). There was no 'Southern Problem', but rather, a national problem in Sudan (Garang 1992:125-129). This broader definition and analysis of the problem led to the problem being one of exclusion and marginalisation at the centre. Garang understood the problem of Sudan as related to the form of power that ruled in the country. The problem was political and demanded a political solution. This ability to contextualise the problem of violence in Sudan and articulate a comprehensive solution by developing an inclusive solution made the New Sudan Concept attractive in all peripheral regions in Sudan. The importance of Garang's leadership, ideological platform and his New Sudan Vision was acknowledged by Hassan al-Turabi, leader of the Popular Congress Party and architect of the National Islamic Front (NIF), who noted that Garang was 'the man around whom all the political forces and the Sudanese have built consensus for the first time in Sudan's history… his departure will greatly affect the issues he has raised and on which the Sudanese have agreed with him' (ICG 2005:7). Garang's understanding of the national problem paved the way to the Conceptual Framework of the New Sudan, the CPA, and the current Constitution in the Republic of South Sudan (Zambakari 2012b:10-11).

The New Sudan model was developed to solve the national problem in Sudan. It has been adopted and framed into the Constitution in South Sudan. With regard to citizenship right and the problem of forced displacement, the New Sudan is consistent with regional and international frameworks dealing with citizenship rights. The ideology behind the New Sudan is similar to the one behind the American notion of E-Pluribus Unum.[17]

The New Sudan is a radical departure from colonial legacy reducing citizenship to the question of nationals. It is premised on two key fundamental shifts that together constitute a paradigmatic transformation in the conceptualisation of citizenship. The first shift is departure from the colonial policy of distinguishing between citizens and subjects, one based in the urban areas while the second is based in the countryside.

The colonial administration in Sudan racialised the urban centres and ethnicised the rural peasantry. It turned tribe into an administrative unit and built its edifice on managing these tribal units as semi-autonomous entities. It locked the peasant onto the tribal homeland and enforced the separation in law.[18] The effect was to move away from developing a uniform, secular citizenship framework to manage the diversity within the country. This was a displacement from citizenship to the national question.

In redefining the problem in Sudan from the problem of the South, Garang effectively included all marginalised regions in the struggle for liberation and reform of power at the centre (Garang 1992). The national identity crisis of whether Sudan is African or Arab is a contested issue today. In the North, the emphasis has been placed on the Arab/Islamic character of the state. With the secession of the South, the tendency in the North has been to consolidate the Arab identity while silencing all marginal identities within the North.

The opposite phenomenon is taking place in the South where the elites have moved quickly to shape the identity of the country as African, secular and Black. Sharif Harir noted that this struggle for national identity has been one of the contributing factors to the violence in Sudan. He wrote: 'This multiple denial of a Sudan which is uniquely Sudanese and not an appendage to Arabism, Islamism or Africanism lies at the root of the political problems of the "Sudan"' (Harir 1994:14). Most scholars dismiss the easy and simplified answer, which is characteristic of the way the problems in Sudan have been reported in the media. Norman Anderson rightly dismissed the notion that the problem is 'Arabs' against 'Africans' and claimed that the relationship between the 'Arab' and the 'African', north and south, is complex (Anderson 1999:65). Sudan has a historical relationship with the outside world, including the Mediterranean and Arabia, predating recorded history. During the Islamic era, Muslim Arabs chose to intermarry and assimilate rather than rely on conquest and force.

Garang took this vision a bit further in his analysis of what constituted the problems of Sudan and offered a model of nation-building, rooted in the concept of unity in diversity, respect for human rights and rule of law, equitable distribution of national resources, devolution of power from the centre to historically marginalised regions, and value of multiple identities. Sudan is a melting pot of nationalities, religions and languages. There will be no peace if some groups feel marginalised, intimidated and territorially besieged. The problem can be seen in regions which have people who have multiple identities: Abyei, Kordofan, Nuba Mountains and Blue Nile. This dilemma was captured recently in the Sudan Tribune by Dr Amir Idris, Associate Professor of African Studies and Associate Chair of the Department of African and African American Studies, FordhamUniversity. He wrote:

> I was born and raised in the North by two parents who came from two different worlds. My father came from southern Sudan and my mother was born and raised in the North. I married a woman who is a southern Sudanese. Our two children are proud to define themselves as Canadian (Idris 2010).

Despite the independence of the South, South Sudan is still linked to the North socially and economically. The South is so inextricably linked to the North that it can be argued that the South cannot find peace if the North is unstable, and the opposite is true for the North. The difficulty can be seen in the attempt to solve the problem in Abyei. The referendum on self-determination did not undo relationships forged historically over thousands of years, and it did not change the social and cultural fabric of the country.

Rather than delink prematurely all relationships between the North and South, Sudan can learn a lesson from the South African experience where violence was effectively brought to an end; and an inclusive political community, which accounts for the diversity within South Africa created and inaugurated with the first election in 1994. South Africa, like Sudan, had the option to perpetuate an endless war or reach a political settlement. It opted for the latter. The terms of the settlement are instructive in settling the crisis in the Disputed Regions and all marginalised areas in Sudan. The solution in North and South Sudan demands a similar political imagination like the one in South Africa. This imagination is noted by a Senior Research Specialist in South Africa:

> It was the fact that the contending political forces imagined the future of what South African citizenship might look like after apartheid, and that this imagination was shaped by the historical particularity of state formation in South Africa, by both its limits and its possibilities (Pillay 2010:35).

This political imagination, crucial in propelling South Africa forward was summarised in South Africa's Freedom Charter of 1955. The Charter presented a vision of South Africa that is similar to what Garang envisioned for Sudan and declared: 'that South Africa belongs to all who live in it, black and white, and that no government can justly claim authority unless it is based on the will of all the people' (African National Congress [ANC] 1955). In 1994, Mandela reiterated the concept and premise of the 'New South Africa'. He identified what appears to be the Achilles heel of the nation-building project throughout Africa in noting that the challenge today for political leaders was 'to build a nation in which all people – irrespective of race, colour, creed, religion or sex – can assert fully their human worth; after apartheid, our people deserve nothing less than the right to life, liberty and pursuit of happiness' (Mandela 1994). Mandela also warned that failure to properly manage diversity within an inclusive framework was recipe for disaster, which destroys the human capital and the potentials of citizens. The New Sudan vision as presented at the Koka Dam Conference on 20 March 1986, was a conceptual framework for a country which was inclusive of all its multiple ethnic groups, pluralistic and embracing all nationalities, race, creeds, religion and genders. It was a country in which all Sudanese were equal stakeholders.

In South Africa, for example, the African National Congress realized that victory was not possible. It also acknowledged that apartheid South Africa was a racially exclusive state. The solution was not in re-racialising the post-apartheid state through a demand for a black majority, but rather, de-racialising and reforming the state. The limit of the South African transition from apartheid to a post-apartheid democratic system is that it managed to deracialise the civil services and the state at the centre, but it continues to uphold the customary sphere without reforming it in the name of tradition. Such is the limit in South Africa, but that is a problem that it is working out as it moves forward.

The lesson of South Africa is 'it recognized that all belonged and that the creation of a single political community was the goal. Race, ethnicity and history defined the answer in the past, but will not define it in the future' (Pillay 2010). For North and South Sudan, those who will pay allegiance to the national flag, those who choose to have a common future not bound by the past, those Sudanese who chose to live side-by-side as friends and neighbours, will have to put the past aside and work for a peaceful common future. That the living must be prioritised over the dead is the lesson of South Africa. South Africa belongs to South Africans. North and South Sudan belong to North and South Sudanese.

Conclusion

This chapter started by demonstrating the successes of the Comprehensive Peace Agreement (CPA), which established the Interim Constitution of Southern Sudan, and effectively ended the war between North (NCP) and South Sudan (SPLA/M). The CPA, enacted in 2005, formed the semi-autonomous Government of Southern Sudan (GoSS) in the southern part of the Republic of Sudan and effectively ended violence, which has devastated Sudan since 1955. A brief history of Sudan was offered to provide a background to the rest of the paper.

Next, the plight of Internally Displaced Persons (IDPs) and refugees was presented, illustrating the daunting task of managing the inflow of displaced people in the various parts of Sudan. The number of South Sudanese living in the North ranges from 1.5 million to 2 million, and a large number of them will not return to the South due to the difficult living conditions in the South and current instability in the region. Among the key issues that affect both the Government of South Sudan (GoSS) and the Government of Sudan (GoS) are the proliferation of ethnic violence, a Disputed Border Region pending consultation, millions of IDPs stranded throughout the country, and over half a million refugees yet to find a permanent home.

A case study was presented to illustrate the tendency for the proliferation of counties in South Sudan. It was argued that this mode of organising the mass of peasantry pre-empts the creation of a true inclusive state and focuses on a mode of governance which produces many smaller 'nation-states' within the larger states in South Sudan. The division is built on the assumptions that the political map must follow the cultural map of a region at the national level and at the county level. The real problem with this logic is that no matter how many counties are created and how much the map of the county and region is redrawn, the political crisis will remain. This political crisis always leads to political violence.

The proliferation of ethnic violence is best understood as an indispensable component of the process of state formation, colonial governmentality, deployed to colonise African colonies in the late nineteenth century. To move forward and pre-empt future violence requires political imagination to rethink an alternative future based on a common future rather than a common past and descent. The solution for both governments in North and South Sudan is found in Garang's conceptual framework of the New Sudan, which is consistent with the other successful case in the African context, South Africa's transition from apartheid to a democracy. The lesson of South Africa is the creation of a single political community inclusive of the diversity within the country.

The New Sudan vision is the most progressive attempt at reforming the state in Sudan. It theorises a political reform of the colonial state in Sudan, the building of an inclusive community where citizens will not be discriminated based on race, colour, creed, religion, ethnicity or sex. Race, ethnicity and history defined the solutions in the past, but race and ethnicity will not define solutions in the future. For North and South Sudan, those who will pay allegiance to the national flag, those who choose to have a common future that is not bound by the past, those Sudanese who will choose to live side-by-side as friends and neighbours, will have to put the past aside and work for a peaceful, common future. The solutions to Sudan's problems cannot be imposed by force; they cannot be imposed upon Sudanese from outside. Any forceful and externally enforced solution has not worked in the past and will not work in the future.

Notes

1. I would like to thank Divine Muragijimana (Brooklyn College), Ana Afsharina-sab (Arizona State University), Pamela Gutman (University of Phoenix) for their insightful comments and constructive feedback on an earlier draft of this essay. An earlier version of this essay was presented as a paper at the International Workshop on the Consequences of the South Sudan Self-Determination Referendum), sponsored and organised by The Council for the Development of Social Science Research in Africa (CODESRIA), Dakar, the United Nations Economic Commission for Africa (UNECA), Addis Ababa and the Africa Research and Resource Forum, Nairobi, Kenya.
2. The Disputed Regions mentioned in the Comprehensive Peace Agreement for special status include Abyei, Southern Kordofan and Blue Nile.
3. After 9 July 2011, Khartoum will remain the capital city of North Sudan while Juba will become the capital city of South Sudan. There is an ongoing discussion about moving the capital city out of Juba but as of the date of the writing of this essay, Juba remains the capital in South Sudan.
4. Internally Displaced Persons (IDPs).
5. Figure includes approximately 400,000 IDPs living in four sites recognized by Sudanese authorities. Most IDPs in northern Sudan live in informal settlements in and around Khartoum.

6. UN Office for the Coordination of Humanitarian Affairs (OCHA).
7. Office of the UN High Commissioner for Refugees (UNHCR).
8. According to UNHCR, as of 13 February 248 Sudanese refugees had returned to Southern Sudan since 30 October 2010.
9. Represents International Organization for Migration (IOM) verified returns at point of arrival; does not include 7,665 registered but unverified returns to the Three Areas.
10. This was the Second Sudanese Civil War. The First Civil War started in 1955 and was brought to an end with the Addis Ababa Agreement in 1972. The controversies following the agreement in 1972 led to the second phase of the Southern rebel movement. Between the First Civil War and the SPLA/M uprising in 1983, there was another group which referred to itself as Anyanya II. The movement started shortly after the Addis Ababa Agreement and initiated military operations starting in 1978 in Eastern Upper Nile on the Ethiopian border.
11. Constitution of Nigeria (1999), § 14(3). "The composition of the Government of the Federation or any of its agencies and the conduct of its affairs shall be carried out in such a manner as to reflect the federal character of Nigeria and the need to promote national unity, and also to command national loyalty, thereby ensuring that there shall be no predominance of persons from a few State or from a few ethnic or other sectional groups in that Government or in any of its agencies." Id. §153(1)(c) establishes the Federal Character Commission. The Third Schedule, Part 1, §7 states: "The Federal Character Commission shall comprise the following members: (a) a Chairman; and (b) one person to represent each of the states of the Federation and the FederalCapitalTerritory, Abuja." Id. The Third Schedule, Part I, §8(1) empowers the Commission and states: "In giving effect to the provisions of section 14(3) and (4) of this Constitution, the Commission shall have the power to: (a) work out an equitable formula subject to the approval of the National Assembly for the distribution of all cadres of posts in the public service of the Federation and of the States, the armed forces of the Federation, the Nigeria Police Force and other government security agencies, government owned companies and parastatals of the states." Id.
12. Minasse Haile, 'The New Ethiopian Constitution: Its Impact Upon Unity, Human Rights and Development', 20 SuffulkTransnat'l L. Rev, 1, 19-20 (1996); Mahmood Mamdani, Columbia Univ., 'Political Identity, Citizenship and Ethnicity in Post-Colonial Africa', Keynote Address at the Arusha Conference: 'New Frontiers of Social Policy' 16 (12-15 December 2005) [hereinafter Mamdani, Keynote Address at the Arusha Conference].
13. The three leading factors accounting for the killing are inter-tribal conflicts, various armed incidences, and intra-tribal clashes. Jonglei, Warrap, Unity, Lake and Upper Nile states are the most affected areas.
14. Together, North and South Sudan have one of the largest numbers of IDPs in the world. For the global overview for people internally displaced by conflict and violence, see IDMC and NRC(2012).

15. The exception was the period between 1986 and 1989, known in Sudan as the second democracy, when Sudan experimented with a democratic system of governance. The share fell to 47 per cent of the total.
16. This is an aggregation of government expenditures.
17. Latin phrase that means 'Out of Many-One'. It is a motto that is featured on the Great Seal of the United States of America.
18. For more on the Closed District Ordinances in Sudan refer to Beshir (1968); Garang (1994:15-16).

References

African National Congress (ANC),1955,'The Freedom Charter', Retrieved 10 March 2011, from http://www.anc.org.za/show.php?include=docs/misc/1955/charter.html

Alex, C., 2005, 'Causes of Conflict in Sudan: Testing The Black Book', European Journal of Development Research, 17(3), 462.

Anderson, G. N., 1999, *Sudan in Crisis: The Failure of Democracy*, Gainesville, FL: University Press of Florida.

Bassiouni, D., 2010, 'Keynote Address by Dr. David S. Bassiouni to ESCA-USA 10th Annual Conference', 4-5 September 2010, Washington, DC.

Beshir, M. O., 1968, *The Southern Sudan: Background to Conflict*, London, UK: C. Hurst & Co.

Beshir, M. O., 1975, *The Southern Sudan : From Conflict to Peace*, New York Barnes & Noble Books.

Brosché, J., 2007, 'CPA - New Sudan, Old Sudan or Two Sudan?- A review of the implementation of the Comprehensive Peace Agreement', Journal of African Policy Studies 13(1), 1-25.

Brosché, J., 2009, 'Sharing Power--Enabling Peace? Evaluating Sudan's Comprehensive Peace Agreement 2005'. Uppsala, Sweden.

CODESRIA, 2003, 'Identity, Security and the Renegotiation of National Belonging in West Africa: Reflections on the Cote d'Ivoire Crisis and its Repercussions on the West Africa Region', Retrieved March 10, 2011, from http://www.codesria.org/spip.php?article582&lang=fr

DCHA and OFDA, 2011, 'Sudan – Complex Emergency: Fact Sheet #2, Fiscal Year (FY) 2011', Washington, D.C.: Bureau for Democracy, Conflict and Humanitarian Assistance (DCHA) and The Office of U.S. Foreign Disaster Assistance (OFDA).

Deng, F. M., 1997, 'Ethnicity: An African Predicament', The Brookings Review, 15(3), 28-31.

Deng, F. M., 2006, 'Divided Nations: The Paradox of National Protection', *Annals of the American Academy of Political and Social Science*, 603, American Academy of Political and Social Science, 217-225.

Deng, F. M., 2010, *New Sudan in the making? : Essays on a Nation in Painful Search of Itself*, Trenton, NJ: Red Sea Press.

Fanon, F., 1963, *The Wretched of the Earth* (Preface by Jean-Paul Sartre) (C. Farrington, Trans.), New York: Grove Press.

Garang, J., 1992, *The Call for Democracy in Sudan*. New York: Kegan Paul International.

Garang, J., 1994, 'Speech of the Chairman and Commander-in-Chief to the First SPLM/SPLA National Convention', Nairobi, Kenya: Sudan People's Liberation Movement/Army: Secretariah of Information and Culture.

Garang, J., 2005, 'Garang's speech at the signing ceremony of S. Sudan peace deal', Retrieved 9 March 2011, from http://www.sudantribune.com/TEXT-Garang-s-speech-at-the,7476

Haile, M., 1997, 'The new Ethiopian Constitution: its impact upon unity, human rights and development', *Suffolk Transnational Law Review*, 20(1).

Harir, S. T., Terje, eds,1994, Short-cut to decay : the case of the Sudan. Uppsala, Sweden: Nordiska Afrikainstitutet

ICG, 2005, 'Garang's Death: Implications for Peace in Sudan', *Africa Briefing* N°30, Nairobi, Kenya/Brussels, Belgium: International Crisis Group. Available at <http://www.crisisgroup.org/~/media/Files/africa/horn-of-africa/sudan/B030%20Garangs%20Death%20Implications%20for%20Peace%20in%20Sudan.pdf>.

IDMC & NRC., 2012, 'Global Overview 2011: People internally displaced by conflict and violence', Geneva, Switzerland: Internal Displacement Monitoring Centre and Norwegian Refugee Council. Available from <http://www.internal-displacement.org/publications/global-overview-2011>.

Idris, A. H., 2001, *Sudan's Civil War: Slavery, Race, and Formational Identities*, Lewiston, N.Y.: Edwin Mellen Press.

Idris, A. H., 2005, *Conflict and Politics of identity in Sudan*, New York, NY Palgrave Macmillan.

Idris, A. H., 2010, 'I hate to Choose: Personal reflections on the referendum', Retrieved 9 March 2011, from http://www.sudantribune.com/I-hate-to-Choose-Personal,37003

IRIN, 2011a, 'Sudan: Managing the great trek southwards', Retrieved 10 March 2011, from http://www.irinnews.org/Report.aspx?Reportid=92150

IRIN, 2011b, 'Sudan: Thousands displaced by Abyei violence "at risk"', Retrieved 9 March 2011, from http://www.irinnews.org/Report.aspx?ReportID=92129

Johnson, D. H., 2003, The root causes of Sudan's civil wars,Bloomington: Indiana University Press.

LSE, 2010, 'Southern Sudan at odds with itself: Dynamics of conflict and predicaments of peace', London, UK: London School of Economics and Political Science.

Lugard, F. D., 1929, *The Dual Mandate in British Tropical Africa*, Edinburgh & London: William Blackwood & Sons Ltd.

Mamdani, M., 1989, 'Social Movements and Constitutionalism in the African Context', CBR Working Paper, No. 2, Kampala.

Mamdani, M., 1996, *Citizen and Subject: Contemporary Africa and the Legacy of Late Colonialism*, Princeton: Princeton University Press.

Mamdani, M., 1998, 'When Does a Settler Become a Native? Reflections on the Colonial Roots of Citizenship in Equatorial and South Africa', Cape Town, South Africa: University of Cape Town.

Mamdani, M., 2001a, 'Making Sense of Non-Revolutionary Violence: Some Lessons from the Rwandan Genocide', Text of the Frantz Fanon Lecture Given at the University of Durban, Westville, Westville, South Africa: University of Durban.

Mamdani, M., 2001b, 'Understanding the crisis in Kivu: report of the CODESRIA mission to the Democratic Republic of Congo 1997'. Dakar: Council for the Development of Social Science Research in Africa.

Mamdani, M., 2001c, *When Victims Become Killers: Colonialism, Nativism, and the Genocide in Rwanda*, Princeton: Princeton University Press.

Mamdani, M., 2005, 'Political Identity, Citizenship and Ethnicity in Post-Colonial Africa: Keynote Address', Paper presented at the Arusha Conference: New Frontiers of Social Policy, Arusha, Tanzania. http://siteresources.worldbank.org/INTRANET-SOCIALDEVELOPMENT/Resources/revisedMamdani.pdf

Mamdani, M., 2007, 'The Politics of Culture Talk in the Contemporary War on Terror', Hobhouse Memorial Public Lecture, London, UK: London School of Economics and Political Science. Available at <http://www2.lse.ac.uk/PublicEvents/pdf/20070308_HobhouseMemorial.pdf>.

Mamdani, M., 2009, *Saviors and Survivors: Darfur, Politics, and the War on Terror*, New York: Pantheon Books.

Mamdani, M., 2011, 'The Invention of the Indigène', London Review of Books 33(2), 31-33, http://www.lrb.co.uk/v33/n02/mahmood-mamdani/the-invention-of-the-indigene.

Mandela, N., 1994, 'The Future of South Africa', The Asian Age. Retrieved March 11, 2011, from http://www.sahistory.org.za/pages/people/special%20projects/mandela/speeches/1990s/1994/1994_future_of_SA.html

Nyaba, P. A., 2010, 'SPLM-NCP Asymmetrical power relations jeopardise the implementation of the CPA and the future of the Sudan', International Journal of African Renaissance Studies, 5(1), 138-147.

Nzongola-Ntalaja, G., 2004 'Citizenship, Political Violence, and Democratization in Africa', *Global Governance*, 10(4), 403-409.

Nzongola-Ntalaja, G., 2006, 'Challenges to state building in Africa', African Identities, 4(1), 71-88. doi: 10.1080/14725840500268374.

Pillay, S., 2010, 'The Political Imagination of State Reform: Reflections on the Making of Political Community after Apartheid in South Africa', CODESRIA Bulletin (1 & 2), 1-55.

Small Arms Survey, 2011, 'George Athor Rebellion, Jonglei State', Sudan Human Security Baseline Assessment (HSBA), Geneva, Switzerland.

SSRC, 2011, February 10, 2011, 'SSRC Announces Final Referendum Results' Retrieved 10 February 2011, from http://www.ssrc.sd/SSRC2/

Sudan Tribune, 2011, 'South Sudan army clashes with rebel group, over 100 dead', Retrieved 9 March 2011, from http://www.sudantribune.com/South-Sudan-army-clashes-with,38227

The US Department of State, 2010, 5 November, 'Background Note: Mozambique', Retrieved April 20, 2011, from http://www.state.gov/r/pa/ei/bgn/7035.htm#history

The World Bank, 2011, April, 'Sudan: Country Brief', Retrieved May 05, 2011, from http://web.worldbank.org/WBSITE/EXTERNAL/COUNTRIES/AFRICAEXT/SUDANEXTN/0,,menuPK:375432~pagePK:141132~piPK:141107~theSitePK:375422,00.html

UN News Centre Home, 2011, 'Abyei conflict could derail Sudan's north-south peace process, UN expert warns', Retrieved 14 March 2011, from http://www.un.org/apps/news/story.asp?NewsID=37754&Cr=Sudan&Cr1=

UNOCHA, 2012, 'Statement Attributable to the United Nations Humanitarian Coordinator in South Sudan, Ms. Lise Grande. Juba, South Sudan', UN Office for the Coordination of Humanitarian Affairs in South Sudan. Accessible from <http://reliefweb.int/sites/reliefweb.int/files/resources/HC%20Statement%20Jonglei%207%20January%202012.pdf>.

UNSC, 2010, 'Report of the Secretary-General on the Sudan (S/2010/681)', New York, NY: United Nations.

USA Today, 2011, 'More than 100 killed in disputed Sudan region', USA Today, Retrieved 9 March 2011, from http://www.usatoday.com/news/world/2011-03-03-Sudan_N.htm

Wai, D. M., ed., 1973, *The Southern Sudan: The Problem of National Integration*, London: F. Cass.

Zambakari, C., 2011, 'South Sudan and the Nation-Building Project: Lessons and Challenges', *International Journal of African Renaissance Studies*, 6(2), 32–56.

Zambakari, C., 2012a, 'South Sudan and the Nation-building Project: Lessons and Challenges', in S. Adejumobi, ed., *Two Decades of Democracy and Governance in Africa: Discourses and Country Experiences*, New York, NY: Palgrave Macmillan.

Zambakari, C., 2012b, 'South Sudan: Institutional Legacy of Colonialism and the Making of a New State', *The Journal of North African Studies*, 1-18. doi: 10.1080/13629387.2012.671996.

7

Factors Shaping the Post-Referendum Nation-Building in Southern Sudan in Relation to the Sudan

B.F. Bankie

Introduction

Ancient Kush, located in present-day northern Sudan was strongly influenced by Egypt for some 1,000 years beginning in 2,700 BC. Subsequently, Egypt's power in Sudan waned. In the sixteenth century Muslim religious brotherhoods spread through northern Nubia in the area adjoining current-day Egypt. These, plus the Ottoman Empire, ruled the area through military leaders for some three centuries. In 1820 Muhammad Ali, who ruled Egypt on behalf of the Ottoman Turks, sent 4,000 troops to Sudan. This invasion resulted in the Ottoman-Egyptian rule of Sudan from 1821 to 1885. Slavery in the Sudan took hold during this period, when it was made state policy. Slavery became a cash commodity when the Europeans started making incursions into the continent to procure slaves. 'Jallaba' means of mixed race from the North of the Sudan. The Jallaba were the procurers of slaves who led raiding squads backed by formidable armies. As Egyptian rule faltered, the Jallaba hoped to inherit the governance of the Sudan. The late Dr John Garang de Mabior (2008) refers to the Jallaba as Afrabians, a hybrid of different races and nationalities, including black Africans, immigrant Arabs, Turks, Greeks and Armenians, that first evolved during the fifteenth century and have since always chosen to identify themselves as Arabs, even though many are black. Hashim states that the political Right, descendants of the Jallaba, has ruled the Sudan since self-government in 1955.

The present-day misunderstandings between Khartoum at the centre and the marginal peripheral areas such as South Sudan, creating tension and war, find their roots in slavery, Arabisation and the Islamisation drive south into tropical Africa. In a filed confidential report of the Juba Conference of 1947 dated 21 June 1947 addressed to M.F.A. Owen, the Deputy Governor of Bahr El Ghazal Area, in Wau, which was signed by B.V. Marwood, Governor of Equitoria, which conference brought together senior British colonial administrators, traditional Chiefs of southern Sudan as well as leaders from northern Sudan, for the purpose considering 'the unification of the two parts of the country', we find the quote from Owen to the northern Sudanese present that they were still suffering from the 'sins of Zubeir Pasha and the slavers'. Owen goes on to state:

> The sins of the Fathers shall be vested upon their children even unto the third and fourth generation.

Owen went on to say that the South had not forgotten the days of oppression even if the North had done so, and that the southerner's view was dominated by fear and suspicion.

When the northern elite was installed in power in Khartoum by the departing Anglo-Egyptian Condominium, they considered the Sudan as consisting of their fellow noble Arabs of the centre north area; the Muslim Africans of the periphery (with possible Arab blood) undergoing rapid Arabisation; and the slaves, being blacks with no authority to rule.

The institution of slavery in the Afro-Arab borderlands and Sudan is a matter on which information is either suppressed or not available. Both Arabs and Africans are reluctant, unwilling or unable to bring the facts to the common knowledge of the two peoples, either by way of curriculum reform or academic research. The approach has been (Laya 2005) to not raise questions of legitimacy of the state, and in the name of 'national unity' reference to slavery is prohibited. Laya affirms there were close relationships between the trans-Atlantic and the trans-Saharan slave trades.

In a paper on the impasse of post-colonial relations, Simone (2005) refers to the legacy of Afro-Arab slavery as having distorted the relations between two major nationalities in Africa and in our world, the African and the Arab.

This, he explains, is because the descendants of the slavers have never publicly condemned or even admitted the abuses of the past, to the descendants of those who were abducted and whose lands were raided. This is a major factor in explaining why slavery continues today. Despite the adoption of the Arab Charter on Human Rights by the Arab League in September 1994, slavery abides. In December 2005, the Organisation of the Islamic Conference (OIC) adopted a Ten-Year Program of Action, promoting issues such as tolerance, moderation and human rights. This has not affected the lives of the people living in Islamic states such as the Sudan and Mauritania. The issue of slavery cannot be divorced from that of reparations and restitution, as stated in the Declaration of the Conference on Arab-Led Slavery of Africans, held Johannesburg on 22 February 2003 (CASAS Book Series No. 35, Cape Town).

Arabisation and Islamisation

Gregory. A. Pirio in his book *The African Jihad – Bin Laden's Quest for the Horn of Africa*, provides some background information on the 'Arab Project in Africa', being the expansion of Islam and Arabic culture in Africa, by defining some basic terms, which have application today from Nouakchott on the Atlantic Ocean to Port Sudan on the Red Sea. The term 'Islamist' is used to describe those groups that seek the establishment of an Islamic state, which theologically promotes a fundamentalist approach to Islam known as the Wahabist or Salafist version of Islam. 'Islamisation' is a set of political ideologies that hold that Islam is not only a religion, but also a political system that governs the legal, economic and social imperatives of the state according to its interpretation of Islamic law. Islamists, such as those ruling in Khartoum, Sudan, advocate that Sharia, a legal system based on the Koran and the Islamic tradition of jurisprudence, should determine public and some aspects of private life.

Pirio explains the term Jihadist as describing those Islamists who espouse violent action, whether military action or terrorism, to achieve their aims. Jihadists see themselves as waging war against 'Kafirun' or unbelievers. They see their struggle as a just war legitimised by religious, political and military interpretations of the Islamic concept of Jihad. Jihadists often see their actions as part of a local and global struggle to decentre the West in world affairs in order to establish 'Hakimiyyat Alklah' or 'God's rule' on a global scale. In Islam, Jihad refers to peaceful inner spiritual striving, which is a widely respected Islamic ideal. Jihadi have misappropriated the word Jihad to sanction the use of violent struggle against non-believers and Muslims, who disagree with their version of Islam. Terrorism is the antithesis of the real meaning of Jihad.

In 1989, by way of a military coup d' état, Colonel Hassan Ahmed al-Bashir took power in Sudan and retains power to this day. The ideological driving force behind the new regime to promote political Islam was Hassan al-Turabi and his National Islamic Front (NIF). It was Hassan al-Turabi who articulated a grand vision for the Arabisation of Africa. Working with Ben Laden, who was then resident in Sudan, they plotted to Islamise South Sudan, Somalia and areas south of the Republic of Sudan, to be used as a launching pad to take control of Yemen and ultimately Saudi Arabia. Not only did they seek to control the Horn of Africa, but also East Africa, stretching into Tanzania. It is important to bear in mind that in those days Khartoum saw South Sudan as a corridor to the capture of Kampala in Uganda.

In 1991 Bin Laden moved his Jihadist fighters from Afghanistan to Sudan at the invitation of al-Turabi. In May 1996 Bin Laden left Sudan for Jalalabad, Afghanistan. At some point he was resident in Juba, fighting on what was considered by Jihadi as part of the global front of Jihad. He left due to pressure from al-Bashir, who was then struggling to take the de facto leadership of Sudan from al-Turabi. It was during Bin Laden's residence in Sudan that Islamic fundamentalist structures were planted in Eritrea, Ethiopia, Kenya, Somalia, Uganda and Tanzania. Sudan's attempts to set up a Jihadist mobilisation in Tanzania were thwarted by the Tanzanian government. Apart from seeking to Arabise and Islamise Africa, Khartoum sought to cut-off Ugandan support for the Sudanese People's Liberation Movement/Army (SPLM/A) of South Sudan. This then is the context of southern Sudan's conflict with Khartoum, which was and remains a formidable war machine with extensive capacity outside its borders. Southern Sudan lost some two million plus lives in the years of war starting with the Torrit Rebellion in 1956 and the Anya-Nya rebellion.

Sudan, historically speaking, was the land of black people. Later it was impacted by slavery and Islam. The ambitions of the current Bashir government to create an Islamic state were not well received by those living in the margins of the country and led to a sustained war between Khartoum at the centre and South Sudan, Darfur and other outlying areas of the periphery, whose populations were considered by Khartoum to be insufficiently Arabised and Islamised by those in the centre. The writer of this chapter lived in Juba from 2006 to 2008, working at the social science research centre, the Kush Institution, within the Office of the President of South Sudan, observing at close hand developments in the South, Darfur and the region in general.

Nhial Bol in his piece dated 15 April 1998 entitled 'Religion- Africa: Countries of the Horn urged to apply Sharia', states:

> An ideology of expansionist Islamic fundamentalism, which sought to' Arabise' all of Sudan and the Horn, underpinned Sudan's regional aggression.

The International Scenario

The President of the Sudan, Omar Hassan Al Bashir in his address to the Organisation of Islamic Conference (OIC) in Abuja, Nigeria (November 1989) declared that the destiny of Islam in Africa is to win. This represents a direct challenge to African sovereignty and was a calculated threat of interference in the internal affairs of all the states of Africa. In 1998 Bashir introduced an Islamic Constitution to Sudan, making the Sudan a *de jure* Islamic Republic. Sharia Islamic codes became applicable to non-Muslims. Islam was used to Arabise all the people of the Sudan. Al Bashir stands indicted by the International Criminal Court (ICC) for crimes against humanity and war crimes in Darfur, in western Sudan, a region of some seven million people. The conflict in Darfur which involved Khartoum fighting Darfuri Africans (some Darfuri identify themselves as Arabs) has left some 200,000–450,000 black Africans dead and over 2.5 million displaced. The resolution of the Darfur conflict, like that in South Sudan which preceded it, and upon which it was modelled, represents a challenge in terms of peace mediation not only to Africans, but to humanity.

The reaction of Africa to Bashir's indictment has created unease amongst those of Africa descent in the global African community. The majority of African states, at a meeting in Libya, apparently took the position that the issue of the indictment was targeted and unfair and they refused to implement it, despite being signatories to the Rome Statutes, establishing the ICC. These states say that leaders in the West have committed worse offences in places like Iraq and Afghanistan.

Outsiders who have researched first-hand what is in fact going on in the Afro–Arab borderlands have concluded that events there are not a product of chance. They are the calculated result of forces from within and without the region that see it as an area that is off-limits to public scrutiny, in which they can, with impunity, pursue their ambitions. There are few attendant risks of exposure, which allows the borderlands to be utilised for human trafficking and smuggling, the testing of new weapons systems (including nuclear) and other inhumane practices, in complete disregard of the welfare of the inhabitants. Of late, the place has become an area for international hostage-taking by groups, one of which goes by the name of Al-Qaeda, a product of the Salifista armed rebellion from Algeria.

It is South Sudan's emergence as new state in Africa that poses the first major challenge to the post-, or we should rather say, neo-colonial geopolitical status quo in north east Africa. In historical perspective, the states in Africa were the product of a deliberate policy of decolonisation.

Having attended and monitored the South Sudan Referendum in January 2011 with its large turnout and its 98. 83 per cent vote for secession, and the independence day on the 9 July being more of a formality,neither of these events, in the opinion of the author, changed the overall intent of Khartoum to 'call the shots' throughout the old Sudan. Nothing has changed in Khartoum's tactic to rule by the sword, when unable to manipulate by peace agreement. To think otherwise would be an exercise in self-deception and a break with historical precedent.

The 'New Sudan' and State Secession

In southern Africa and Africa in general, as well as its western Diaspora, such is the level of collective amnesia about the borderlands in general that many believed the Independence of South Sudan marked the end of violence in Sudan. State secession is a sort of taboo in Africa in general, where the current architecture of multi-state formation is a work in progress jealously defended by the AU. It requires hard work to explain the Sudan realities, in the face of the fear of the unknown and indifference. Some persons in the area, who know better, did nothing to dispel expectations of peace and a negotiated settlement in Sudan. Nothing could be further from reality. Indeed, informed opinion is that in the coming period the Republic of Sudan will be rendered ungovernable with war becoming more generalised in the country than in living memory. This is the reality of relations between the Republic of Sudan and the new state of South Sudan

One needs to keep centred, when seeking to come to terms with the South Sudan reality, the Late Garang's vision of a 'New Sudan', which remains the guiding light of the new state. Secession was not an option for Garang, who apart from leading the Sudan revolution, was a visionary and a Pan-Africanist, whose horizon stretched further afield than Sudan. The ultimate objective of Garang was the creation of a democratic state in Sudan, ruled by law, with its separation of powers enshrined in its constitution. Until this is achieved war will continue in Sudan, with the 'marginalised' striving to achieve Garang's vision, whatever the human costs. Despite the 'independence' of South Sudan, it is now in Blue Nile, southern Kordofan and adjoining areas that the Sudan Revolution Forces (SRF), constituted by the SPLM-North, forces from Blue Nile, southern Kordofan and Darfur fight on to achieve the 'New Sudan', lead by the associates of Garang, who participated in the Navaisha Talks, which lead to the signing of the CPA. These are persons such as Yassir Arman and Malik Agar.

What we have seen since the flag went up in Juba is Khartoum actively assisting the installation of the Transitional Government in Libya; its attempt, with the assistance of the United States of America, to escape the isolation of sanctions by negotiating its removal from the list of states sponsoring terrorism; attempts to ingratiate itself with the African community so that the ICC warrant is waived and desperate attempts to conclude any peace agreement on any terms in Darfur, even by way of internal consultation within the captive community in the Darfur camps.

From the Republic of South Sudan we witnessed the visit of the Israeli Likud Parliamentarian, Danny Danon to Juba and were informed that South Sudan would position its Israel embassy in Jerusalem. The South announced the establishment of embassies around the world commensurate with what it perceives as its status as a sovereign nation.

Continuous observation of western actions in Sudan indicates that although the country enjoys pariah status, none are ready for regime change in Khartoum as happened in Libya. US Sudan envoys had wavered on Sudan secession but in the end respected the will of the South to be 'free'. On security co-operation, and this is where best to make real assessment of real interests, the US is working well with Khartoum.

The new state has been unable to develop as it had planned to during the transitional period after the signing of the CPA. Khartoum kept Juba on the defensive by invading Abyei, by the border demarcation uncertainties, by interfering with the flow of oil from the South to Port Sudan on the Red Sea, by the expulsion of southerners from Khartoum, by raising tax issues and creating a general crisis scenario and tensions between the North and South.

In the Sudan theatre all actors, be they from the North, South, East or West, are locked into a struggle without end in sight. The intermittent talks in Addis Abba and elsewhere between Khartoum and Juba hosted by the AU, moderated by the AU High Level Panel chaired by Thabo Mbeki have yielded little fruit. There should be no illusions. It is not possible to discern any changing attitudes amongst the African governments vis-à-vis Sudan.

Traditionally, the policy has been 'hands off'. Many came to Juba to pledge their alliance to the new state on 9 July 2011. It may be too early to draw conclusions. The fatigue induced expectations of peace after 9 July 2011 were expectations devoid of foundation and indicate that many have yet to come to terms with Sudanese realities.

Ultimately, the majority of the Sudanese will determine their destiny. However, in the absence of the input of their experience, the rest of Africa will be much poorer in its policy formation. The experience from the Afro-Arab borderlands represents the 'missing link' in the logical framework for unity.

Lessons from the Sudan Experience and the Relations Between the Republic of Sudan and South Sudan

The OAU came about at the end of a long historical process which saw a structural manifestation of the quest for Africa national unity. By that is meant that shortly after Africa began to decolonise, the vision of a united Africa, ruling itself with dignity and respect, led to the formation of the OAU. This historical process had begun with the abduction of African slaves from Africa to the western hemisphere, where the incubation of Africans in the 'new world' was built on crude capitalism with the elimination of the indigenous people of America and the harnessing of black labour from Africa for development. This led to a conscientisation around common experiences of enslavement, racism and exploitation (Sibanda 2008), culminating in the Garveyist 'Back to Africa Movement' and the Pan-African Congress series organised by the African American scholar, W.E.B. Du Bois. In some measure the trans-Atlantic slave trade replicated the experience of Africans – especially women and children – who were the principal victims of the trans-Saharan slave trade and those taken into Arab bondage. The fundamental difference was that the Europeans, apart from attempting conversion to Christianity, did not succeed in denationalising the Africans taken to the western Diaspora (Caribbean, North/South America or Europe). In contrast, as seen in the Sudan today and graphically illustrated in Darfur (where the conscientisation around African identity is recent and its future uncertain), Africans in the eastern Diaspora ceased to be Africans and became Arabs. It is this loss of identity under the Arab system, which renders the reconnection of the African eastern Diaspora in the Gulf, Arabia, etc, with Africa a major cultural challenge with deep psychological implications.

Cultural solidarity within the Arab League stressed the concept of a single Arab nation. This nation looked back to the ancient Arab empires of the

Umayyads and the Abbasids, noting that Arabs had 'civilised' Europe in the Middle Ages. Such a cultural collective for sub-Saharan Africa was promoted by Cheik Anta Diop in his work on the cultural unity of black Africa. Indeed, it is astonishing that little serious effort has been made to establish a culturally based African League/Nation, given the respect accorded Diop and his conclusions, the basic premises of which had been advanced by 1885, if not earlier, by the Haitian, Antenor Firmin in his book published the same year, entitled *The Equality of the Human Races*.

There is much information available in situ about what has happened in South Sudan. Darfur developments can be tracked daily, as can those in other parts of the Sudan, such as Nubia. News availability is a recent development. Because of the distortions and silencing of history, Africans have, in the past, chosen to not interest themselves in the problems of this part of Africa. Indeed, it was only in February 2009 that the AU appointed its High-Level Panel on Darfur, which concluded that, 'Africa has no choice but to assume a leadership role with respect to the Sudan, it being 'a bridge between North Africa and sub-Saharan Africa'. The High-Level Panel declared that the Sudan 'is Africa's crisis and, as such, Africa has a duty to help the people of Sudan to achieve a lasting solution'. Prior to this, Sudan including the South, was considered by the OAU as an Arab issue, Sudan being a member of the Arab League as well as the OAU. It took that body dedicated to continentalism, some 35 years to arrive at a conclusion that southern Sudanese nationalists, such as Aggrey Jadeen, had reached, through blood, before the OAU was born (*The Sudan Mirror* 2007:21).

Conclusion

The late John Garang de Mabior (2008) opted for a 'New Sudan' with its place in Africa and the world, coming out strongly for a unity of Africans south of the Sahara. His African Nation concept was to be an ideological weapon to arm the African youth. He asked:

> Are all parts of continental Africa parts of this African Nation? Arabia has its own Nation incorporated in the Arab League. Do we want in our African Nation people belonging to another Nation? The time has come for the African youth to determine who will lead the national movement (Bankie and Mchombu 2007:214).

Prah (2006:230), in his discursive reflection on nationalism in a substantial work about what he terms 'The African Nation', defines this as follows: 'I speak of and mean nationalism, based on the unity of Africans as a whole

– Pan Africanism.' Prah is of the view that the states in Africa are stillborn and will never be viable. He refers to the work of the Egyptian scholar, Samir Amin, towards the achievement of the Arab Nation, which organizational framework is represented by the Arab League. He opts for a unity of Africans based on the African Diasporas, plus sub-Saharan Africa.

The future of South Sudan and its relations with the Republic of Sudan are interlinked with the trajectory of history. The emergence of the new state of South Sudan is but a stepping stone in a bigger picture whose implications are of importance to north-east Africa in general. More attention is being given to this area, located between the Middle-East and Africa, as it now attracts intense international media attention.

References

Bankie, B.F., 1995, *Pan-Africanism or continentalism*? African Opinion Series Number 4, Cape Town: Harp Publications.

Bankie, B. F. and Mchombu, K. 2008, *Pan-Africanism/African Nationalism --Strengthening the Unity of Africa and its Diaspora,* Trenton NJ: The Red Sea Press.

Diakite, S., ed., 2006, 'Racial prejudice and inter-ethnic conflicts: The case of the Afro-Arab borderlands in the Western Sahel', in *Racism in the global African experience*, Prah K., ed., Cape Town: CASAS.

Esedebe, P. O., 1964, *Pan-Africanism: The idea and movement, 1776–1991*, Washington, DC: Howard University Press.

Firmin, A., 2002, *The equality of the races*, Urbana and Chicago: The University of Illinois Press.

Garang, J.D., 2008, 'Pan-Africanism and African Nationalism: Putting the African Nation in context – the case of Sudan', in *Pan-Africanism/African Nationalism: Strengthening the unity of Africa and its Diaspora*, Bankie B.F. & Mchombu, K. J., Eds., Trenton, NJ: Red Sea Press.

Hashim, J.M., 2004, 'To be or not to be: Sudan at the crossroads', Unpublished paper.

Hashim, J.M., 2007, 'The policies of de-Nubianization in Egypt and Sudan: An ancient people on the brink of extinction', *Tinabantu Journal of African National Affairs*, 3(1), Cape Town: CASAS.

Laya, D., 2005, 'Soudanais 'sans Dieu ni maitre': Esclavage et traite trans-Saharienne dans le Soudan Senegalo-Nigero-Tchadien, avant 1800', *in Reflections on Arab-led slavery of Africans*, Cape Town: CASAS.

Marwood, B.V., 1947, http://www.gurtong.org/resourcecentre/documents/articles/juba_conference_1947.pdf

Nabudere, D.W., 2007, 'Cheik Anta Diop: The social sciences, humanities, physical sciences and transdisciplinarity', *International Journal of African Renaissance Studies*, Vol. 2 No. 1. Pretoria: UNISA.

Nyaba, P.A., 2002, 'The Afro-Arab conflict in the 21st century, A Sudanese viewpoint', *Tinabantu Journal of African National Affairs* 1(1), Cape Town: CASAS.

Nyaba, P.A., 2007, 'What is African liberation?' *South Sudan Post*, November 2007, Juba: Centre for Documentation and Advocacy.

Pirio, G.A., 2007, *The African Jihad - Bin Laden's quest for the Horn of Africa*, Trenton NJ: The Red Sea Press.

Prah, K.K. 2006, *The African Nation: The state of the Nation*. Cape Town: CASAS.

Sibanda, S., ed., 2008, 'Pan-Africanism and Afrikan Nationalism: Putting the Afrikan Nation in context', in *Pan-Africanism, African Nationalism: Strengthening the unity of Africa and its Diaspora*, Trenton NJ: Red Sea Press.

Simone, S., ed., 2005, 'Addressing the consequences of Arab enslavement of Africans: The impasse of post colonial cultural relativism', in *Racism in the global African experience*, Cape Town: CASAS.

PART IV

Economic Policy for the New State

8

South Sudan's Priority Development Programmes, Projects, and Policies

Benaiah Yongo-Bure

Introduction

One of the main reasons South Sudanese voted overwhelmingly for separate statehood from North Sudan is the quest for socio-economic development. Although many foreign commentators imply that the poverty of South Sudan makes it an unviable separate country, virtually all South Sudanese believe that the present poverty of Southern Sudan will persist and never begin to be tackled as long as South Sudan is ruled from Khartoum. Consequently, all South Sudanese are looking forward to a government of the Republic of South Sudan that puts socio-economic development as one of its priorities.

To sustain peace and national solidarity, the government of the new country must put in place short, medium, and long-term development programmes and policies. Most of the past and current problems of instability and violence can be attributed largely to the poverty and limited opportunities in South Sudan. With expanding opportunities, a hopeful future becomes possible and antagonisms may be greatly reduced. The intra- and inter-ethnic conflicts are not new and are not inherent in the nature of the people but are largely a result of extremely limited socio-economic development in South Sudan since its incorporation into the present Sudanese and world systems. With equitable transformative socio-economic programmes and policies such conflicts will be greatly reduced. Hence, the government of the new country must pursue policies that bring optimism to the majority of South Sudanese. The population should be able to see that there are concrete projects in the pipeline which will soon alleviate their poverty. For basic educational, health, and water projects, deliverables should be available within two to three years. Domestic food production can be substantially increased within one to two seasons, especially if the peasants are given incentives through attractive producer prices and availability of marketing, transportation, and storage facilities.

Fortunately, the Government of Southern Sudan (GoSS) has already initiated some of these activities during the Interim Period of the Comprehensive Peace Agreement (CPA) and will not have to begin from zero as was the case in 2005. Furthermore, GoSS has founded some of the institutions of a state and gained experience during the six-year Interim Period.

Given the dearth of development and pervasiveness of poverty in the new country, both quick-impact and long-term development activities need to be embarked on immediately. The quick-impact activities are to alleviate poverty and lay the foundation for long-term development, while the long-term programmes will bring about cumulatively self-sustaining development. The quick-impact projects must include those in agriculture, education, health and sanitation, water supply, transport and bridges, and small-scale off-farm activities.

The long-term projects will be in the same sectors as well as in energy, mining, and manufacturing, which will eventually lead to an integrated industrial economy. Such projects must include the building of oil refineries and the oil-pipeline to the Kenyan port of Lamu, speeding up of large-scale gold exploitation, the construction of major hydro-electric projects, the establishment of the three major Southern universities, and the construction of modern secondary schools, teacher training colleges, and modern referral and research hospitals. Serious initiation of some of these projects under a five-to-ten-year programme will give the citizens an optimistic view of the future as they will have something to hope for. The projects should be sequenced appropriately so that they are not just meant for political appeasement of the population. The political leadership, at all levels of government, must continuously explain to the people what is being done, why things may not be happening as expected, and what corrective measures are being put in place.

Short-run and Medium-term Programmes

A growth strategy that is aimed at reaching the bulk of the population is essential for improving the living conditions of the majority and giving them a hopeful future. Given that the majority of the South Sudanese are scattered in the countryside, rural development and decentralised administration should be the basis of such a strategy. With lack of so much pre-requisite physical and social infrastructure and limited agricultural production, little manufacturing industry should be expected in South Sudan in the next few years. Hence, absorbing the urban population in gainful employment will be a daunting problem in the near future. However, the creation of many productive activities in the rural areas will slow the rate of urbanisation. Thus, John Garang's strategy of 'taking the towns to the people instead of the people coming to the towns', at leastfor now, should be interpreted as putting emphasis on rural infrastructure, peasant agricultural production, crop marketing (cash payments and storage facilities), cottage industries, and the development of education, health, and water supply in the counties, payams and bomas.

With at least some rudimentary roads now linking the urban and rural areas, import substitution of food production should be seriously embarked on. This needs prioritisation on rural roads, bridges, lorries (trucks), bicycles, storage facilities, paying farmers cash on delivery, etc. Both the public and private sectors should be involved. Domestic food supply should displace much of the imported food as transport cost will be lower if roads and bridges are reconstructed or constructed. Rising incomes in the rural areas will have multiple beneficial effects such as ability to undertake community self-help activities, reduce dependence and corruption as the rural population will earn their own incomes instead of depending on government-employed relatives whose income cannot take care of all relatives; and are hence induced to supplement their salaries illegitimately. Taxes on internal trade in South Sudan have to be abolished. Local governments can supplement their revenues by charging minimal poll taxes, based on the incomes of their residents but not on quantities of particular commodities produced, as taxes on specific commodities tend to stifle production.

As most food imports from Kenya and Uganda will increasingly come to be produced in South Sudan, these countries, among others, will be propelled to trade with South Sudan in higher-value manufactures, which will take time for South Sudan to produce. With abundant and cheaper food supply in urban areas, the cost of living will fall and so will the cost of production in industry and other sectors. The tax bases of state and local governments will also be enhanced and so will their abilities to undertake their programmes in fields such as education, health, and water supply. Raw material for agro-industry and export earnings for servicing and expanding the economy will be ensured, thus reducing overdependence on oil for foreign exchange and domestic revenue.

For a long-term strategy to minimize reliance on exhaustible resource such as petroleum, South Sudan should begin to develop a variety of export crops. In addition to oil seeds, coffee, cotton, tea, and palm oil have been grown for cash in South Sudan. In the 1990s, other crops had demonstrated their potential for supplying the local and export markets. These crops included shea butter, chillies, sunflower, gum Arabic, soybeans, vegetables, fruits and honey. In the shortrun, expansion in the production of these crops should be encouraged. But in the medium and longrun, research into these crops for varieties that are high-yielding, pest and disease resistant will be important (Yongo-Bure 2007:33-50 & 204-206).

Availability of consumer goods gives the peasants incentives to earn more income. Since there is hardly any domestic manufacturing in South Sudan, imports of consumer goods should be biased towards the basic needs and wants of the peasants. Importation of household utensils, basic textiles, blankets, bicycles, sewing machines, farm implements, baggage, building materials, etc will spur higher development effort. In the meantime, South Sudan should be planning to eventually produce these products.

There should be continuous programmes to vaccinate livestock. Also essential for the animal industry are the provision of dry-season watering points, and the creation of large reservoirs or mini-lakes for dry-season watering and grazing. Training of many veterinarians and veterinary assistants must be greatly expanded. Research and cross-breeding will have to be restarted. Veterinary laboratories for vaccine production and testing have to be constructed. Local government taxation of cattle could help speed up the controlling of chronic animal diseases and provision of watering points as well as improvement of rangelands and primary education. A one-pound tax per head on half of one's herd of cattle, and the tax revenue used in the local community, would probably be acceptable to the majority of the livestock owners.

Construction of local access rural roads should be among the priorities of quick-impact programmes. In the light of the constraints on construction capacity, there is need to institute labour-intensive public works programmes at the county level to begin work on rural infrastructure. Each county should be equipped with a basic package of road construction equipment with maintenance capacity. The county road equipment will be complemented with rural manual labour, thus increasing employment opportunities and reducing instability as many cattle-rustling youth will have alternative fields of productive employment. The use of local labour will infuse more cash into the rural economy and raise income and trade, in addition to raising the general productivity of the economy.

Oil refineries should be built in the oil producing areas, with pipelines linking the refineries to the major national consuming areas. Large oil storage depots should be built in every county. All these measures will ensure reliability of fuel supply at lower prices. The multiplier effects of the construction and operation of refineries and pipelines will considerably contribute to the alleviation of poverty.

GoSS has done substantial work in the area of providing social services such as education, health, and rural water supply. However, there is need for a functioning hospital in each county. Each state should have at least a modern referral and research hospital in the next five years. Sending government officials abroad for medical care is too expensive and discriminates against the ordinary citizen. Let South Sudan create its own modern facilities such as those in Kenya, South Africa, Uganda, etc, to which government officials go for better medical treatment. The national facilities with have far greater impact on health in South Sudan than the foreign ones.

The problems of water-borne diseases can be most effectively addressed by supplying clean water in both rural and urban areas. More boreholes should be drilled in the rural areas so as to eventually cover all the rural population. Piped water supply should be available to all residents of cities in the long run. In the short run, boreholes should supplement urban water supply. In the long run, however, boreholes are not appropriate means for urban water supply given seepage from pit latrines and sewage systems. Sewage systems should be developed in urban areas beginning with the large cities.

Facilities and spare parts for the servicing and maintenance of water supply machinery, equipment, and vehicles should be available at the county level. Other important long-term policy issues, regarding drinking water, include the building of community capacity to maintain the installed facilities as well as the extension of the services to cover all the population. This will involve training of servicing and maintenance capacity at the county and eventually at the community level. Local sources of funds, to be supplemented with central resources, will have to be developed.

To achieve the goal of universal primary education, higher education will have to be greatly expanded to produce the necessary number of teachers and other human resources. Even though there has been a substantial expansion in primary and alternative education during the Interim Period, the gross number includes young adults. This is fine, but it also means that many children of school age are not yet able to attend school. Hence, primary education needs more expansion and improvement of quality in terms of teachers, buildings, school supplies, etc.

Secondary education needs a major boost. As of 2009, there were about 44,027 students attending secondary school (grades 9-12) in the whole of South Sudan (MOEST 2010). Yet it is from this number that the universities and training institutions will recruit in the near future. Given the paucity of properly educated and trained human resources in South Sudan, this figure is very low. Hence, great efforts should be exerted in secondary school expansion. In any case, such a policy should be inevitable given the recent substantial increase in primary school enrolment. In the 1960s, the International Development Association (IDA) availed loans for the development of education in many newly independent countries. South Sudan should explore this avenue given that IDA's loans are not expensive to service and repay. After about a generation, the organisation charges an interest rate of 0 to 2 per cent (World Bank 2009).

The universities of Juba, Upper Nile, and Bahr el-Ghazal should be considerably expanded in both student-intake and the variety of courses dependent on the needs of the country. For the various developments envisaged and for the efficient running of both the public and private sectors, South Sudan needs a basic stock of well-educated and trained people. Beginning at a low level of stock, a big push has to be made to fill the wide gap otherwise whatever development is initiated in the short run will not become sustainable. The implementation, management, monitoring, and evaluation of all programmes and projects need well educated and trained human resources. While importation, especially from neighbouring countries, may fill in the gaps, in the long run local human resources will be important for the sustenance of development. There must be a conscious and genuine effort to recruit and encourage the South Sudanese in the Diaspora to return home to contribute. Recruitment for available posts in South Sudan can be undertaken in the country's embassies where there are large South Sudanese communities instead of requiring those in the Diaspora to return home before being considered for employment.

In fact, to enhance productivity in the public sector as well as to boost the indigenous private sector, redeployment of South Sudanese human resources is necessary. Veterans and aged civil servants should be deployed to productive activities in the private sector and be substituted with new graduates who are trainable in current technologies and processes. If given some handsome retirement packages, which they deserve, South Sudanese war heroes can have substantial positive impact on the private sector through investing their pensions and gratuities in construction and housing, farming for the market, security, trade, trucking, and so many other activities in the private sector. Institutions should be established to train and guide them in transitioning to productive private-sector activities. If given some training in various types of commercial enterprises, they can pick up areas of activities consistent with their aptitudes, interests, and locations. A productive private sector dominated by war heroes will give it respectability with the general public.

As much as a number of foreign banks have moved into South Sudan, the country needs to develop its own banks, which in the long run will come to dominate its banking industry. Considerable efforts must be made to develop such a vital sector. It will take time before the habit of banking becomes widespread. Therefore, it must be consciously developed. The persistent problems that the Nile Commercial Bank has been experiencing must be seriously addressed. Each state should establish its own bank(s) with the capital contributed by the central, state, and county governments. The citizens of each state should also buy shares in their state bank(s). This will reduce future complaints about unfairness in the functioning of the national banking system. At least an insurance and re-insurance company/corporation must be set up. States may also establish their own insurance companies, again with shares from the citizens of each county and state. Plans should be devised to educate and train human resources for the establishment of the nucleus of a financial system.

Manufacturing should focus selectively on those activities relevant to rehabilitation and construction, using as much local material as possible. The building materials industry is among the priority sectors. There is need for carpentry at the local level for the manufacture of furniture. Repair and manufacture of farm implements will enhance the growth of the agricultural sector. The manufacturing of packaging materials will gain in prominence as agricultural production and exports increase (Yongo-Bure 2007:62-63). Other products that can easily be produced in the early stages of manufacturing and are essential include hosiery, aluminium utensils, cardboard boxes, sanitary fittings, nails and screws, toothpaste, and many others.

Textile and leather industries have strong linkages to the national economy as the raw materials either already abound (animals) or can be produced annually (cotton). With rapid urbanisation, the manufacturing of sanitary products and fittings will be urgent. To expand education at as low cost as possible, many educational supplies will have to be manufactured in South Sudan. Hence, there is need to develop the pulp and paper industry from the abundant local papyrus as well as from agricultural (e.g., sugar cane and sorghum stalks) and wood by-products. The manufacturing of various spare parts for vehicles and industry will improve the overall performance of the economy, as high capacity utilisation will be made possible. Given the low level of entrepreneurship in the modern manufacturing sector, government policy will have to play an important role in the acquisition of skills and the development of local entrepreneurship.

Small-scale Cottage Industries

Small-scale and handicraft industries can make a significant contribution in generating employment, supplying inputs, and consumer goods. Most of cottage industries usually consist of activities already being undertaken, but due to lack of some complementary inputs, their full potentialis not being realized (Yongo-Bure 1992). Therefore, public policy support to these activities could considerably improve the quality and quantity produced. The importance of this sub-sector in the reconstruction and development of South Sudan arises from the fact that this is the only industrial sub-sector that has had greater role than large-scale urban manufacturing in the new country. The skills for the revival and expansion of this sub-sector exist. Given the fact that this sub-sector requires less demanding complementary facilities and inputs, it could respond much more quickly to the recovery and development of South Sudan. Moreover, this sub-sector is of immediate direct benefit to the rural population through agricultural production, employment, and incomes as well as poverty alleviation and minimisation of rural-urban migration. Furthermore, together with peasant-based agriculture, it provides a sound basis for further development, as rising rural incomes will provide the necessary market for the other economic activities to be undertaken domestically.

Rural industry also contributes to food security as it supplies and repairs the farm tools and implements. It increases the market for agricultural output, leading to increased food production as well as the ability to purchase food for those not directly engaged in farming. In case of crop failure, rural non-farm employment can provide earnings for food purchases from other areas and/or imports. Part-time rural non-farm activities reduce underemployment and therefore increase the income of the rural population and enhance their ability to purchase food and have a diversified food basket.

Some of the various activities that have been carried out at the subsistence level, both in the rural and urban areas consist of pottery, fibre weaving, leather works, carpentry, wood-carving, iron-mongery, home-made yarns, building materials, carpet making, cheese, granary, and musical instruments. Small-scale rural and urban industries undertaken mainly on commercial basis include tailoring, grinding mills, brick laying, brewing, crop processing such as tobacco curing, and repair works – especially of bicycles. While assistance to handicraft activities in the urban centres is not in dispute, greater efforts should be directed at encouraging these activities in the rural areas. Dispersed small-scale industries can reduce the rate of rural-urban migration. This effect would minimize the problems resulting from urban population concentration with stagnant employment opportunities in the towns.

Brick production is already widespread all over South Sudan. It should be promoted in every community as it is important for both public and private sector construction in terms of building schools, health centres, stores and houses. The making of large granaries for crop storage, from durable local materials such as bamboo, will contribute considerably to easing some constraints in the marketing system before large modern silos can be substituted for them.

Tailoring is of considerable significance in scope, employment, value added and income. Most of the rural population buys made-to-order instead of ready-made clothing. However, the cost of both second-hand and new sewing machines has risen beyond the means of most peasants. The high cost of sewing machines limits the number of tailors in the rural areas, which forces the rural population to walk long distances to purchase clothing and other modern necessities. This is largely because tailoring in rural South Sudan has been undertaken jointly (in the same premises) as retailing. This leads to the reduction in the supply of farm labour due to the time and effort spent walking long distances to obtain these services. The introduction of a hire-purchase system all over South Sudan can ease the constraint on sewing machine ownership.

To realize the production of adequate food supply and agricultural exports, the peasants must have plenty and reliable supply of farm tools and implements such as hoes, axes, pangas, matchets, slashers, etc. While most of the inputs will continue to be imported, facilities for repair and maintenance will be a local responsibility. Given the scattered nature of the population in the vast area of South Sudan, it will not be possible to establish repair and maintenance centres for most peasants. The local blacksmiths will be crucial in providing the bulk of these services. This sub-sector should be given financial, technical and material support to enable it to upgrade the quality of its products and increase its productivity. Acquisition of information on farm tools and equipment from neighbouring countries or from countries at similar level of development is important. Examples include the FAO agricultural equipment improvement project in Kenya, the FAO village workshop project in Zambia, and the UNIDO project on village production of agricultural implements by local blacksmiths in Tanzania (ILO/JASPA 1983).

For easier rural transport and to increase competition in crop marketing, repair facilities and spare parts for bicycles must be widespread in the rural areas. Availability of grinding mills and water boreholes at the village level will enhance labour productivity as more time and effort will be released for other activities. Hence, the availability of tools and spare parts for the maintenance of these facilities as well as the training of local maintenance personnel at the village level is a must. Carpentry for chairs, tables, trays and cupboards at the village level can supply the local needs for these household items. The village carpentry will be necessary for the maintenance of the local school furniture.

Although processing of farm products for export will require modern facilities, local processing is important in such sub-sectors as fishing and hides and skins. In the remote fishing villages, fish not eaten or sold fresh is smoked, sun-dried or salted and sun-dried. The third method of local fish processing is the most efficient. Hence, availability of salt is critical for boosting food supply in the local fishing industry. The quality of hides and skins can be greatly improved through the way they are treated by the local herdsman during drying and storage. Shade and frame drying techniques should be expanded. New and better methods of treating hides and skins will raise the value of these raw materials for the tanning and leather industries. Consequently, South Sudan will be able to produce large and high quality leather products such as shoes, suitcases, belts, purses, etc. The thrust in this sub-sector is to raise productivity by supporting what is already being undertaken instead of introducing new activities.

Medium to Long-term Programmes

While most of the actions, projects and programmes discussed above are mainly short to mediumterm, GoSS also needs to initiate plans for the long-run strengthening of the new country's economy. Where does GoSS want to see the new country ten to twenty years from now? This calls for projects which will have transformative impact on the country. This is where the major projects in industrialization, energy and power, irrigation, mining, and training of various specialists become pertinent. GoSS should give an indication of its plans for the development of the Fulla and Bedden

There is need for new hydroelectric projects as well as the development of transmission lines to the central, eastern, northern, and western parts of South Sudan, given that the hydroelectric potential of the country is concentrated south of Juba. The adaption of solar and wind energy technologies should also be seriously pursued. The extraction of alluvial gold, from Kapoeta and southern Bari was said to be important during the war. Can these goldfields be exploited on a large scale and help reduce South Sudan's overdependence on oil for foreign exchange and domestic revenue? What other Southern mineral deposits are commercially viable? What are the country's long-term plans for building a diversified self-sustaining economy and its relationship to the neighbouring countries' economies? What are the plans for an integrated transportation network in the next ten-to-fifteen years (major roads and railways, etc)? Indications of serious actions in these fields will give people some ideas about their future and get engaged in productive dialogue with optimism.

While GoSS may have already developed and appraised its post-referendum projects, this chapter suggests a look at a number of projects that were planned in the past but were halted because of the war. Some of these projects can be re-evaluated and incorporated in any of the short, medium, and long-term programmes of the new country (Yongo-Bure 2007:61-74).

Mefit's Projects

In the second half of the 1970s, the Regional Government of Southern Sudan contracted Mefit, an Italian consulting firm, to undertake a comprehensive analysis of the Southern Sudanese economy (Mefit 1979). Mefit produced a number of reports including one on projects that could produce goods for export, for the South Sudan market, as well as for local markets. There were eleven export market projects, seven for the Southern market, and nine local market projects.

Most of the projects were agro-industrial. The same pattern of development is still relevant for the predominantly rural economy of South Sudan. However, given the time that has elapsed since Mefit undertook its comprehensive surveys and analyses of various aspects of the economy of South Sudan, GoSS should commission a similar study that should come up with a number of implementable programmes and projects, and/or undertake a re-evaluation of the feasibilities of Mefit's projects so that those which are still profitable may be implemented with appropriate adjustments for the changes over time. With increase in population and incomes, most of the South Sudan market and local markets projects will have to be up-scaled and/or duplicated. Increased agricultural production and development of the power sector will fasten the implementation of many such projects.

Export Market Projects

The eleven export market projects were all in the crop and livestock production subsectors. They dealt with the processing of groundnuts (peanuts), pineapple, tea, cocoa, tobacco, and sorghum; cattle, sheep, and poultry raising centres; and egg, milk, and beef production. Maize (corn) production and processing should be included in this group. These projects were essentially medium-sized estate schemes each with an out-growers peasant component. The peasant out-grower component of each of these projects is important for a broad-based poverty reduction development strategy.

Mefit argued that increased production and processing of groundnuts and sorghum would be among the fastest industries that can be developed in South Sudan. Except for the areas of water-logging, both crops are grown all over South Sudan. Mefit suggested an integrated project for the two crops. The objectives of Mefit's groundnut project were to: (i) increase the availability of edible oils for the Sudanese and export markets; (ii) substitute export of groundnuts with those of its products such as oil and flours, which have higher values; and (iii) produce highly nutritive flour so as to improve the quality of both human and animal nutrition in South Sudan.

The project was to consist of: (i) a groundnut mill; (ii) specialized farms to be cultivated in groundnuts, sorghum and/or maize; and (iii) the improvement of productivity in peasant farms.[1] The annual output of the mill was to consist of flour and shells. While Merfit's preferred location of the mill was Juba, the farms can be located anywhere in South Sudan where there is no water- logging.

The sorghum project was to consist of specialised farms to be located near the major population centres, and improvement in the productivity of peasant production around the specialised farms. With extension services to raise peasant productivity, the whole project would eventually become profitable. In the shortrun, the importance of the project results from its social benefits of providing basic food, and the profitability of the groundnut project integrated with it.

Thesorghum would be grown both for marketing and for seed. Seed production must be integrated by a functioning agricultural extension service so that peasants can effectively take advantage of it. The specialised farms would have flour processing and packaging plants. The sorghum varieties would be short enough for mechanical harvesting. They would have to be resistant to birds, contain a high percentage of proteins, and meet consumers' taste.

Mefit proposed an integrated pineapple export project to be located in the Meridi area. This is one of Mefit's projects which is being implemented in the post-second war period. The key project components were to include a factory capable of processing more than 20,000 tonnes of fruit a year, a specialised farm managed directly by the factory, and a system of family-managed farms. The family farms were to be situated around Meridi, Ibba, Mamba and Eidi. The total annual output of the project was estimated at 42,000 tonnes of fresh fruit. The canning plant would have a processing capacity of 22,000 tonnes of fresh fruit, which are approximately 12 to 15 thousand pineapples in eight months per year.

To increase the acreage and productivity of the family farms, it would be necessary to improve the road system and extension services as well as to extend loans to the farmers. Transportation for domestic and export markets would also need to be improved. It was also observed that verification of the appropriate pineapple varieties most suitable for the environment was essential so as to maximize productivity. Otherwise pineapple growing is widely practiced in the area, and favourable soils exist to permit further expansion. In addition to the fruit processing plant, the project would need an accessory plant for the production of metal cans for the export of fresh fruit, a nearby source of packing material (wood shavings, cartons), a refrigerated plant and refrigerated equipment for transporting the fruit. A thermal electric plant was installed in Meridi in February, 2011.

One of the components of Mefit's tea growing and manufacturing project was being implemented at Upper Talanga in the 1980s. Mefit confirmed the Yei area, on the basis of rainfall, as one of the most suitable area for growing the crop. Tea had been produced at Iwatoka, in the Yei area, since colonial times. Mefit envisaged the establishment of four integrated production centres in South Sudan. Each centre was to consist of a factory with a yearly productive capacity of 500 tonnes of dry tea, and a group of family-managed tea farms, located in the factory's surrounding, covering a total cultivated area of 625 to 750 feddans. The Upper Talanga and Yei tea projects are planned for re-activation.

Mefit assessed cocoa as a marginal crop in South Sudan mainly because of rainfall requirements.[2] After providing for supplementary irrigation, the consultant identified the Tombura area as the most suitable location for a cocoa growing and manufacturing project. This project has the longest gestation period. But once all the areas destined for planting are fully developed, the project would give an annual export of 600 tonnes of cocoa beans. Later production of chocolate and powdered cocoa may be considered. The entire agro-industrial enterprise would become fully productive in about 16 years. While low immediate profitability characterizes this experimental project, the smallholders may eventually increase their acreage and productivity when its profitability is proven.

Commercial production of tobacco started in South Sudan in the 1950s. Being a crop of relatively low rainfall requirements, the crop has adapted itself to many areas in South Sudan. Mefit's proposed project consisted of three independent agro-industrial centres. Smallholders were to grow most of the crop. Each centre was to consist of: (i) a factory with a yearly processing capacity of 500 tonnes of dry tobacco leaves; (ii) a specialised farm covering an area of 375 feddans of which 250 would be cultivated in tobacco; the farm would be managed by the factory's administration; (iii) a number of family-managed farms, covering a total area of 900 feddans growing tobacco; these farms would be located in the area surrounding the factory; (iv) a total area of 1,150 feddans of tobacco plantations.

The annual yield provided by each specialised farm was estimated at 125 tonnes of dry tobacco leaves. Each family-managed farm should produce 360 tonnes of dry tobacco leaves per year. The factory would have to guarantee the purchase of tobacco from private growers. It would have to process it and supervise its marketing both domestically and abroad.

The cattle and sheep raising centres and related processing plants were to take advantage of the large livestock industry of South Sudan. However, in spite of the readily available raw materials, the project would take some time due to the need to train personnel and establish a steady supply of young livestock. The faster peasants would respond to raising and marketing of calves and lambs, the shorter the gestation periods for both projects. The rate of return on the beef and lamb processing plants can be higher if the feeds can be supplied without irrigation as the investment costs would be lower. Still a better rate of return can be obtained if both processing plants can be merged into one unit with two processing lines, one for beef and the other for lamb. This should permit great saving with subsequent reductions in both investment requirements and operating expenses for the same level of production.

Each of thebeef and lamb processing projects consisted of three distinct sections: an agricultural section for the production of fodder, an animal husbandry section for fattening of livestock or sheep, and an industrial section for slaughtering and meat processing. The project aimed at raising 30,000 heads of cattle per year, to yield 5,250 tonnes of meat (in half carcasses) for export, and the production of feed and fattening of livestock on five farms, each with an area of 3,000 feddans. In each of the five farms, 2,750 feddans would be irrigated for the production of maize and sorghum, a fattening centre for 6,000 heads of cattle, and silos and warehouses would be constructed for stocking the forage. The 30,000 cattle per year would be slaughtered in a location as central as possible to all five farms.

The production process would include the processing of the maize and sorghum into silage as maize, maize cakes or mash, and sorghum flour. Calves would be purchased on the South Sudan market for fattening. These would consist of male calves with average weight of 70 kg (one year old). These calves would be raised for an average period of 300 days, until they reach a medium live weight of 350 kg. The 30,000 heads of cattle would be slaughtered in one slaughtering-refrigerating processing plant. The annual output of the plant would consist of beef in half carcasses, hides, a variety of meats (entrails), and protein flour.

The sheep project aimed at raising 120,000 lambs a year to produce 1,800 tonnes of carcasses of meat. The lambs to be fattened would be purchased locally, with a live weight of 15 kg (six to eight months of age). Production of feed and fattening of stock would take place in four farms, each with a size of 850 feddans. In each of the four farms, 790 feddans would be irrigated for the production of maize and sorghum. Each farm would have a fattening centre with a capacity of 10,000 lambs capable of completing three fattening cycles a year, giving a total of 30,000 lambs altogether. Silos and warehouses would be constructed for stocking the feed. The 120,000 lambs fattened every year on the four farms would be sent to a butchering-refrigerating processing plant to be built near the farms. The annual output of the plant would consist of lamb in carcasses, kip (hides), protein flour and pluck (entrails).

Mefit suggested the area north of Malakal, particularly the Renk area for the location of both projects because, by then, the Middle East oil exporting countries were the markets targeted. However, during the second war, cattle from southern Bahr el Ghazal were exported to Uganda. Moreover, the tsetse infested Green Belt and western Bahr el Ghazal are protein deficient regions. Kapoeta is another area with plenty of raw material, especially sheep. Kapoeta is also closer to the Kenyan market and other export markets. Furthermore, the potentially large market of the Democratic Republic of Congo and to a lesser extent the Central African Republic (CAR) markets are available for meat exports from South Sudan.[3] Moreover, population growth, economic growth and development, and increasing urbanisation will result in greater demand for food and meat, particularly by the non-farming population.

Egg and poultry consumption is the cheapest sources of animal protein. Egg and poultry production can be undertaken almost anywhere in South Sudan. Hence, Mefit proposed the establishment of poultry raising and egg production centres. These centres were to be located in the agricultural areas around Juba as Juba was/is the largest market in South Sudan. Moreover, Juba was linked by good transportation to the other towns of South Sudan as well as to North Sudan, and neighbouring countries. Furthermore, Juba Airport was being upgraded to international standards. However, now the project can be located in many centres in South Sudan as population and incomes have grown.

For the Mefit project, an integrated poultry breeding system was to be established. A poultry company would be responsible for the feeder mill, brood-stock raising, incubator, the processing plant (slaughtering, dressing and freezing), and the marketing of the finished products. Individual farmers would be responsible for raising poultry for fattening. A contract system would be established between the farmers and the poultry company. The company was to supply the farmers with one-day-old chicks, feed, medicine and disinfectants, technical and veterinary assistance. The farmers would attend to the chicken raising and bear the costs of labour, litter material and operation expenses. At the end of each raising cycle, the company would buy the chicken from the farmers for processing. The processing would involve slaughtering and refrigeration. The raw material for the feeds would be from the local production of maize, sorghum, groundnut flour, cottonseed cakes, and sesame-seed cakes. Hence, the project would lead to increased production in other sub-sectors. Training and organising the integrated farmers would play an important role in raising the productivity and profitability of the project.

The egg-processing project was initially to depend on the import of one-day-old female chicks from Italy to produce 55.5 million eggs per year (or 153,000 eggs per day). This was because of the modest capacity of the project that could not justify the implementation of a brood-stock raising system.[4] The project was to consist of six brood-stock raising centres, 12 laying centres, one egg grading and packaging centre and one droppings dryer plant. A feed mill, which could be integrated into the poultry fattening system, would take care of processing and supplying the feed stuff. The droppings should be dried to produce high-value organic fertilizer.

South Sudan Market Projects

The main consideration Mefit took into account for the selection of projects for the South Sudan market included increase in employment, a better and more efficient use of local resources, and greater integration of existing productive resources. Therefore, the consultant recommended projects that would use wood, quarries, hides and skins. The bicycle and soap projects were included due to the need to facilitate mobility in South Sudan and the necessity of lowering the cost of raising hygiene and sanitary standards. A factory for making blankets should be included in this list.

The building components industries project was basically the production of prefabricated panels of reinforced concrete to be used for private homes, industrial sites, road building, and public buildings such as schools, hospitals, administrative buildings, etc. The importance and hence the scope of this project would increase with population and economic growth and development. With increasing urbanisation and industrialisation there will be an increased need for housing, industrial, and other productive units such as warehouses, livestock and breeding farms, etc. The project has also strong backward effects as it has strong linkages to the brick, cement, and wood industries. Hence, its impact on production, employment and income in South Sudan would be substantial. Moreover, its products would increase the longevity of capital goods in South Sudan, particularly in the construction sector.

The construction phases of the project would last about two years. Depending on the availability of the required labour and other complementary inputs and services, the prefabricated panel industry would take about three years to generate its maximum employment and a fully productive working schedule.

The building material industries project was proposed to furnish the construction components necessary for the building of low-cost housing, including do-it-yourself. The simplicity of assembly of the selected components would guarantee rapidity of construction, as well as a high grade of building quality. This project would complement the building components' project, as it would also include the prefabrication of reinforced concrete panels for public and industrial buildings.

The project was to consist of two plants. The first plant was to handle the acquisition and processing of raw materials, that is expanded clay. The second project was to prepare prefabricated blocks of diverse types in relation to the various mains and supporting masonry, partitions and coverings. The production process was to be flexible such that, the dimensional pattern could easily be amplified and reproduced according to the needs of the building materials of the area. With the growth in population and income, this project can be replicated in many locations.

The wood processing industry was to include products such as doors, windows, office furniture, and components of kitchen furniture. With increased economic growth and development, and population growth, there would be an increase in demand for housing and public buildings, which in turn would lead to increase in demand for the products of the industry. Furthermore, there would always be demand for all and various types of restructuring and repairing activities for existing homes.

The bicycle project was included in the development plans of the Southern Regional Government in the 1970s, but was not executed. Bicycles of various types and sizes were to be produced. Mefit foresaw on-the-spot construction of bicycle frames, painting of the same, and the assembly of imported accessories. The project was to be expanded to the assembly of motor cycles; and the manufacture of chassis, parts for agricultural and industrial machines as more skills were gained. The bicycle has been an important means of cheap peasant haulage of produce to local markets and can play an important role in crop marketing. The motor-cycle has become a major means of passenger transportation in the post-second war period. Special designs of both the bicycle and motor-cycle could be developed to suit the local conditions and purposes.

The manufacture of matches was an import substitution project aimed at taking advantage of South Sudan's abundance of the main raw material, wood. After meeting the national market, in the first phase, expansion in the second phase would lead to production for export to North Sudan as well as to other countries. Two different groups of machines were to be installed: one for the production of small wooden pieces of the match base, and the other for the production of matches. Two types of matches were to be produced:

a family type made up of 100 matches with rough phosphorous, and the Swedish safety match, in boxes of 50 matches.

The manufacture of leather products was to be transformed from traditional to more efficient industrial processes. The products of the modern manufacture were to include purses, shoes, suitcases, etc. The presence of plenty of skins and hides, as well as the development of the animal industry and the processing of animal products provides ample supplies of raw materials. After meeting the needs of South Sudan, the capacity of this industry would be expanded for the export market.

The soap-manufacturing project was aimed at improving the living conditions of the population by raising hygiene and sanitary levels. A locally-made product would be relatively cheaper than imports, and would lead to a more intense use of these products. The plant was to produce several types of soap – in bars, flakes and powder – so as to satisfy the various family-level requirements such as personal hygiene, washing clothes, kitchen use, etc. The plant was also to be able to produce more sophisticated products as basic chemicals became plentiful. Products such as detergents were/are only imports in South Sudan. The project was to make the import substitution of such projects possible, both for family as well as for handicraft and industrial use.

Local Market Projects

Mefit's proposed nine local market industrial projects were sheet metal fabricating, paint and varnishes, wire products, bakelite electrical accessories, hosiery, aluminium utensils, corrugated cardboard boxes, sanitary fittings, and a tooth paste unit. Mefit envisaged that the local market projects would be located in district/county headquarters. These projects could easily be undertaken, as the investment on them would be quite limited. All these projects would be executed in about 12 months, except for the paint and varnishes plant, which would take 16 to 18 months to construct. Furthermore, the goods can be made with local inputs. Finally, these projects would help in the transformation of such existing activities that use inefficient traditional methods, through the introduction of modern techniques and forms of labour organization. On the whole, the projects Mefit proposed are based on very simple technological processes, do not require very qualified human resources, use mainly local resources, and are highly remunerative. Each of these projects can be replicated in many counties on scales dependent on the population.

The sheet metal fabrication project was to produce laminated metallic material for use in the production of tables, chairs, tanks and similar products. The annual productive capacity of each plant was projected to range from 100 to 120 metric tonnes. The raw materials were to be made up of 150 metric tonnes of steel per year, and 4,000 litres of water per day.

The paint and varnishes project was to supply the building industry with an annual output of 300 metric tonnes. This plant may be replicated in other areas. The input requirements for each plant would include 30,000 litres of dry oils, 30,000 litres of solvents, 25 metric tonnes of colour pigments, 100 kW of electric energy and 80,000 litres of water per day.

The wire products project was to produce nails, screws, clips, and other metallic products, designed for use in the building and construction sector, including office and housing. The productive capacity of the plant was planned at about 25 metric tonnes of metal parts per year. The necessary raw materials include about 30 metric tonnes of steel and 10 to 15 kW of electric energy, glues, lubricants, etc. The output of this unit was to be about 25 metric tonnes of metal parts annually. With the boom in the building industry in the post-second war period, many plants of this project would be necessary.

The aim of the bakelite electric accessories unit was to produce electrical materials such as plugs, switches, etc., for the building industry. The projected annual output was 80 to 100 thousand switches, 40,000 plugs, 10,000 junction box plates and 20,000 lamp holders. The raw material consists of four to five metric tonnes of formaldehyde powder, seven to eight metric tonnes of brass sheets, and 250 to 300 pounds of polystyrene moulding powder. Once again, more plants of such a project would be needed to meet the increased demand for its products.

The hosiery unit was to produce clothing and knitwear of simple types and broad consumption. Its annual production was to consist of 300,000 units of cotton dresses and robes, and 350,000 units of personal knitwear. The base raw material for these products was placed at about 50 metric tonnes of spun cotton per year, and 15 to 20 kW of electric energy per day. With increased demand and an increasingly sophisticated market, large quantities of a diversified product would have to be manufactured. Increased cotton production should be encouraged.

The aluminium utensils unit was to produce kitchen utensils for the local market. The utensils were to include plates, pans, knives, forks, spoons, etc. It was geared to produce 30 metric tonnes of utensils annually. Its daily consumption of electricity was estimated at 40 kW, while a total of 32 metric tonnes of aluminium raw materials would be required per annum. This is another project whose production capacity would have to be greatly expanded in consistence with population increase.

The corrugated cardboard box unit was meant to produce cardboard boxes, paper envelopes, and similar objects for wrapping and boxing products such as soap, clothing, electrical products, and the like. The plant was to produce 170 metric tonnes of corrugated cardboard cartons, and 85 metric tonnes of kraft paper and straw paper; 90 metric tonnes of cardboard or millboard; and 25 metric tonnes of adhesives. More such projects are needed in the post-second war period.

Conclusion

The hope for improved living conditions in South Sudan, under a separate nationhood, was one of the major factors in the overwhelming vote for secession. Consequently, the government of the new country is expected to immediately initiate a serious programme of socio-economic development. The programmes, projects, and policies outlined in this chapter constitute some of the feasible activities that can substantially reduce poverty in South Sudan within a few years. Not all the projects and programnes outlined above are to be undertaken by the government, but the various levels of government are to play leading roles in organising and coordinating all the actors: public, private, and co-operative sectors; NGOs, bilateral, and multilateral donors. Given the great need for physical and social infrastructure, the public sector will have to play a very important role in the economy since the private sector rarely undertakes infrastructural projects. The private and co-operative sectors should play important roles in undertaking the directly productive activities.

Redeployment of veterans and old civil servants to more remunerative activities in the private sector will allow for the recruitment of new trainable civil servants, with the relevant levels of education, in key positions in the public sector. Such a policy will enhance the efficiency and productivity of the public sector. At the same time, it will infuse both capital and relatively experienced and trained domestic human resources into the private sector.

The largest private sector in South Sudan, at this stage of its development, is the peasant sector. Tapping this potential through appropriate policies will impact considerably on South Sudan's medium and long-term development. More efforts should be exerted on the development of this domestic sector rather than on the present vigorous hunting for foreign investors. Foreign investors will not need much effort to attract when the profitability of the economy will have been enhanced through investing in the local factors. Profitability of the domestic economy will depend largely on improving its productivity and enlarging the domestic market. Permanent improvement in productivity will depend on investment in human resources and infrastructure; while growth in the domestic market will depend on cumulatively rising gross domestic income. The latter is dependent on raising the incomes of the majority of the population who, at the present moment of South Sudan's development, are predominantly peasants.

Notes

1. 1 feddan = 1,038 acres= 4,200 m2.
2. The rainfall requirements for ideal cocoa growing were not available in southern Sudan at the time of the study (late 1970s). These requirements include 1,500-2,000 mm annual rainfall, uniformly distributed. However, supplementary irrigation can correct for the natural rain in parts of South Sudan such as Yambio.
3. The areas of Central African Republic and the Democratic Republic of Congo (DRC) are also infested with tsetse fly, and hence have limited livestock industries. The DRC, with its huge resource potential and large population is a large potential future market for the countries surrounding it; and especially for animal products in the case of South Sudan.
4. With growth in population and rise in incomes, a large plant(s) may be possible; and hence, a national brood-stock raising system may become economical.

References

International Labor Office (ILO/JASPA), 1983, *Appropriate Farm Equipment Technology for the Small-Scale Traditional Sector, Synthesis Report*, Addis Ababa/Geneva.

Mefit S.P.A., 1979, Regional Development Plan, Vol. 1-Part Two: Key projects, Rome.

Ministry of Education, Science and Technology (MOEST), 2010, *Education Statistics for southern Sudan 2009 Statistical Booklet*, Juba.

World Bank, 2009, *Sudan: The Road Toward Sustainable and Broad-Based Growth*, Washington, D. C., December.

Yongo-Bure, B., 1987, 'Prospects of Socio-Economic Development in the South', in Francis M. Deng and Prosser Gifford, eds, *The Search for Peace and Unity in the Sudan*, Washington, D. C.: The Wilson Center Press, pp. 36-55.

Yongo-Bure, B., 1988, *North-South Relations in Sudan since the Addis Ababa Agreement*, Khartoum: Institute of African and Asian Studies and Khartoum University Printing Press, (Co-edited with Mom Kou N. Arou).

Yongo-Bure, B., 1989, *Economic Development in Southern Sudan: An Overview and a Strategy*, Sudan Research Group, Institute for World Economics and International Management: University of Bremen.

Yongo-Bure, B., 1992, 'The Role of Small-Scale Industry in the Recovery and Development of the Southern Sudan', in Martin Doornbos, Lionel Cliffe, Abdel Gharffar M. Ahmed, and John Markakis, eds., *Beyond Conflict in the Horn: Prospects for Peace, Recovery and Development in Ethiopia, Somalia and the Sudan*, The Hague and London: The Institute of Social Studies and James Currey, pp. 165-171.

Yongo-Bure, B., 2005, *Peace Dividend and the Millennium Development Goals in Southern Sudan*, Sudan Economy Research Group, Institute for World Economics and International Management, University of Bremen, Germany, September.

Yongo-Bure, B., 2007, *Economic Development of Southern Sudan*, Lanham, MD: University Press of America, February.

Yongo-Bure, B., 2007, *Human Capital Policy in Southern Sudan in the Post-Second War Period*, Policy Brief # 53, The William Davison Institute at the University of Michigan: Ann Arbor, April.

Yongo-Bure, B., 2007, 'Southern Sudan: A Macroeconomic Perspective on Development Priorities, Challenges and Opportunities', in Philip Ochieng, ed., *Building a New and Prosperous Society in Southern Sudan in the Post Conflict Period*, Nairobi: African Research and Resource Forum, pp. 57-83.

9

Southern Sudan: Monetary and Financial Policies and the Case for a Separate Currency

Benaiah Yongo-Bure

Introduction

Money is anything a society accepts as a means of payment. It is accepted universally in the community as a medium of exchange, a store of value, and a unit of account to measure the value of transactions. Money is important to the smooth functioning of an economy. The development of money facilitates trade, which in turn facilitates specialisation and the division of labour; consequently, promoting economic development. The amount of money in the economy has influence on economic growth, employment, inflation, exchange rate, and balance of payments. Hence, monetary policy should be judiciously managed by an independent central bank. The issuance of fiat money has a substantial revenue component for the national treasury. This consists of seigniorage and inflation tax. While caution should be exercised on the amount of inflation tax, the seigniorage revenue is a net benefit of issuing a national currency. Channeled to productive sectors such as the rural economy, seigniorage can substantially contribute to the growth of a predominantly subsistence economy.

Monetary policy is the regulation of money supply and the amount of credit by the central bank so as to influence the level of economic activity. Its effectiveness varies from economy to economy, depending on the existence of a developed financial infrastructure. The financial system should be well intergraded and flexible to changes initiated in any of the economic sectors. Currently, there is hardly any financial infrastructure in Southern Sudan.

The building of a financial infrastructure should take precedence over the pursuance of a narrow monetary policy. Monetary policy should be conducted in consistence with the state of development of Southern Sudan.

If, after separation, the two Sudans will have a common currency, they will effectively be in a monetary union. This will have consequences for their fiscal policies as no one country will be able to use monetary policy to regulate its own economy given the fixed exchange rate of the common currency vis-a-vis the two countries. The use of a common currency by a number of countries in a region is based on the theory of optimal currency area.[1] But is Sudan an optimal currency area?

The Revenue Component of a Currency

Government derives significant amount of revenue from the use of fiat money. The cost of printing the currency is very insignificant compared to its market value. This difference is referred to as seigniorage. Seigniorage is the most important fiscal factor in the desire to issue a separate national currency (Buiter 2007:1-4, Fry 1995:393-404). The seigniorage revenue is equal to the amount of goods and services that the government obtains by printing money in a given period. It is equal to the differences between the value of the printed amount of money and the cost of printing it. For example, if it costs $0.06 to print a $1.00 or a $100.00 note, the seigniorage value of each note is $0.94 or $99.94 respectively. A country at its early stage of development, with a very narrow tax base needs this source of revenue. A government that cannot control itself in issuing currency might want the discipline of using foreign money. But in such a case, the seigniorage will go to the foreign country issuing the currency.

In many countries, the central bank prints the money and credits the government account less the central bank's cost of operations. Where open market operations are effective, as in many developed countries, the central bank buys secondary securities with the new printed money. The interest on the securities the Treasury would have paid to the public is now owed to the central bank and is written off (retired) from the central government's domestic debt. The interest the central bank is paid for its loans to the financial intermediaries is also another source of seigniorage. The more cash the central bank sells to the financial intermediaries, the larger the amount of seigniorage.

If the currency is used in other countries, it represents a large gift of seignioprage to the issuing country. This is how countries with hard currencies that are used internationally as foreign exchange acquire real foreign resources by just printing more of their currencies. The foreign banknote is retained because it is valued as a store of value as a result of mistrust of the local currency.

A larger economy has more capacity to generate greater amount of seigniorage. However, if the larger economy is formed of different political entities, the cooperating groups must have a high degree of trust among themselves. They should trust that any agreement on issues such as agreed formulae of seignorage sharing is faithfully implemented. The experience between northern and southern Sudan, as evidenced in their revenue sharing in accordance with the 2005 Comprehensive Peace Agreement (CPA) is not encouraging (Global Witness). Given the many urgent funding needs of both governments of northern and southern Sudan, divergences in monetary and fiscal policies will be inevitable. Hence, let each country issue its own currency, at least in the early years of disengagement.

Furthermore, a common currency automatically means a common market for the two countries. But given the fact that all the manufacturing industry is currently concentrated in central Sudan, northern Sudan will be the beneficiary of the common market. The backwash (negative) effects of the established industry in northern Sudan will kill any effort towards industrialisation in Southern Sudan. Usually, infant industries are far less efficient than already established ones. Unless Southern Sudan expects a radical change in the mindset of the Khartoum policy-makers, a common market is not the immediate arrangement Southern Sudan should enter into with northern Sudan.

In addition to seigniorage, many governments obtain inflation tax as another form of revenue by issuing more printed money than the amount that can be issued at a zero rate of inflation (Fry 1995:206-255, Gills et al. 1987: 323-340). The inflation tax reduces the purchasing power of the currency for the general public. However, the inflation tax cannot be generated indefinitely. The inflation tax will rise with inflation up to a certain point, beyond which it actually can decrease. This occurs when inflation rises so high that the societal demand for money falls. This point is reached when people place vast amounts of their wealth into hard currencies, or when cash incomes are rapidly converted into real goods, hoarding critically needed goods for self-consumption, or for bartering and avoiding cash transactions altogether.

Falling real balances require larger infusion of cash, and higher inflation levels for the government to finance the same levels of fiscal deficits. This could precipitate an upward spiral as the inflation tax rises even as the tax base falls. Hyperinflation can be the result. This could lead to the collapse of the currency and the whole financial system. Beyond a certain point, as real balances fall, the real trade-off between inflation and inflation revenue becomes increasingly unfavourable to the government and the country.

Optimal Currency Areas

Mundell developed the theory of optimal currency area in the 1960s (Mundell). A number of countries that use a common currency experience both advantages and disadvantages. The area that maximizes the net benefits of using a single currency is referred to as an optimal currency area. The potential benefits of using a common currency include reduced transaction costs, and enhanced policy credibility. Uncertainty about future changes in exchange rates may discourage international trade and financial activity between the member countries if they were to use separate currencies. A common currency eliminates this uncertainty and allows firms to specialise according to comparative advantage and to plan imports and exports without worrying about losses due to future exchange rate movements and without having to hedge in forward markets. A common currency eliminates the fees paid to banks or to currency brokers that arrange the conversion of currencies. It simplifies accounting and book-keeping, and it enables consumers and investors to compare prices across international boundaries more accurately. A single currency eliminates price fluctuations that are caused by changes in the exchange rate (Gerber 2011:237-242). A common currency also can provide an advantage to policy makers by allowing them credibility commitment to a future course for monetary policy. However, an important cost of a common currency is that countries lose the ability to pursue independent monetary policies. A common currency also eliminates exchange rate devaluations or revaluations as a policy instrument in the currency area.

The criteria for an optimal currency area include synchronised business cycle, complete factor mobility, regional development programmes for lagging areas, and a desire to achieve a higher level of economic and political integration. A region is likely to gain from a common currency if (i) a large share of members' trade occurs with other members, (ii) the region is subject primarily to common shocks that affect the entire area similarly and not to shocks that affect sub-regions differently, (iii) labour is mobile within the region, and (iv) a tax-transfer system exists to transfer resources from sub-regions performing strongly to those performing poorly.

The higher the share of intra-group trade the greater the transaction-cost saving of a single currency. If different shocks buffet sub-regions, policy-makers in those sub-regions may need to follow different monetary policies or to allow their exchange rate to move to offset the shocks' short-run effects. When some sub-regions of a currency area grow quickly and others grow much more slowly, movements of labour between sub-regions represent another possible adjustment mechanism. If cultural or institutional factors restrict such labour flows, then differential monetary policies and exchange rate realignment may be needed, ruling out a common currency. An alternative means of dealing with differential regional growth involves fiscal transfers from growing regions to stagnant ones (Yarbrough 2006:695-697).

Even as one country, Sudan fell short of a single currency area. The border states of northern and southern Sudan may have approximated an optimal currency area. As one country, labour mobility was relatively free, although at times migrants from the periphery were deported to their home regions from the cities of central Sudan. There were no regional development programmes for poor regions when Sudan was still one country. Infrastructural links between the various regions are weak or absent. While underdeveloped countries have usually experienced similar economic conditions, these experiences can be altered in the long-run depending on the long-term development strategies of a country. An opportunity was lost for creating an integrated Sudan economy that could have led to strong interdependencies and thus creating, as closely as possible, an optimal currency area.

Monetary and Financial Policies

For developed industrial economies, the terms financial and monetary policies are synonymous as the financial sector is well developed and integrated into virtually all sectors of the economy. However, for underdeveloped counties, the two concepts mean quite different things. Financial policy embraces all measures intended to affect the growth, utilization, efficiency, and diversification of the financial system. It also includes measures intended to encourage the growth of savings in the form of financial assets, to develop money and capital markets, and to allocate credit between different economic sectors (Fry 1995:299-313; Gills et al. 1987:323-362).

On the other hand, monetary policy means changes in the growth of money supply and credit aimed at reducing instability induced by cyclical fluctuations arising from either internal or external markets. The instruments of monetary policy include open market operations, changes in legal-reserve requirements of commercial banks, changes in central bank (re)discount rates to commercial banks, and moral suasion. Hence, for an underdeveloped economy, the term financial policy has a broader meaning. Monetary policy is only a part of financial policy.

A country's financial system consists of a variety of interconnected financial institutions, both formal and informal. In most countries, a central bank lies at the core of the formal financial system. The central bank is responsible for the control of the money supply and the general supervision of the formal financial activities. Virtually in all countries, and particularly in underdeveloped countries, the commercial banking system is the most visible and vital component of the formal financial system, as acceptor of deposits and grantor of shorter-term credit. Other elements of the formal financial system include savings banks, insurance companies, pension funds, development banks, and nascent securities markets. Coexisting with the formal sector are the informal and largely unregulated systems of finance, including local moneylenders, trade credit, family lending, and cooperative credit (Fry 1995:344-352; Todaro and Smith 2006:741-759).

In many underdeveloped countries, substantial portion of economic activity is conducted through barter. The monetisation ratio is relatively low in many underdeveloped economies. The effective use of monetary policy instruments for combating cyclical fluctuation is difficult enough in monetised economies. In largely subsistence economies it would hardly work. While the use of monetary policy in developed countries is aimed at influencing the utilisation of existing capacities through changing aggregate demand, the main problem of underdeveloped economies is the creation of productive capacities through long-term investment. Hence, the traditional functions and tools of monetary policy applied in developed countries have to be considerably adjusted to be consistent with the development issues of underdeveloped economies.

The financial system is a vessel for mobilising and allocating funds, and gathering savings from numerous savers and channelling them to investors, a process called financial intermediation. The system provides a means of transferring and distributing risk across the economy. Finally, a well developed financial system allows for an effective monetary policy to be pursued by providing a set of policy instruments for stabilisation of economic activity.

Thus, in an underdeveloped economy such as the one of Southern Sudan, the building of a sound financial infrastructure should be one of the major focuses of the central bank. The financial system consists of financial markets and financial institutions. Financial markets are the markets where surplus spending units (SSUs) lend their funds directly to the deficit spending units (DSUs). Examples of these are markets for bonds and stocks (Stock Exchanges). Financial institutions provide financial services to SSUs and DSUs. The most important financial institutions are the financial intermediaries such as banks, credit unions, microfinance institutions, etc. They serve as go-between the SSUs and the DSUs (Cecchetti 2008:39-59, 172-192,247-268).

The process of financial intermediation involves the gathering of savings from multitudinous savers and channelling them to a smaller but still sizable number of investors. At early stages of economic development a preponderant share of intermediation activities tends to be concentrated in one type of institution: *commercial banks*. As development proceeds, new forms of financial intermediaries begin to appear and gradually assume a growing share of intermediation function. These include development banks, insurance companies, and ultimately, securities markets (Fry 1995:393-419; Gills et al. 1987:323-362). Plentiful intermediaries, however, do not always guarantee successful intermediation.

The effects of monetary policy on economic growth, employment and income are transmitted to the economy through an integrated financial system. As the money supply changes, the key interest rate changes leading to general changes in interest rates and spending levels and patterns in the whole economy. Without an integrated financial system, the effects of monetary policy will be localised as there is no flexibility in the system. Consequently, the economy may become prone to inflation. Idle funds may not be channelled to productive undertakings as SSUs may not be aware of such opportunities or they may not be willing to risk their surpluses. Financial markets and intermediaries' pool funds, take risks, and channel these funds to productive ventures, large and small.

Monetary Policy and Fiscal Policy

Responsible fiscal policy is a precondition for successful monetary policy in a monetary union. For a common central bank to do its job effectively, all member countries' governments must behave responsibly and not play of games. However, central banks remain independent at the pleasure of politicians. Fiscal policy is the responsibility of elected officials, and is not controlled by the central bank. Instead the central bank, in most underdeveloped countries, is under the politicians through the ministry of finance and the presidency. When conflict arises between them, it is usually the politicians who win, thus sacrificing the basic objectives of the central bank.

Fiscal policy-makers are responsible for providing national defense, education, health, building and maintaining transportation, etc. They need resources to pay for these services. Thus, funding needs create a natural conflict between monetary and fiscal policy-makers. Central bankers, in their effort to stabilise prices and provide the foundation for high sustainable growth, take a long-term view, imposing limits on how fast the quantity of money and credit can grow. On the other hand, fiscal policy-makers tend to ignore the long-term inflationary effects of their actions. Their time horizon often extends only until the next election.

Fiscal management is especially important in the context of a monetary union because once a common currency is adopted fiscal policy will be the main macroeconomic policy available to individual countries after giving up independent national monetary policy. Excessive spending in one country may cause inflationary pressure on the common currency that would negatively impact the other country as well. Thresholds on government deficits and debt have been instated in all the existing monetary unions to address the negative externality and moral hazard issues.[2] However, such thresholds are challenging to implement in practice. Whether fiscal commitments are implemented through self-discipline, surveillance and persuasion, or centralised enforcement, the examples of monetary unions around the world are replete with unsuccessful efforts to prevent excessive deficits and debt crises (Anand et al. 2011:6).

In underdeveloped economies, some governments simply order the central bank to print more money, even if the level of money supply would not be consistent with the health of the economy. This would result in inflation or even hyperinflation. This led to the idea of independent central banks. The independence of central banks is to ensure that such a key national policy-making body is run on sound professional economic judgment of the health of the national economy. The independence of the central bank would leave fiscal policy-makers two options of financing government spending: taxation and borrowing. Because politicians fear angering the electorate by raising taxes, they tend to rely on borrowing. But in most underdeveloped countries, bond markets are either non-existent or at their infancy with hardly any secondary component. Hence, the government will sell new bonds directly to the central bank, thus expanding the money supply, even up to inflationary levels.

In the European monetary union, before a country can join the common currency area and adopt the euro, it must meet a number of conditions. Two of the most important are that the country's annual deficit cannot exceed

3 per cent of its gross domestic product (GDP) and the government debt cannot exceed 60 per cent of GDP (Yarbrough 2006:691). Once the country gains membership in the monetary union, failure to maintain these standards can lead to pressure from other member countries and possibly even to substantial penalties. Yet in such a monetary union of developed economies, with elaborate and well integrated financial systems, the convergence criteria are still very difficult to adhere to.

However, fiscal limits must be realistic and in line with recent and current deficit levels. Furthermore, underdeveloped countries depend on foreign borrowing for their investments and development. Hence, the fiscal deficit criteria have to include grants to best account for the realities of domestic revenue generation challenges and reliance on donor support in such countries.

Aid flows indicate that budget assistance can have significant and volatile effects on domestic liquidity. Both northern and southern Sudan receive foreign aid flows, including budget support, limiting discretion in spending of budget aid for them can help ensure that problems managing aid flows do not have negative economic consequences for either country. How will both countries address these issues? Should an automatic tax be applied to a country that runs excessive deficits, surpassing agreed upon-deficit levels? How will they meet such penalties if they cannot meet their budgetary expenditures? Will oil revenues last and be shared to take care of each other's budgetary requirements?

Sudan's Budgetary Performance

Until 1958, Sudan financed most of its operations with domestically generated revenue. However, from the late 1950s to the beginning of the twenty-first century the Sudan Government increasingly depended on foreign finance and bank credit for most of its operations. The country accumulated a lot of unspent balances during the Second World War. Britain granted Sudan L S 2.0 million (L S – Sudanese Pound) at the end of the war. From 1947 to 1951, Sudan experienced an unprecedented boom, brought about by a rise in the value of cotton exports. The already high cotton prices rose sharply in 1951/52 as a result of the war in Korea. However, from 1958, the country began to experience financial crisis. Cotton exports began to experience problems in the midand late 1950s. Official foreign capital inflow began to play an important role in financing Sudanese development. For example, an American aid programme to Sudan was started in 1958 with grants of L S 1.1 million. This amount was increased to L S 3.1 million and L S 4.1 million in

1959 and 1960 respectively. As a result of the construction of the Aswan High Dam, Sudan received compensation from Egypt for the flooding of Wadi Halfa and the subsequent resettlement of its inhabitants in Khasm el Girba (Yongo-Bure 2002).

Available figures for 1965/66-1969/70 indicate that external finance was L S 72.2 million, public sector savings financed L S 16.8 million, and deficit finance constituted L S 48.7 million. The dependence of Sudanese development, and even current operations, on foreign resources intensified from the 1970s until the late 1990s when Sudan became an oil exporter. The available data on the degree of Sudanese financing on foreign resources and deficit financing is summarized in Table 9.1.

From the early 1970s, it became increasingly difficult for the government to provide adequate funds for the public sector. Foreign aid and borrowing from the banking sector, largely from the Bank of Sudan, became the main ways of meeting public sector operations. Foreign commodity aid became the main non-inflationary means of generating local currency for public sector operations. Commodity aid was sold in the local market to generate local funds for the government. Even public corporations that were supposed to remit profits to the public treasury came to rely on credit from the Bank of Sudan.

With an external debt of approximately $40 billion, foreign aid and borrowing will be crucial in Sudan's fiscal policy and consequently on monetary and exchange rate policies. How the two Sudans will resolve the issue of debt repayment will have important bearing on any agreement they may make on convergence criteria should they decide to have a common currency.

Table 9.1: Actual Central Government Operations (L S millions)

Items	1970/71-72/73	1973/74-75/76	1976/77-78/79	1979/80-81/82	1982/83-84/85	1985/86-87/88	1993-94/95	1994/95-1996	1997-1999
Revenue	168.0	270.7	448.9	734.9	1,410.6	2,922.8	252,000	426,700	1,569,700
Current Expenditure	149.0	236.9	440.4	768.2	2,211.8	5,722.0	268,300	460,300	1,537,700
Development Expenditure	21.1	85.7	168.6	275.5	501.8	1,078.2	42,300	61,000	190,300
Other Expenditures	0.0	0.0	24.9	181.0	0.0	0.0	19,300	63,300	0.0
Total Expenditure	170.1	322.6	633.9	1224.4	2,713.6	6,800.2	347,000	604,700	1,728,000
Overall Balance	-2.1	-51.9	-184.9	-489.8	-1,303.0	-3,877.1	-93,700	-178,000	-158,300
External Financing	-4.1	65.6	71.5	347.6	1,003.2	2,490.9	32,000	32,300	48,300
Central Bank Financing	11.5	20.4	139.4	155.1	286.4	1,334.5	63,700	145,000	110,000
Other Financing	-5.4	-33.4	-26.0	-12.8	13.3	51.7	2,000	700	0.0
Deficit as % of GDP	0.2	12.0	6.1	9.3	9.9	12.3	3.0	2.8	0.5

Figures for the 1990s were originally recorded in billions of Sudanese pounds (L S). The three-year moving averages are calculated from the given sources.
Source: IBRD, Reports on Sudan Economy, 1982, p. 223, 1985, p. 152, &1990, p. 113; *and IMF, Reports on the Sudan Economy, 1998, p. 6, 1999, p. 63, &2000, p.19.*

The Sudanese Financial System

The Sudanese financial system is not well developed. Commercial banks dominate it. It is heavily concentrated in the urban areas of central Sudan and Port Sudan. It has been characterised by heavy government interventions and regulations. Apart from establishing its own public sector banks, the Bank of Sudan lends directly to public corporations. Table 9.2 gives an overview of the geographical and political spread of Sudan's banking network.[3]

Table 9.2: The Distribution of the Banking Network in Sudan (%)

Province	1959	1981	1991	1994	1997	1998	1999	2000	2001
Khartoum	41	34	30	29	32	32	32	33	33
Central	25	21	22	22	23	24	23	22	23
Eastern	19	17	13	14	14	13	15	14	11
Northern	6	8	14	13	12	11	12	11	10
Kordofan	6	8	9	11	9	9	8	9	10
Darfur	0	7	8	8	7	8	7	8	7
Southern*	3	7	4	3	3	3	3	3	3
Total	100	100	100	100	100	100	100	100	100

* Southern Sudan was composed of three provinces, each comparable to each of the six original provinces of the North as at independence. The southern provinces were Bahr el Ghazal, Equatoria, and Upper Nile.
Source: Bank of Sudan, Annual Report (various years) and UNDP, *Macroeconomic Policies for Poverty Reduction: The Case of Sudan,* (2006), p.63.

The uneven distribution of the banking services, both private and public, has not changed over the last fifty years of independence. Even in favoured areas, bank branches are concentrated in the urban areas of Atbara, El Obeid, Khartoum, Port Sudan, and Wad Medani; and their surrounding satellites. The rural areas and small towns have no banking facilities. Even the Agricultural Bank of Sudan (ABS) is urban-based; mainly lending to absentee landlords whose hired workers do the entire farm work.

A relevant feature of the Sudanese financial system to the issue of common or separate currencies for northern and southern Sudan is the Islamisation of the financial system of northern Sudan while southern Sudan operated on the conventional banking system during the Interim Period of the Comprehensive Peace Agreement (CPA) (2005-2011). The Islamic Instruments of monetary policy such as *murabaha* and *musharaka* are equity-based with a variable yield according to profit and loss sharing, unlike the interest-based securities of a conventional financial system.[4]

According to Bekkin, Sudan is the only country in the world that has a wholly Islamic financial sector. The Islamisation of the Sudanese financial system started in the late 1970s with the setting up of the Faisal Islamic Bank in 1977. In 1992, the government established a High Shariah Supervisory Board (HSSB) to oversee the progress of economic and financial reforms and their compliance with Shariah. This body comprised scholars, jurists and economists, including the governor of the central bank (the Bank of Sudan). The members of the HSSB can combine their membership in the board with membership of the Shariah boards of commercial banks. Their appointments were not term-limited. The HSSB also acts as an appeal authority for disputes between various Islamic banks, Islamic banks and the Bank of Sudan, and an Islamic bank and its customers.

However, like the conventional banks, the Islamic banks concentrated their loans on trade and other short-term commercial activities. They hardly extended much of their services to the agricultural and livestock sub-sectors. Specialised banks were set up to lend to the farming community, but agriculture did not receive any better services from the Islamic banks than under the conventional banking system. In addition to the Agricultural Bank of Sudan (ABS), the Farmers' Commercial Bank and the Animal Resources Bank were set up in the 1990s to focus on the two sub-sectors (crop and animal production).

The Islamised ABS did not perform any better than before it was Islamised. From its inception in 1957 to its Islamisation in the 1990s, the ABS was supposed to focus its activities on the achievement of self-sufficiency in the production of basic food crops, raising the standard of living of the peasant farmers and equitable regional development. Instead, the ABS concentrated its resources on financing large-scale mechanised farms, owned by absentee landlords resident in the cities of central Sudan. The ABS has been characterised by its absence in the areas with sufficient rainfall for reliable rain-fed agriculture (Yongo-Bure 2005).

In addition to extending direct loans to public corporations, the Bank of Sudan extended short-term loans and foreign aid funds to the ABS for extension to farmers. The ABS expended the bulk of these public resources on funding large-scale mechanised farming. In 2001, total lending to the agricultural sector in Sudan amounted to SD 44 billion (Sudanese Dinar): (1US$= SD 260). The irrigated scheme received about 60 per cent, the mechanised schemes received about 39 per cent, and the peasant sub-sector received only about one per cent (Mohamed :7; Yongo-Bure 2005:84).

Sudan's insurance sector has also been Islamised. Faisal Islamic Bank initiated the idea of establishing an Islamic Cooperative Insurance Company in 1977 (Bekkin; UNDP). In 1979, the new venture, Islamic Insurance Company of Sudan, obtained public company status. The Islamic banks needed Islamic insurance; hence, they promoted the Islamisation of the insurance sector. In 1992, the government passed a decree on the control and supervision of the insurance sector, making all insurance operations in Sudan comply with Shariah principles. In 2001, more detailed legislation was adopted, and in 2003, the government expanded it further and passed an Islamic Law of Insurance. In 1990, the first Islamic bond was issued.

In 1994, the Khartoum Stock Exchange was set-up, operating on Islamic principles (Ali 2007; Hearn et al.: 15-18). The central bank created the Central Bank Musharaka Certificate (CMC) as a market-oriented instrument compatible with Shariah law.[5] The Sudan Financial Services Company (SFS) on behalf of the Bank of Sudan and government ownership in commercial banks issued these securities in July 1998. The authorised primary bidders are all the commercial banks having accounts with the Bank of Sudan. The CMC can be traded in the secondary market.

In 1999, the Ministry of Finance and National Economy (MoFNE) issued Government Musharaka Certificate (GMC) with the primary goal of financing the budget.[6] Part of the GMC was transferred to the Bank of Sudan in 2000 to be used as additional tools for open market operations. Most securities are being marketed, and new ones issued, most notably the newly issued Government Investment Certificate (GIC). GICs are a form of Murabaha issued by the government to finance particular outlays for ministries of education, health and department of medical supply.

The Financial Infrastructure of Southern Sudan

Before the outbreak of the second war in 1983, there were about ten branches of the Khartoum-based Unity Bank in southern Sudan (Yongo-Bure 2007:144). These bank branches mainly collected savings from the South and channelled them for utilisation in the North. The Bank of Sudan had a branch in Juba, which became the Bank of southern Sudan in 2005. However, the Bank of Sudan extension of credit to agriculture and public corporations was confined to the North where public corporations operated the irrigated schemes. The Agricultural Bank of Sudan (ABS) had branches in Juba, Renk, and Wau in the South. But most of the ABS's lending in the South was concentrated in Renk, where the mode of mechanised farming had extended from the North. For example, between1982-1984, the total agricultural credit extended by the ABS was L S 72 million. The share of the South out of this total was L S 9.6 million. Renk received 82 per cent of the share of the South, Wau17.7 per cent, and Juba 0.3 per cent (Yongo-Bure 2005:82-83). There was only one insurance company in the South, performing a limited number of functions such as motor vehicle insurance. By then motor vehicle ownership was very limited in the South.

During the war, Faisal Islamic Bank and Omdurman National Bank were established in southern Sudan. From the 1990s to 2005, these Khartoum-registered banks, operating in the government-garrison towns in the South, were also Islamic. In 2007, these Islamic banks were told by the Bank of southern Sudan to either change to conventional operations or quit the South. They chose to quit. By February 2009, Faisal Islamic Bank, Omdurman National Bank, and the Agricultural Bank of Sudan announced the closure of their branches in the South.

By 2011, a rudimentary financial system had been established in southern Sudan. The Nile Commercial Bank, created during the war, plus the Buffalo Bank, Ivory Bank, and the Sudan Microfinance Institution (SUMI) are local banks now operating in southern Sudan. Other banks operating in southern Sudan include subsidiaries from neighbouring countries such as the Kenya Commercial Bank, Equity Bank, and Ethiopia Commercial Bank. Three insurance companies from eastern African countries provide insurance services in southern Sudan. These are the National Insurance Corporation, the Renaissance Insurance Company, and UAP Insurance (www.gurtong.com 2011).

Monetary and Exchange Rate Policies in Sudan

Sudan adopted a fixed-exchange rate regime from 1957-1978, first pegged to Pound Sterling until 1971 and then to the United States Dollar. From 1978 to 1987, a series of devaluations, controls, and multiple exchange rates were pursued, each unsuccessfully. As part of liberalisation policy in 1992, there were attempts to unify the official and parallel exchange rates. With further deterioration in the country' balance of payments, more devaluations were undertaken through 1996 when another unification effort was pursued until 1997. Commercial banks and private exchanges continued to fix the selling and buying rates, while the central bank calculated a weighted average of the private sector rates as its own rate.

In 1998, a more comprehensive strategy exchange rate reform was introduced to unify the rate. The official rate was replaced by a moving average of market rates and exchange controls were progressively lifted. The mandatory immediate surrender of foreign exchange receipts from exports was extended to six months. Existing restrictions on means of payments for foreign trade and on financing imports were lifted. In May 2002, the Sudanese dinar was changed from a de-facto fixed rate to a managed-float. A formal band of ±1.5 per cent was introduced and later broadened to ±2.0 per cent around the official rate. The Bank of Sudan began to auction its foreign exchange within this band.

Sudan's monetary policy has been drawn and executed to achieve macroeconomic objectives, which included raising the growth rate of GDP and maintaining monetary and exchange rate stability through controlling monetary aggregates. The Bank of Sudan takes monetary policy decisions in coordination with the Ministry of Finance and National Economy (MoFNE). While the stated policy of the Bank of Sudan is that the target of monetary policy is to maintain price stability and low inflation, in actual fact the operations of the central bank have been to finance the government budget deficit, including lending to public enterprises, and to prescribe credit ceilings for priority sectors. To attain these objectives, the Bank of Sudan uses a set of direct and indirect instruments of monetary and credit control. In addition to moral suasion and quantitative measures, the Bank of Sudan experimented with several instruments: Statutory Reserve Ratio (SRR); Internal Liquidity Ratio (ILR); Financing Windows, Credit Ceilings; Open Market Operations; Foreign Exchange Operations; and Setting Minimum Rates (UNDP 2006:55).

The SRR was raised from 20 per cent in 1992 to 30 per cent in 1997, but steadily declined after that. Sub-ceilings were maintained for credit to priority sectors, but were then gradually abandoned in the wake of liberalisation of 1997, except for the imposition of 10 per cent of total private sector credit for social development activities.

From the early 1990s, all sectors were subdivided into priority sectors, non-priority sectors, and sectors excluded from credit. In 1996, the government issued a list of 13 priority sectors, which were intended to receive 90 per cent of total credit. Up to 40 per cent of commercial banks' total credit was to be allocated to agriculture, and within agriculture certain amounts were prescribed to various subsectors. In addition, the cost of credit was regulated and differentiated depending on the nature and financial adequacy of the lending institution. (UNDP 2006:53-56).

But against the escalation of inflation to historically unprecedented levels during the first half of the 1990s, accompanied by a sharp deterioration in the balance of payments, a strengthened programme focusing on macroeconomic and price stabilisation was formulated for the period 1997-2001. This was supported with a tight fiscal policy from 1997, which restricted central government resort to deficit spending from the central bank. The Bank of Sudan became more active in conducting a market-oriented monetary policy and started engaging in open market operations using indirect instruments based on Islamic modes of finance. The Islamic open market operations instruments included central bank Musaraha certificates (CMCs) and government Musaraha certificates (GMCs). A strengthened economic reform programme aimed at consolidating and modernising the macroeconomic management regime, was activated in 2002 as Sudan switched to indirect Islamic monetary policy management and broad monetary targeting, and introduced a managed float exchange rate system.

The main aim of monetary and credit policy during this reform period centred around achieving positive rates of growth in real GDP and stabilising prices to acceptable levels, concomitant with a general reduction in the rate of growth of broad nominal money supply to specified levels. The CMCs were used for both liquidity control and increasing government revenue, while the GMCs and GICs were basically aimed at meeting government need for revenue.

After the signing of the CPA, the country moved to a dual banking system: an Islamic system for the North and a conventional one for the South. From 2005, the Dinar continued to function anywhere in Sudan while other currencies operated side-by-side with the Dinar in the South, until 2007, when a new unified Sudanese Pound (SP) was introduced to replace the

Dinar at an exchange rate of 1US$=2SP. Hence, just before its split, Sudan implemented one monetary policy under two different financial systems. Was this willingly accepted by Juba? Or did Juba tolerate it just because it was sure the South would soon separate and have its own system?

Foreign exchange operations were used as a monetary policy instrument during 1997-99 for the purpose of controlling liquidity. With oil, foreign exchange operations lost their liquidity control function but continued to be used to stabilise the exchange rate. The Bank of Sudan stood ready to buy and sell foreign exchange on demand, targeting exchange rate stability. Banks were also instructed to ensure that the total amount of credit advanced to rural areas, at any given time by any of their branches, was not less than 50 per cent of total deposits received from these areas.

With increases in petroleum exports, the persistent exchange rate crisis of the Sudanese currency was somehow resolved. Soon the Comprehensive Peace Agreement (CPA) was signed in 2005. Then a new currency was issued in 2007. With all the foregoing experiences, can the two Sudans sustain a common currency or should each one have its own currency?

Conclusion

From the historical experiences of Sudan with monetary, exchange and fiscal policies, it will be extremely difficult for the two Sudans to manage a common currency. Their financial systems are at different levels of development. Although the North's system is relatively more developed, it is still far from the ideal integrated system. The South has just started to set up a financial system. Each of the two Sudans aims at developing a different financial system: a conventional one for the South and an Islamic one for the North. The enthusiasm of the North for an Islamic system and southern Sudan's persistent opposition to a religious system makes it unfeasible for them to manage a common currency. They hardly worked cooperatively during the six years they were implementing the Comprehensive Peace Agreement (CPA). They quarreled over the sharing of oil revenue. Will they cooperate on sharing of the seigniorage revenue? Will they be able to agree on convergence criteria and cooperate on their enforcement?

As one country, they did not devise polices for regional development. How will they address their marked economic inequalities in their development policies as separate countries? A common currency also means a common market. In a united Sudan, it was the northern industry that benefited from the common market as southern Sudan had no industrial products to export to the North. It is always very difficult for a new industry to compete with established ones unless there is a deliberate policy to alter the historical relationship. In the case of a united Sudan it would be an uphill battle for southern Sudan to overcome northern Sudan's early-start advantages due to the backwash effects of the established northern industry. The same backwash effects will operate if the two countries continue to have a common currency. A common currency is only useful in a relationship in which the partners do care for each other's welfare and therefore institute measures that can bring about justice and equality through balanced regional development.

Countries that have sought to establish a monetary union have initially been separate. Their quest for adoption of a common currency has been in the process of moving towards cooperation and even integration. But the two Sudans are moving in the opposite direction. Will the forces that pull them apart politically withstand the maintenance of a single currency? Would confederation not have been the preferred political arrangement, if maintenance of a single currency was seen as crucial?

Therefore, northern and southern Sudan should have a separate currencies and monetary policies, given their different levels of development and degree of mistrust. This mistrust will not allow for harmonious handling of the major economic challenges the two separate countries will be encountering. The central bank in a developing economy plays more and difficult roles. The Bank of Sudan has experienced many problems throughout its history, especially from 1978. Northern Sudan and southern Sudan will undergo many economic challenges before they eventually stabilise. It is preferable that each one addresses these initial challenges individually otherwise their mistrust of each other will be deepened in the process of antagonistically managing difficult situations jointly. As their economies develop and stabilise, they may be able to see their mutual benefits of working cooperatively as neighbours with a very long border. That will be when they may pursue common policies cooperatively.

At the present level of development of southern Sudan, the major component of money supply consists of cash. Demand deposits are limited as the habit of banking is not widespread. Financial institutions such as commercial banks, development banks, insurance companies, social security and pension schemes, that play an important role in development, are either in their infancy ornon-existent. Therefore, the effects of monetary policy on sustained economic growth and development will be very limited. Consequently, policy-makers for an independent southern Sudan should continue to focus on the building of a financial infrastructure and spreading the habit of banking throughout the population instead of spending time on fruitless negotiations and management of a common currency with a never-caring supposed partner.

Through judicious use of its *seigniorage*, southern Sudan will benefit from having its own currency before it is able to diversify its tax base. Of course, the Bank of Southern Sudan (BoSS) should not over-print the currency because of the inflationary consequences of an overprint. Macroeconomic stability, particularly price stability, is essential for sustained economic growth and development. Inflation tax should not become a significant part of the revenue of the Government of Southern Sudan (GoSS) regardless of how hard-pressed the country is with financial difficulties.

The South should allocate its *seigniorage* to cash purchases of crops from the peasant farmers as the crop production will liquidate the inflationary consequences of the newly printed money. *Seigniorage* channelled to rural development will generate production and will have minimum inflationary consequences. It will also increase employment, income, and reduce abject poverty as the bulk of the population will share in it.

As much as a number of foreign financial institutions are providing services in southern Sudan, the South needs to develop its own financial infrastructure, which in the longrun will dominate its financial industry. Considerable efforts must be made to develop such a vital sector. It will take time before the habit of banking becomes widespread. Therefore, it must be consciously developed. The persistent problems that the Nile Commercial Bank has been experiencing must be resolved permanently and the lessons learned from it must be used to help in the development of other financial institutions.

Each state should establish its own bank(s) with the initial capital contributed by GoSS and the state governments. More capital should be raised from county governments and the citizens of each state by selling shares to them. Such a policy will reduce future complaints about the functioning of the national financial system. At least a national insurance and re-insurance company/corporation must be set up. States may also establish their own insurance companies, again with shares from the counties and citizens of the state. Counties should establish credit unions. The cooperative movement should establish a bank with branches in all counties and payams in medium and the longrun. The Government of southern Sudan, the Bank of Southern Sudan, and the southern universities should cooperate in devising plans to educate and train human resources for the establishment of the nucleus of a financial system. About 15-20 per cent of intake to highereducation should be in the disciplines of economics, commerce and statistics.

Although a larger developing economy has more potential for development than a smaller one, which is extremely dependent on changes in the world economy, cooperation and integration has to be among countries with common aspirations and goals. Can South Sudan develop its financial sector along the East African lines, with the hope of realizing the benefits of a common currency under future East African Monetary Union? Unlike North Sudan, which is developing an Islamic financial system, the East African Community member countries have operated on the conventional financial system. Furthermore, the East African economies, especially the Kenyan and Ugandan ones, and the South Sudanese economy have become closely integrated since 2005.

Notes

1. The concept of optimal currency area is discussed in the following pages.
2. A moral hazard arises as some members of the monetary union borrow unsustainably with the hope that other members of the union or the union central bank would bail them out in case of debt crisis.
3. Southern Sudan is approximately three times each of the original provinces of the North. For the figures on southern Sudan to be comparable to those of the six provinces of the North at independence, the figures of the South should be decomposed to the three comparable original provinces of Bahr el Ghazal, Equatoria, and Upper Nile.
4. Both instruments of Islamic finance are based on profit-loss-sharing. The investor (Islamic Bank) shares profits or loss generated by funds invested in an enterprise. There is no automatic interest earned by lending to an undertaking. Under a Mudaraba contract, the bank contributes the capital and the borrower provides labour and expertise. The borrowers do their best to make productive use of the funds. The lender and borrowers share profit in predetermined percentages. Any loss is borne by the lender unless the borrower causes it through willful acts, negligence, or breach of contract.
Musharaka is similar to a partnership. Each of the party to the contract contributes a percentage of the capital and her/his obligations toward any liability are stated. Profits and losses are shared according to a partner's contribution of capital, service, or expertise to the enterprise.
5. The Central Bank Musharaka Certificates (CMCs) were shares in a special fund composed of government investments in nine commercial banks. The CMCs allow their owners to share with the Bank of Sudan and the Ministry of Finance the benefits of investing in banks wholly or partially owned by them. If the Bank of Sudan wants to reduce liquidity of the commercial banks, it will sell certificates up to the amount of money it wants to withdraw from the banks. If it wishes to increase liquidity in the economy, it will buy certificates accordingly.

6. The Government Musharaka Certificates operate in a similar manner as the CMCs. They allow their buyers to share the profit or loss resulting from the operation of government corporations and companies whose equity capital constitutes the fund from which these certificates are issued. The GMCs work as open market operations, managing overall liquidity in the economy. They also contribute to covering part of budget deficit instead of printing money by the Bank of Sudan. The Government Investment Certificates (GICs) also play the same role as the GMCs, except that they are limited to particular ministries whose services are considered essential.

References

Ali, Abdalla Ali, 2007, 'Khartoum Stock Exchange: Who should oversee its operations?', *Sudan Tribune*, June 25, 2007. (http://www.sudantribune.com/, Accessed on 05/11/2012).

Anand, Shriya, John Anderson, Rochelle Guttmann, Ruiwen Lee, Matthew Mandelberg, Samuel Maurer, Kristy Mayer, Shawn Powers, Caitlin Sanford, Mary Yang, 2011, *Moving Toward a Monetary Union and Forecast-Based Monetary Policy in East Africa*, Princeton University: Woodrow Wilson School of Public and International Affairs.

Bank of Sudan, *Annual Reports*, various years.

_____, *Central Bank of Sudan Policies for the Year 2011*.

Bekkin, Renat, 2012, 'Country Focus: Sudan – Forgotten center of Islamic finance',in http://www. newhorizon-islamicbanking.com/index.cfm?section=features&action=view&id… Acceessed: 05/11/2012.

Buiter, Willem H., 2007, 'Seigniorage', www. *Economics-ejournal.org/economics/journalarticles*.

Burton, Maureen and Ray Lombra, 2003, *The Financial System & The Economy: Principles of Money and Banking*, Mason: Thompson South-Western.

Cecchetti, Stephen G., 2008, *Money, Banking, and Financial Markets*, New York: McGraw-Hill/Irwin.

Feist, Holger, 2001, 'The Enlargement of the European Union and the Redistribution of Seigniorage Wealth', CESifo Working Paper Series No. 408,www.SSRN.com

Fischer, Stanley, 1982, 'Seigniorage and the Case for a National Money', *The Journal of Political Economy*, Vol. 90, No.2, 295-313.

Fry, Maxwell J., 1995, *Money, Interest and Banking in Economic Development*, Baltimore: The John Hopkins University Press.

Gerber, James, 2011, *International Economics*, New York: Addison-Wesley.

Gills, Malcolm, Dwight H. Perkins, Michael Roemer, and Donald R. Snodgrass, 1987, *Economics of Development*, New York: W.W. Norton & Company.

Global Witness, 2009, *Fuelling Mistrust: The Need for Transparency in Sudan's Oil Industry*, London.

Hearn, Bruce, Jenifer Piesse, and Roger Strange, [No date], *The Role of the Stock Market in the Provision of Islamic Development Finance: Evidence from Sudan*, King's College, London.

Hess, Peter and Ross, Clark, 1997, *Economic Development: Theories, Evidence, and Policies*, Forth Worth: The Dryden Press.

Hansen, Jorgen Drud and King, Roswitha M., 2004, "How to Cut the Seigniorage Cake into Fair Shares in an Enlarged EMU", *Jorgen-drud.hansen@ef.vu.lt* and *vitaking@eurofaculty.lv* , December.

Mohamed, Sufian Eltayeb and Sidiropoulos, Moise, [No date], *Finance –Growth Nexus in Sudan: Empirical Assessment Based on an Application of Autoregressive Distributed Lag (ARDL) Model*, Aristotle University of Thessaloniki and LEAP (Greece).

Mundell, R. A., 1961, 'A Theory of Optimum Currency Areas', *American Economic Review*, 51 (4): 509-17.

Todaro, Michael P. and Smith, Stephen C., 2006, *Economic Development*, New York: Pearson Addison Wesley.

United Nations Development Programme, 2006, *Macroeconomic Policies for Poverty Reduction: The Case of Sudan*.

Yarbrough, Beth V. and Yarbrough, Robert M., 2006, *The World Economy: Trade and Finance*, Thomson: South-Western.

Yongo-Bure, Benaiah, 2002, *Development Financing in Sudan, 1946-1999*, Kettering University.

_____, 2005, 'The Agricultural Bank of Sudan and the Sudanese Peasant', *Journal of Development Alternative and Area Studies*, Vol. 24 No. 3 & 4,(Sept.-Dec., 2005): 74-93.

_____, 2007, *Economic Development of Southern Sudan*, Lanham, Md: University Press of America, Inc.

10

South Sudanese Pound Managed Under Floating Exchange Regime: Prospects and Challenges

Andrew Ssemwanga

Introduction

South Sudan voted overwhelmingly for secession from Sudan and became a new independent African nation on 9 July 2011. South Sudan has already enacted key laws to ensure the smooth running of the country, e.g. Transitional Constitution, a Central Bank law and others. A managed float exchange rate regime to ensure macroeconomic stability has been adopted and a new currency in the name of the South Sudanese Pound (SSP) is already in circulation. South Sudan is faced with a lot of social and economic problems that include limited access to basic education, healthcare, food, water, high inflation, sovereign debt, low level of national revenue and others. Most of the problems have been *exacerbated* by suspending oil production during January 2012. The Government of South Sudan has come up with a number of measures to address the shortfall in oil revenue and also the overdependence on oil revenue by establishing a Non-Oil Revenue Action Plan as well as instituting austerity measures that relate to Government expenditure.

Basing on studies carried out by the IMF and World Bank as reported by Simwaka (2010), a number of Sub-Sahara African countries performed well in terms of GDP and exports for the period 2002 to 2008. These include Kenya and Nigeria which were using a managed float exchange regime for the whole period. However, their annual average percentage changes in consumer prices were rather high. Results from Dynamic Stochastic General Equilibrium

Model (DSGE) which were done by Vencatachellum (2007) show that for a median net oil exporting country, a doubling in the price of oil would increase its gross domestic product while a rate of inflation would increase and there would be an appreciation of exchange rate. A number of studies carried out to show the effectiveness of monetary policy and fiscal policy on economic activity show mixed results. Some indicate that monetary policy is more effective than a fiscal policy as in the cases of Ajayi (1974), Eliot (1975), Ajsafe and Folorunso (2002), while others indicate the opposite, as in the cases of Andersen and Jordan (1986) and Chowdhury (1986).

In the following paragraphs, the author discusses possible challenges and prospects that the managed float exchange regime could have for the economy of South Sudan and provides possible policy recommendations that could help the infant economy to overcome them. The author has consulted different materials, e.g., textbooks, reports, research papers and numerous websites.

Facts on South Sudan

South Sudan voted overwhelmingly for secession from Sudan with about 99 per cent of voters in favour of it. The referendum was held from 9 to 15 January 2011 (Goitom 2011). Subsequently, on 9 July 2011, a new independent African nation, South Sudan, was born. It became the 54th African nation and 193rd member of the United Nations (Richmond 2011). The referendum was the result of a Comprehensive Peace Agreement which was signed between the Government of Sudan and the Sudan People's Liberation Movement (SPLM)in 2005. South Sudan covers an area of 644,329 sq km (Southern Sudan Bureau of Standards, 2010). The Gross Domestic Product (GDP) of South Sudan in 2010 was 30.5 billion South Sudanese Pounds (SSP). The biggest chunk of GDP was from the oil sector under which oil exports amounted to 71 per cent of the value of GDP in 2010 (Ngai 2012). The Gross National Income in 2010 was 19 billion Sudanese Pounds which was equivalent to USD 8 billion. The GNI per capita was 2,267 Sudanese Pounds or USD 984 (Republic of South Sudan, National Bureau of Statistics 2010). The Consumer Price Index (CPI) has been high and rising throughout 2011, reaching a peak of 79 per cent in November 2011 (Ngai 2012). As a result of stopping of oil production, South Sudan will have a high rate of inflation. For example, inflation went to 50.9 per cent from 21.3 per cent from February to March 2012 according to South Sudan's Statistics Office (Ferrie 2012).

The South Sudan CPI increased by 79.5 per cent from May 2011 to May 2012 (Republic of South Sudan, National Bureau of Statistics 2010). The price of the South Sudan Pound (exchange rate) which is under a managed float exchange mechanism by the Central Bank of southern Sudan was at a rate of 2.95 SSP per United States dollar by the end of March 2012 (Ngai 2012). In 2010, trade amounted to over 100 percent of the value of GDP. Export and import shares were 72 and 40 per cent of the value of GDP respectively (South Sudan, National Bureau of Statistics, 2010). Exports consist of timber from teaks, mvuba and other trees. According to a report from Human Rights Watch, millions of South Sudanese do not have access to basic education, healthcare, food and water; while the Government estimates that 47 per cent are undernourished and the maternal mortality of 2,054 per 100,000 live births is regarded as the highest in the world (Sudan Tribune 2012). There are currently some 162,500 people who have fled conflict and related food shortages in Sudan and have taken refuge in neighbouring South Sudan (New Times of Rwanda 2012). The whole region has less than 60km of paved road (Guardian 2012). The good news is that during April 2012, China reached an agreement with South Sudan for a US$ 12 billion deal to construct roads, bridges, telecoms networks and to develop agriculture and hydro-electric power (BBC News Africa 2012).

South Sudan faces a highly volatile economic situation due to its overdependence on oil exports for foreign exchange. Oil accounted for 98 per cent of South Sudan's Government revenue for its budget of 2011 (Mpyisi, 2010). Both South Sudan and Sudan were sharing oil revenue on an equal basis, i.e., 50 per cent for each side from 2005 to 2011. After South Sudan became independent in July 2011, southern and northern negotiators were not immediately able to reach an understanding on how to share the revenue from the southern oilfields. While Sudan believes that South Sudan should pay between US $ 32 and US $ 36 per barrel, South Sudan does not agree to this as it would mean paying over ten times the international average price of a barrel of oil (Woolf 2012). South Sudan believes that the cost should be closer to US $ 1 to US $ 2 per barrel to transport the oil through the pipelines (Sudan Tribune 2012) and (El-Sadany et al. 2012). During January 2012, South Sudan suspended oil production (Sudan Tribune 2012) after Sudan had seized South Sudanese's oil worth a lot of million dollars (US $ 815) because Sudan claimed that South Sudan had failed to pay oil transit fees which had accumulated over months (Woolf 2012). South Sudan plans to lay a new pipeline that could take oil from Juba to the Indian Ocean port of Lamu in Kenya through Uganda (Woolf 2012). However, the plan might take a long time to implement as an investor for the project has not yet been identified (RT 2012). In Chart 1, there are projections of oil revenues for South Sudan from 2011 to 2035 (Ministry of Finance and Economic Planning, Republic of South Sudan (2011). The picture is not rosy as oil revenues will start decreasing from 2013. The upper line shows the total oil revenues for South Sudan before any transfers/payments to the North. The lower line indicates the total revenues to South Sudan with the continuation of the CPA wealth sharing agreement. Possibly, the future will lie between the two lines.

Chart 1: Projected oil Revenues for South Sudan

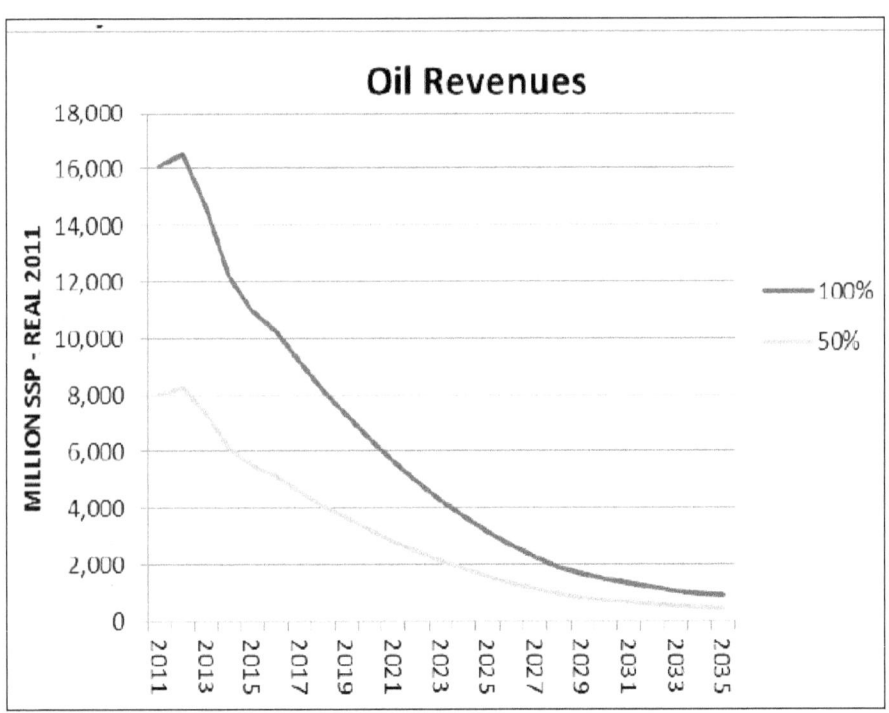

Source: Ministry of Finance and Economic Planning, Republic of South Sudan (2011)

Monetary Issues in South Sudan

During July 2011, the President of South Sudan signed a Central Bank law to formally establish the Bank of southern Sudan as the Central Bank of South Sudan. The Central Bank Law empowers, among other things, the Central Bank of South Sudan to monitor all issues related to monetary policy, e.g. prices, exchange rate, interest rate, money supply etc. to ensure that there is macroeconomic stability in the country (Central Banking Newsdesk 2012). The Bank of South Sudan which is now the Central Bank of South Sudan is a key player in the monetary policy of southern Sudan. It is located in the city of Juba, the capital of South Sudan. The Bank of South Sudan (BoSS) which became the central bank of South Sudan was originally established in 2005 as a branch of the Bank of Sudan until 9 July 2011 when South Sudan seceded to become an independent republic. It is headed by a Governor. The Bank is the only institution that is constitutionally mandated to issue the South Sudanese Pound (The New Sudan Vision 2011). On 9 July 2011, the Bank of South Sudan (BoSS) took over monetary management from the Central Bank of Sudan (CBoS) for the South; issuing the currency, monitoring money supply and regulating financial institutions. BoSS has replaced all the SDG notes it is responsible for with the notes of the new currency, the South Sudanese Pound (SSP) at par rate, i.e., 1 SDG = 1 SSP. During the time of enacting the Central Bank Law, it was announced by the South Sudan's Central Bank Governor that the Central Bank planned to operate a managed float exchange regime and that the exchange rate would be set depending on the price of oil and the value of regional currencies (Central Banking Newsdesk 2012).

Fiscal Issues in South Sudan: Expendintures and Revenues

The South Sudan Development Plan (SSDP) (2011-13) outlines government's response to core development and state building challenges in the next three years, and outlines priority programmes for achieving these objectives. It emphasizes channelling resources towards development, basic education and health service delivery and development of a vibrant agricultural sector. The SSDP will follow the requirements of an interim Poverty Reduction Strategy Paper (iPRSP) and will build on the existing GoSS policy positions (Vision 2040 and GoSS Growth Strategy) and the various existing sector plans and the 2010 Action Plan to address core government functions (Kameir 2011).

Total amount of revenue which was collected from January to the end of September 2010 was Sudanese Pound (SDG) 4.47 billion. Of this amount, oil revenue accounted for SDG 4.37 billion (97.6%), whilst non-oil revenue accounted for SDG 106 million (2.4% of total revenue). Revenue estimates in the supplementary budget for that period were SDG 4.22 billion due to changes in the price of oil. Actual expenditures to the end of September amounted to SDG 4.11 billion. Budgeted expenditure for the period was SDG 3.83 billion. This means that a small amount of savings was made during the period between actual revenue and actual expenditure, i.e. SDG0.36 (Athorbei 2011). The total available resources which had been budgeted for 2011 amounted to SDG 5,719 million. Oil revenues for 2011 were estimated at SDG 5,608 million, and accounted for 98 per cent of the estimated resource envelope. Non-oil revenues were estimated at SDG 111 million. An amount of SDG 40 million was estimated to come from Personal Income Tax and a sum of SDG 71 million from other Government of southern Sudan revenues. Total allocations for 2011 amounted to SDG 5,719 million. Those allocations were equal to total expected revenues. In 2011, a sum of $719 millionhad been expected from development partners. Actual spending from January 2011 to June 2011 was SDG 4.4 billion. Between July 2011 and January 2012, a sum of South Sudanese Pound (SSP) 5.95 billion was spent. On 17 February 2012, the Council of Ministers approved an initial set of austerity measures to maximise the use of existing public resources by immediately reducing government spending in an attempt to compensate for the loss of oil revenue as a result of stopping oil production (Ngai 2012). Operating and capital budgets had been cut by 50 per cent for most agencies and State transfers were to be cut by 10 per cent (Ngai 2012).

Non-oil Revenue Action Plan

The Government of South Sudan, through the Ministry of Finance and Economic Planning, has formulated a non-oil revenue action plan that aims at reducing revenue volatility as a result of surges in oil prices on international markets. The plan entails a short-term measure in form of an oil-revenue stabilisation fund and widening the base for more stable sources of revenue. The latter involves the establishment of a non-distortionary tax regime that is private-sector driven. The plan also envisages a medium to long term solution to oil revenue volatility by establishing a strong and broad-based non-oil economic growth (Athorbei 2011). For the purpose of increasing government revenues, the Government of South Sudan enacted the Taxation Act 2009 which requires that all businesses operating in South Sudan register as taxpayers. The largest source of non-oil revenue would be customs revenue. The Government of South Sudan plans to establish a National Revenue Authority in the future (Athorbei 2011). The Government of South Sudan plans to secure external funding through loans on concessional terms. Such loans would be geared towards stimulating economic growth in form of roads and other infrastructure. The Government would not print money to meet expenditure (Ngai 2012).

Exchange Rates in Theory

A Fixed Exchange Rate Regime

Exchangerate regimes range from fixed (hard peg) regimes at one end and floating (fully flexible) regimes at the other (Simwaka 2010). Under a fixed exchange regime, a country fixes its exchange rate to another currency, for instance, the US dollar or a basket of other currencies. Under this policy, a monetary authority does not actively buy or sell currency to maintain the rate. Instead, the rate is enforced by non-convertibility measures, e.g., capital controls, import/export licenses, etc. The monetary authority is normally a currency board and every unit of local/native currency must be backed by a unit of foreign currency. This ensures that the local monetary base does not inflate without being backed by hard currency. If anyone holding a foreign currency wishes to exchange it for a local currency, a currency board must redeem foreign currency at the currency's fixed price. In the absence of a currency board, a central bank could carry out the same function but the central bank's monetary liabilities would no longer need to be fully backed by foreign assets. The principal justifications behind a currency board are threefold:

(a) To import monetary credibility of the anchor nation;
(b) To maintain a fixed exchange rate with the anchor nation;
(c) To establish credibility with the exchange rate.

Currency boards are suitable for small open economies that would find independent monetary policy difficult to sustain (Kasekende and Brownbridge 2010). The virtue of this system is that questions of currency stability no longer apply. Fixed rates provide a non-inflationary anchor for monetary policy and are characterised by lower inflation (Edwards 1996). In some instances, a fixed rate of exchange provides a higher degree of certainty for exporters and importers so that there is less speculation in a market (Tutor2u 2012). In addition, domestic firms and their employees exercise strict financial discipline when an economy is using fixed exchange rate because they have to keep operational costs low in order to compete favourably in international markets (Tutor2u 2012). The biggest disadvantage of a fixed exchange monetary policy is that it allows only limited room for independent monetary policy because the need to defend the fixed exchange rate becomes the overriding objective and other monetary domestic objectives are put aside (Kasekende and Brownbridge 2010). Another disadvantage is that this option involves the loss of monetary autonomy (Williamson 1998). The policy also limits the use of other monetary policy instruments such as interest rate which would be appropriate in a given circumstance to manage, for example, inflation (Goodfriend 2004). Evidence has shown that some economies in Latin America which were using the fixed exchange monetary policy ended up with depleted foreign exchange reserves during financial crisis in their respective countries (Edwards et al. 1999). Argentina abandoned its currency board in January 2002 after a severe recession. There are, of course, some success stories of economies that use currency boards, e.g. Hong Kong, Bulgaria, etc. The success of these economies is based on fiscal discipline and sound structural policies which are necessary to deliver good inflation and growth outcomes. Otherwise, currency pegs quickly become unsustainable (Williamson 1998).

Freely Floating Exchange Rate Regime

Under a freely floating exchangerate regime, authorities in a given country allow an exchange rate to fluctuate according to market forces of demand and supply of foreign and domestic currencies. The demand and supply of foreign and domestic currencies is determined, to a large degree, by foreign trade and international capital flows (Harrigan 2006). One of the advantages of a floating exchange rate is the possibility of providing an automatic adjustment in an economy with a large balance of payments deficit. This happens because a net outflow of currency that takes place in that economy puts pressure on exchange rate and results into a depreciation of the native currency. As a result of a depreciation in exchange rate, the relative price of exports in overseas markets falls which makes exports more competitive in international markets and, at the same time, the price of imports in the home market goes up. Imports become more expensive. This situation could reduce the overall deficit in the balance of trade if price elasticity of demand for exports and price elasticity of demand for imports are sufficiently high (Tutor2u 2012). In addition, a floating exchange rate provides the monetary authority flexibility on the use of other monetary instruments, i.e., interest rate to move towards a desired rate or range of exchange rate (Tutor2u 2012). One of the disadvantages of a floating exchange rate is that it does not provide greater certainty for exporters and importers and that could lead to speculation (tutor2u 2012). A floating rate regime might be too weak to control inflation that could be caused by various shocks (Kasekende and Brownbridge 2010).

Intermediate Foreign Exchange Regimes

Harrigan (2006) has indicated that between the two extremes, i.e., pure fixed exchange rate and pure floating exchange rate, there are a number of intermediate types of exchange rate.

As you move away from a pure fixed exchange rate, there is an adjustable peg which involves a fixed exchange rate but adjustable in exceptional situations. There is a crawling peg which is towards a pure floating exchange rate,but contains a fixed exchange rate andis periodically adjusted in line with a set of indicators, e.g., inflation. A crawling band is a fixed exchange rate regime that allows an exchange rate to fluctuate within a narrow band from a fixed central rate and the narrow band is periodically adjusted to take into account certain economic parameters, e.g., inflation. A managed float exchange rate is a situation where authorities do not have any particular exchange rate or pre-announced path but there is periodic intervention to bring an exchange rate to the desired level. A wide band exchange rate regime allows an exchange rate to float freely over a period of time within a predetermined broad band. According to Bofinger and Wollmershäuser (2003), as shown in Figure 1, exchange rate regimes are best identified using the IMF's International Financial Statistics classification of exchange regimes. The IMF's classification of exchange regimes provides eight categories of exchange rates:

a) Exchange rate arrangements with no separate legal tender (dollarisation, membership in a currency union);

b) Currency board arrangements;

c) Other conventional fixed peg arrangements (formal or de facto peg with a narrow margin of at most ± 1 per cent around a central rate);

d) Pegged rates within horizontal bands (formal or de facto peg with margins that are wider than ± 1 per cent around a central rate);

e) Crawling pegs (the currency is adjusted periodically in small amounts at a fixed, preannounced rate or in response to changes in selective quantitative indicators);

f) Crawling bands (the currency is maintained within certain fluctuation margins around a central rate that is adjusted periodically in small amounts at a fixed, pre-announced rate or in response to changes in selective quantitative indicators);

g) Managed floating (no pre-announced path for the exchange rate; the monetary authority influences the movement of the exchange rate through active intervention in the foreign exchange market without specifying, or pre-committing to, a pre-announced path for the exchange rate);

h) Independent floating (the exchange rate is market determined, with any foreign exchange market intervention aimed at moderating the rate of change and preventing undue fluctuations in the exchange rate rather than establishing a level for it).

Bofinger and Wollmershäuser (2003) decided to add on another category which is the pure floating under which an exchange rate is market determined with no foreign exchange market intervention at all; changes in foreign exchange reserves are due to technical factors only. In Figure 1, Bofinger and Wollmershäuser (2003) portray the different categories of exchange rate regimes that have been highlighted in the preceding paragraphs.

Figure 1: Exchange Rate Regimes

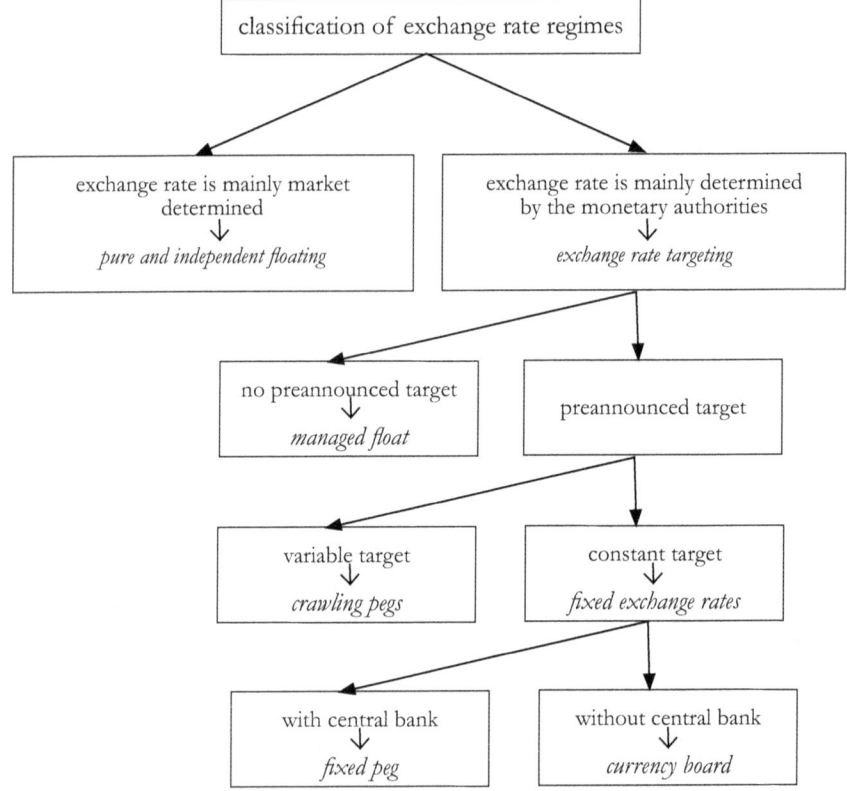

Source: Bofinger and Wollmershäuser (2003)

Choice of an exchange rate regime

The standard theory which underlies a choice of an exchange rate regime is mainly based on the theory of optimal currency areas of Mundell (1961) and Poole (1970). These models of choosing an exchange rate regime normally evaluate such regimes by how effective they are in reducing the variance of domestic output in an economy with sticky prices (Simwaka 2010). The argument by Mundell

(1961) is that an economy cannot simultaneously maintain a fixed exchange rate, free capital movement and an independent monetary policy. An economy could choose two of them for control purposes and the other one would be left to market forces. As the author has already mentioned in the previous paragraphs, each exchange regime has its own advantages and disadvantages. However, in recent times, other considerations have been included in deciding on what type of monetary policy to use, such as price-setting behaviour; the prevalence of foreign debt; the adequacy of reserve levels; and, the credibility of giving monetary policy an exchange rate anchor (Devereux 1998 and 1999).

In a number of theoretical literatures, developing countries are being encouraged to use pegs or exchange rate anchors when their economies face high propensity to inflation with a view to controlling inflation (Dornbusch 2001; Edwards 2001). Mussa et al. (2007) give a list of criteria that favour an economy to have a fixed exchange rate, i.e., low level of capital mobility; has similar trade shocks with a country with which its currency would be pegged; a flexible labour market; a high volume of foreign reserves; its fiscal policy is strong, flexible and able to stand the test of time; there is a high volume of trade between the country and the one with which its currency would be pegged and there is already enough evidence that the two countries use very much the currency that would be used for pegging. Mussa et al. (2007) argue that as economies get more integrated into global markets, it would be wise to use flexible exchange rates. Harrigan (2006) argues that the choice of a particular exchange rate regime will depend on a number of specific factors which are pertinent to a given economy. Some of the factors that are vital in choosing a particular exchange rate are: the attitude of authorities in implementing fiscal and monetary discipline; how elastic prices of imports and exportsare; level of openness to global capital markets; level of maturity of domestic capital and money markets. From the above discussions, one would conclude that for low-income, small and open economies coupled with limited exposure to international capital flow and an undeveloped financial sector as well as inelasticities in tradable markets with a tendency for expansionary fiscal policy, a fixed exchange rate could be ideal for them. As Frankel (1999) has argued, there is no single exchange rate regime that is right for all countries or at all times.

A Managed Float Exchange Rate Regime

The Government of South Sudan decided to adopt a managed float exchange rate policy as has already been mentioned in the previous chapters. Therefore in the subsequent discussion, the author focuses on both the theoretical and empirical evidence which is related to a managed float exchange rate. Bofinger and Wollmershäuser (2003) explain that a floating exchange regime is where monetary authorities do not have a pre-announced path for the exchange rate but intervene as and when it is necessary. Authorities use various policies to counter some short-term movements in the exchange rate and to maintain market liquidity by using limited exchange interventions

In this policy, a central bank manages both the money supply and exchange rate by using monetary policy tools such as open market operations, liquidity requirements, reserve requirements, interest rate and discount window lending, etc. Management of exchange rate could be against one currency or a basket of other currencies. There are quite a number of countries which use this monetary policy, e.g., Bangladesh, Sri Lanka, Tanzania, Uganda and Zambia (Kalyalya 2010). Singapore has been very successful in using the managed float rate regime. Bofinger and Wollmershäuser (2003) argue that the main advantage of managed floating is that it enables authorities to deal with various shocks provided they (authorities) are able to keep the exchange rate on a path determined by the interest rate differential. The managed float provides an opportunity to authorities to decide on the level of intervention in a market. The level of intervention would normally depend on the importance they attach to targets for output, inflation, real exchange rate and real interest rate (Simwaka 2010).The advantage of this exchange regime is that a central bank is directly managing both interest rate and exchange rate.

A central bank tries to smooth out short-term volatility in an exchange market. From time to time, a central bank intervenes by buying or selling foreign exchange for fear of letting the native currency to float freely. The monetary policy, however, suffers from failing to address directly output gaps, inflation and other external shocks (Kasekende and Brownbridge 2010). Some central banks in developing countries find the monetary policy not easy to implement as it combines two monetary policy targets and more than one monetary policy tools that require data which may not be easily available. Bofinger and Wollmershäuser (2003) mention that one of the disadvantages of the regime is that since there is no announced exchange rate path, it could necessitate providing a separate anchor for a private sector's expectations particularly in small economies. Bofinger and Wollmershäuser (2003) go on to say that a central bank could fail to defend an exchange rate path where an economy is faced with strong speculative capital outflows. In some cases, authorities could manipulate an exchange rate in order to improve international competitiveness.

Theoretical Framework for Managed Float Exchange regime

Bofinger and Wollmershäuser (2003) developed a theoretical framework that explains how a managed float exchange is used. It is based on the simultaneous application of exchange rate and interest rate as operating targets of a monetary policy. The tools of interest rate and exchange rate are used to achieve internal and external equilibrium.

Under the policy of managed floating, a central bank has to respect the Uncovered Interest Parity (UIP) condition in order to avoid high costs of sterilisation. The condition tends to maintain profits for short-term investors close to zero and hence removes the incentive for short-term capital inflows. The scenario is given in the following formula.

$$S_{t+1} - S_t = i_t - i_t^f$$

Where St is the nominal exchange rate (a rise is a depreciation), it the domestic nominal interest rate, and itf is the foreign nominal interest rate.

The internal equilibrium is characterised by minimising the central bank's loss function. In other words, combination of the interest rate and the exchange rate has to generate an optimum Monetary Condition Index (MCI).

$$MCI_t^{opt} = r_t - \psi q_t .$$

Where real exchange rate qt, rt is the domestic interest rate and MCIopt is the optimum Monetary Condition Index.

Optimum MCI determines the inflation rate and the instrument variables of monetary policy (it and St) are directly controllable by the central bank and are portrayed in the form of their real counterparts rt and qt.

Figure 2: Monetary Policy in Small Open Economies

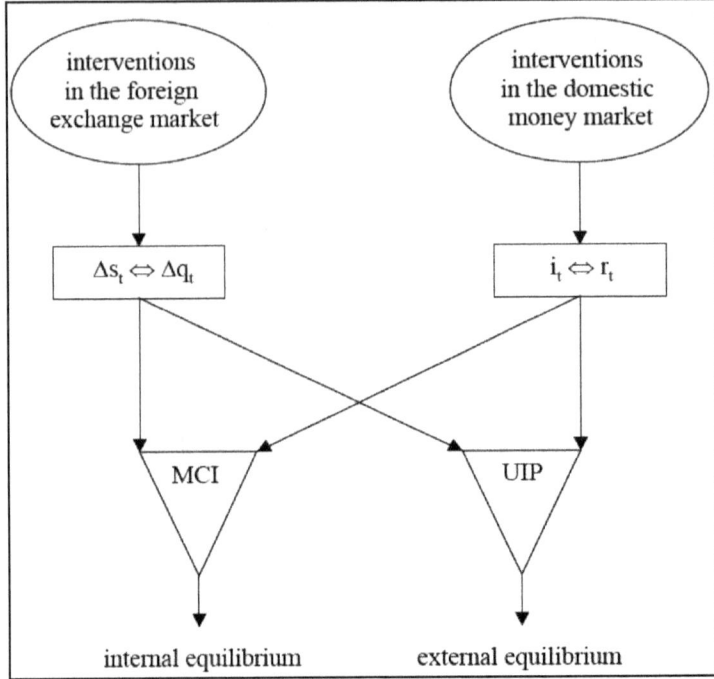

Source: Bofinger and Wollmershäuser (2003)

The simultaneous management of the exchange rate and the interest rate indicates that a central bank is able to target the exchange rate by means of sterilised interventions because it has two independent instruments at its disposal:

(i) With open-market operations (or any other form of refinancing operation) a central bank exchanges short-term domestic notes, etc., against domestic central bank reserves in order to target the short-term interest rate. Due to that transaction, monetary base changes and the central bank balance sheet is extended.

(ii) With foreign exchange market interventions, a central bank exchanges foreign sight deposits against domestic central bank reserves in order to target the exchange rate. If the intervention is sterilised, the monetary base remains constant and also the size of central bank balance sheet; but this will change the structure of the central bank's assets.

The intervention in a foreign exchange market is shown in Figure 3. On the y-axis is the price of foreign exchange in terms of the domestic currency.

Hence, there is an upward-sloping supply curve and an onward-sloping demand curve for foreign exchange. The equilibrium exchange rate is at S0.

In a foreign exchange market intervention, a central bank targets a higher or a lower exchange rate than the market-clearing rate. If a central bank targets a rate S1 that is higher than the equilibrium rate, there is an excess supply of foreign exchange which it has to buy in exchange for domestic reserves/money. Due to that transaction, a central bank's net foreign assets/reserves (NFA) will grow. If a central bank wishes to target rate S2 which is below the market-clearing rate which is mostly likely due to an excess demand for foreign exchange, it has to satisfy that demand by selling foreign assets out of its foreign exchange reserves (NFA<0). As a result, commercial banks' reserves decline.

Figure 3: The Flow Channel of Foreign Exchange Market Interventions

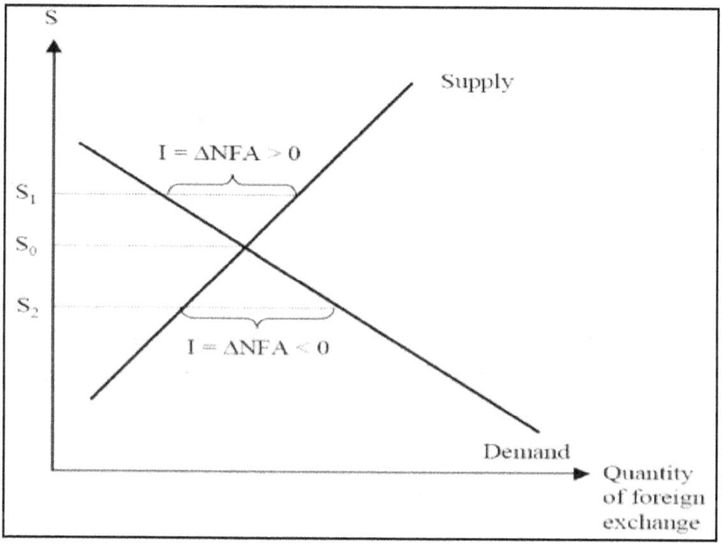

Source: Bofinger and Wollmershäuser (2003)

Dynamic Stochastic General Equilibrium Model (DSGE)

The Dynamic Stochastic General Equilibrium Model (DSGE) has been used to show impact of oil prices on oil exporting economies under fixed and managed float exchange rate regimes. The author of this chapter has found this model to be useful because southern Sudan depends heavily on exports of oil. Vencatachellum (2007) constructed a DSGE with a view to quantifying an effect of an increase in the price of oil on main macroeconomic aggregates in both oil importing and exporting African countries. For the purpose of this chapter, the author has focused on results of the model on oil exporting countries, which South Sudan is. The model is based on a small open economy where oil exports represent roughly 88 per cent of total exports and 35 per cent of total GDP. The macroeconomic aggregates are output, consumption, investment, inflation, the real exchange rate, the government budget deficit and foreign debt. In all simulations, the oil-price shock is assumed to be persistent, with a first-order auto-correlation coefficient of 0.85 as delivered from the data. The simulations are performed both under a fixed exchange rate regime and a managed float. In each case, two different arrangements are considered, i.e., complete and zero pass-through. Results show that for a median net oil exporting country, a doubling in the price of oil would increase its gross domestic product by 4 per cent under managed-float and by 9 per cent under a fixed exchange rate regime. This is mainly due to the larger appreciation of the real exchange rate under the managed float regime. The smaller increase in consumption under the managed float implies that the budget deficit narrows less than under fixed exchange rates.

A sharp appreciation of a real exchange rate that normally follows oil price increase may hinder the competitiveness of a country's exports in international markets. It is therefore important that oil-export revenues be spent in projects that are developmental in nature. Again, a sharp appreciation of the real exchange rate could be harmful if an economy is heavily concentrated in a few industries Vencatachellum (2007). This could happen to the southern Sudan economy because the industries are still few. For oil-exporting countries, government intervention does not seem to affect in a significant way an outcome of the economy, especially in the case of a managed floating. Rate of inflation would increase by a much greater magnitude under managed than a fixed exchange rate regime in a median net oil exporting country.

Effectiveness of Monetary Policy and Fiscal Policy on Economic Activities

Whereas monetary and fiscal policies are deployed in the pursuit of macroeconomic stabilisation in various economies in the world, there is a debate among academicians on the relative effectiveness of each policy on economic activity (Ajisafe and Folorunso 2002). This debate also extends to policy-makers when it comes to implementing those policies. A number of studies have been done to examine the relative effectiveness of monetary and fiscal policies on economic activity. Ajayi (1974), using ordinary least square (OLS) technique with the support of beta coefficients, confirmed that changes in economic activity brought about by monetary policy were greater than those caused by fiscal policy. By examining the relative importance of money supply changes in comparison with government expenditure changes in relation to changes in nominal GNP using OLS technique, Elliot's (1975) results showed that monetary policy had a stronger impact on nominal GNP than fiscal policy. He used the following equation:

> DYt = c + SmiDMt-i + SeiDEt-l + ut where Y represents the change in nominal GNP, M represents the change in money supply while E represents the change in high employment federal government expenditures.

The results from Ajayi (1974) and Elliot (1975) were later confirmed by Batten and Hafer (1983). However, Andersen and Jordan (1986), tested empirically the relationships between the measures of fiscal and monetary actions and total spending for United States. They used Gross National Product (GNP); money stock (MS); high employment budget surplus (R-E); high employment expenditure (E); and, high employment receipt (R). They obtained results that indicated that the influence of fiscal action on economic activity occurred faster than that of monetary action. A study that was conducted by Chowdhury (1986) in Bangladesh that considered monetary and fiscal impacts on economic activity in that country revealed that fiscal rather than monetary action had greater influence on economic activities. He also made use of the ordinary least square (OLS) technique in his empirical investigation by using the following formula:

> Yt = Co + SmiMt-i + SfiFt-i + SeiEt-1 + ut where Y, M, F, and E represent the growth rate of nominal income, money supply, government expenditures and exports respectively.

Olaloye and Ikhide (1995) carried out a study in Nigeria for the period 1986 -1991 and their results showed that that fiscal policy exerts more influence on the economy than monetary policy. Ajisafe and Folorunso (2002) carried out a study for period 1970 to 1998 for the Nigerian economy with the help of econometric modelling techniques of co-integration and error correction as well as PC-GIVE computer package of econometric data analysis and estimation. They used the following empirical model:

> Yt = f(MPt, FPt) where Y is a measure of economic activity in which Gross Domestic Product (GDP) is employed as a proxy, MP and FP are measures of monetary and fiscal actions of the government respectively. Both narrow money (MI) and broad money (M2) are employed as proxies for monetary policy variable while the search for fiscal policy variable is among the government revenue receipts (R), government expenditure (E) and government budget deficits (BD) which is measured as (R -E).

Considering the log-linear specification, the above equation in its explicit form becomes:

> InYt = a0 + b1lnMPt + b2lnFPt + et where all variables are as earlier defined, ln is natural logarithm and et is error term. It is known a-priori that GDP is expected to be positively related to MP and FP. Their results indicated that monetarypolicy rather than fiscal policy exerts greater impact on economic activity in Nigeria.

Conclusion

South Sudan is faced with multi-dimensional economic and social problems as well as others. Most of the problems have been *exacerbated* by suspending oil production during January 2012. The Government of South Sudan has come up with a number of measures to address the shortfall in oil revenue and also the over-dependence on oil revenue by establishing a Non-Oil Revenue Action Plan, as well as instituting austerity measures that relate to Government expenditure.

Findings based on the IMF and World Bank as reported by Simwaka(2010), indicate that an economy under managed float exchange regime is able to achieve good performance in terms of high GDP and exports. However, the findings indicate that under the managed float exchange regime, annual average percentage change of consumer price in both countries was high.

A Dynamic Stochastic General Equilibrium Model (DSGE) designed by Vencatachellum (2007) to show the impact of oil prices on main macroeconomic aggregates of oil exporting economies under fixed and managed float exchange rate regimes shows that for a median net oil exporting country, a doubling in the price of oil would increase its gross domestic product by 4 per cent under managed-float and by 9 perc ent under a fixed exchange rate regime. The results show that when there is an increase in oil prices, oil exporting countries, and more so for those using a managed float exchange, experience high inflation and an appreciation of the exchange rate. In addition, consumption goes up in those countries.

A number of studies carried out to show the effectiveness of monetary policy and fiscal policy on economic activity show mixed results. Some indicate that monetary policy is more effective in stabilising economic activity than a fiscal policy as in the cases of Ajayi (1974); Eliot (1975); Ajsafe and Folorunso (2002); while others indicate the opposite as in the cases of Andersen and Jordan (1986) and Chowdhury (1986).

The author concludes that a managed float exchange regime could perform well in South Sudan provided the authorities take appropriate measures to deal with possible inflationary and exchange rate appreciation tendencies, particulary during a time of oil price boom. The authorities in South Sudan should be aware that the effectiveness of monetary policy in stabilising their economy would also depend on effectiveness of their fiscal policy.

There is still a gap in research to identify the impact of monetary policy (without fiscal policy) on macroeconomic aggregates that relate to an entire economy in a given country or groups of countries that use a managed float exchange regime. There is also a gap in research to identify the effectiveness of monetary policy (in conjunction with fiscal policy) and fiscal policy on macroeconomic aggregates that relate to an entire economy in a given country or groups of countries that use a managed float exchange regime. Future research, using modern techniques of data collection and analysis, should be undertaken with a view to identifying how monetary policy could be complemented by fiscal authority or the other way round.

Policy Recommendations

The theoretical and practical cases discussed in this chapter pave the way for making recommendations for the management of the new currency dubbed the 'South Sudanese Pound'. The socio-economic and political setting in the Sudan and South Sudan are the most important determinants for fiscal and monetary policies, especially for the South Sudanese Pound. Four broad recommendations are advanced to address the problems discussed in this chapter:

Peaceful Co-existence with Sudan

Without a peaceful co-existence between the two countries, South Sudan will not fully achieve its national goals because the ensuing hostility and insecurity discourage long-term investments. It is therefore important that the two countries come together and resolve their differences which cover a number of issues, i.e., oil transit fees, boundaries and others.

Monetary Policy Measures

South Sudan, an oil exporting country and at the same time using a managed float exchange regime, should use oil revenue in case of increase in oil prices on the world market to construct more industries with a view to increasing output in the country. This measure will offset inflationary tendencies and increase GDP in the country. Part of the oil revenue should be put in an oil stabilisation fund to stabilise the exchange rate. The Central Bank should be independent from government pressure to finance its fiscal deficits, i.e. by printing money or borrowing from the Central Bank. It is advisable that the Government of South Sudan finances its deficits through taxes or possible foreign aid. Authorities should strengthen the monetary policy transmission mechanism by widening competition within the financial system through promotion of more commercial banks both in urban and rural areas with a view to increasing accessibility to financial services; set up credit reference bureaux; create a capital market, development bank and others. They should provide supportive structural policies that would strengthen monetary policy, e.g., a good system of corporate governance; build capacity in econometric and structural models; institute high-quality record-keeping and financial reporting within the central bank and entire financial and banking sectors and strengthen the regulatory and monitoring framework of the central bank; establish communication channels with the public and other stakeholders to enhance feedback mechanisms that should enable the central bank to secure market signals about the effects of its monetary policy and improve on the range, reliability and timeliness of macroeconomic data.

Fiscal Policy Measures

A managed float exchange regime will work well if it is fully supported by a strong fiscal policy because both of them are complementary to each other. The Government of South Sudan should strictly implement The South Sudan Development Plan (2011-13); strengthen a Treasury Single Account where all revenues and expenditures of the Government of South Sudan are transparently consolidated and accounted for; strengthen reserve management and ensure transparency in allocations and expenditures. An appropriate parliamentary committee should regularly monitor public revenue and expenditure and report to Parliament and the public. This arrangement will ensure full accountability of public resource management. The Government of South Sudan should continuously focus on capacity-building in areas of planning, budgeting, procurement, audit; management of oil resources, monitoring and evaluation, ICT, Corporate Governance and others.

The Government of South Sudan should ensure that financing of fiscal deficits is not done by a central bank and therefore the Government should strictly institute austerity expenditure measures that aim at fiscal sustainability and low deficits. If deficits occur, they should be financed from other sources, e.g., an Oil Revenue Stabilisation Account and a Generation Account as stipulated in the Transitional Constitution. In other instances, the Government should call upon development partners to finance some deficits. Under no circumstances, should a fiscal policy dominate a monetary policy. The Government should strictly implement the Non-Oil Revenue Action Plan by strengthening and implementing the 2009 Taxation Act. More revenue should be collected from customs, corporation tax, personal income tax and others. In this regard, the Government should streamline the tax administration in terms of collection and accountability. The Government should establish a National Revenue Authority as a matter of urgency. The Government of South Sudan, if necessary, should secure external funding in form of loans on concessional terms from African, Asian and other international development banks. In this regard, a sovereign debt which the Government shares with Sudan should be re-negotiated with a view to providing South Sudan with longer payment periods. South Sudan should concentrate on putting in place and strengthening the necessary institutional structures i.e. offices of Inspector General of Government, Auditor General, anti-corruption commission and others.

South Sudan is facing a bleak future due to the shutting down of oil production. There is an urgent need to re-negotiate for a peaceful settlement of a dispute between South Sudan and Sudan with a view to resuming the production of oil which will boost revenue in South Sudan. In connection with oil, the Government should regulate and monitor the oil sector which should be in line with a robust oil policy framework. In line with the Non-Oil Revenue Action Plan that aims at reducing revenue volatility as a result of surges in oil prices on international markets, the Government should encourage farmers to grow more food for consumption and export with a view to reducing imports of foodstuffs. The government could also encourage large private commercial farmers to invest in agriculture and also enter joint ventures with foreign firms to expand agricultural production. This will help the country to increase non-oil revenue. The main strategy in agriculture is to move towards sustainable agriculture that can both lead to food self-sufficiency and export earnings. The combination and coordination of both monetary and fiscal policy are highly recommended.

Private Sector and other Measures

The private sector should play an important role in providing vital investment in various sectors, e.g., agriculture, industry, transport, wood industry, etc. At the moment, there is a dearth of an entrepreneurial class. The Government should train and provide appropriate opportunities to the private sector. The Government should also provide an enabling environment in form of security, friendly investment regulatory framework and infrastructure in form of road network, water, power and others. The Government should encourage and provide support to young people to create jobs with a view to earning income and preventing crime and conflicts. The Government should provide skills training, microfinance and labour-intensive capital projects. South Sudan is still a young nation and she will do well if she secures membership in organisations, particularly economic ones, with a view to learning, networking, interdependence, getting appropriate support, improving international rankings and attracting foreign investment. South Sudan should vigorously follow up its membership application to the East African Community and others. South Sudan is faced with a lot of social problems that include, among others, limited access to basic education, healthcare, food, water, etc. The international community should provide the necessary humanitarian assistance in this direction.

References

Ajayi S.I., 1974, 'An Econometric Case Study of the Relative Importance of Monetary and Fiscal Policy in Nigeria', *The Bangladesh Economic Review*, Vol. 2, No. 2, 559-576.

Ajsafe and Folorunso, 2002, 'The Relative Effectiveness of Fiscal and Monetary Policy in Macroeconomic Management in Nigeria', *The African Economic and Business Review*, Vol. 3, No. 1, Spring.

Andersen and Jordan, 1986, 'Monetary and Fiscal Actions: A Test of Their Relative Importance in Economic Stabilization',*Federal Reserve Bank of St. Louis Review*, Vol. 80, 29-45.

Athorbei, David Deng, 2011, 'Government of Southern Sudan, 2011 Budget Speech', presented to the South Sudan Legislative Assembly by H.E. David Deng Athorbei, January 2011, Ministry of Finance and Economic Planning, Government of Southern Sudan, Juba.

Batten, D. S. and Rafer, R. W., 1983, 'The Relative Impacts of Monetary and Fiscal Actions on Economic Activity: A Cross-Country Comparison', *Federal Reserve Bank of St. Louis Review*, Vol. 65, 5-12.

BBC, 2012, 'Agrees US$ 8 billion with China',*BBC News Africa*, 28 April 2012, Retrieved on June 18, 2012 from http://www.bbc.co.uk

Bofinger and Wollmershäuser, 2003, 'Managed Floating: Theory, Practice and ERM II', Paper prepared for the CEPR/Deutsche Bank Research Workshop 'Managed Floating

- An Alternative to the Two Corner Solutions?' in Kronberg/Germany, 30/31 January 2003.
Bleany, M. and Fielding, D., 2002, Exchange Rate Regimes, Inflation and Output Volatility in Developing Countries', *Journal of Development Economics* 68 (1), 233-45.
Central banking Newsdesk, 2012, 'South Sudan enacts central bank law', Retrieved on May 23 from http://www.centralbanking.com/central-banking/news/2094427/south-sudan-enacts-central-bank-law
Chowdhury, A. R., 1986, 'Monetary and Fiscal Impacts on Economic Activities in Bangladesh A Note', *The Bangladesh Development Studies*, Vol. XIV, No. 2,101-106.
Devereux, M. B., 1998 and 1999, 'Fixed vs. Floating Exchange Rates: How Price Setting Affects the Optimal Choice of Exchange Rate Regime', NBER Working Paper No. 6867, December 1998, and 'The Optimal Choice of Exchange Rate Regime: Price-Setting Rules and Internationalized Production', NBER Working Paper No. 6992, March 1999.
Dornbusch, R., 2001, 'Fewer Monies, Better Monies',NBER Working Paper 8324. Cambridge, MA: National Bureau of Economic Research.
Edwards S., 1996, "The Determinants of the Choice between Fixed and Flexible Exchange-Rate Regimes," NBER Working Paper No. 5756, September 1996.
Edwards, S., 2001, 'Exchange Rate Regimes, Capital Flows and Crisis Prevention', NBER Working Paper 8529. Cambridge, MA: National Bureau of Economic Research.
Eliot, J.W., 1975, 'The Influence of Monetary and Fiscal Actions on Total Spending: The St. Louis Total Spending Equation Revisited', *Journal of Money Credit and Banking*. Vol. 7, 181-192.
Engle, R. F. and Granger, C. W .J., 1987, Co-integration.
El-Sadany, M. and Ottaway, M., 2012, 'Sudan: From Conflict to Conflict', Carnegie Paper, May 2012, Retrieved June 18, 2012 from http://carnegieendowment.org
Frankel, J. A., 1999, 'No Single Currency Regime is Right for all Countries or at all Times', *Princeton Essays in International Finance No. 215*,Princeton, NJ: Princeton University Press.
Ferrie, J., 2012, 'South Sudan hunts for Loans as Oil-Output Halt Dents Economy', Retrieved on June 10, 2012 from Bloomberg Business Week, 11 May 2012, http://www.businessweek.com
Ghosh, A., 1996, 'Does Nominal Exchange rate Regime Matter?' NEBER Working Paper 5874.
Goitom, H., 2011, 'South Sudan and The Law Library', Retrieved on 10 June 2012, from http://blogs.loc.gov/law/2011/07/south-sudan-and-the-law-library/
Goodfriend, 2004, 'Understanding the Transmission of Monetary Policy', manuscript, Federal Reserve Bank of Richmond, Presented at Joint China-IMF High Level Seminar on 'China's Monetary Policy Transmission Mechanism', Beijing, May.

Guardian, 2012, 'Southern Sudan development hindered by World Bank', Retrieved on 17 April 2012 from http://www.guardian.co.uk/world/2010/feb/18/southern-sudan-development-world-bank

Harrigan, J., 2006, 'Time to Exchange the Exchange Rate Regime: Are Hard Pegs the Best Options for Low-income', *Development Policy Review* 24 (2), 205-223.

Husain et al. 2005, 'Exchange Rate Regime Durability and Performance in Developing Versus Advanced Economies', *Journal of Monetary Economics* 52(25), 35-64.

Kalyalya, D., 2010, 'Monetary policy in Zambia: experiences and challenges', Chapter 17 in Gill Hammond, Ravi Kanbur and Eswar Prasad, eds,*Monetary Policy Frameworks for Emerging Markets*, Edward Elgar Publishing Ltd.

Kameir, E.W., 2011, 'The Political Economy of South Sudan: A Scoping Analytical Study', Retrieved May 23, 2012 from http://www.afdb.org/fileadmin/uploads/afdb/Documents/Project-and-Operations/2011%20Political_Economy_South_Sudan_-_24_October_20111.pdf

Kasekende, L. and Brownbridge, 2010, 'Post-crisis Monetary Policy Frameworks in Sub-Saharan Africa', Research paper, October 2010, African Development Bank publication, Tunis, Tunisia.

Mendoza, E. G. and Uribe, M., 1999, 'The Business Cycles of Balance-of-Payment Crises: A Revision of Mundellian Framework', NBER Working Paper No. 7045, March.

Ministry of Finance and Economic Planning, 2011, 'Guidelines for Draft Budget Sector Plans 2011 -2015', Ministry of Finance and Planning, Republic of South Sudan, 23 November.

Mpyisi, K. and Okello, D., 2012, 'The Cost of Future Conflict in Sudan', Frontier Economics, 2010, Retrieved on 18 June 2012 from http://www.frontier-economics.com

Mundell, R.A., 1961, 'A Theory of Optimum Currency Areas',*American Economic Review*, November.

Mussa, Michael, 2007, 'IMF Surveillance over China's Exchange Rate Policy', Washington, DC:Peterson Institute for International Economics.

National Bureau of Statistics, Republic of South Sudan, 2010, 'Fast Facts', Retrieved on 15 May 2012 from http://ssnbs.org/

National Bureau of Statistics, Republic of South Sudan,2010, "Consumer Price Index for South Sudan, May 2012', Retrieved on June 13, 2012 from http://ssnbs.org/cpi/2012/6/1/consumer-price-index-for-south-sudan-may-2012.html

New Times of Rwanda 2012, 'UN agency seeks funds for 'critical' refugee situation in South Sudan', Retrieved on June 24, 2012 from http://www.newtimes.co.rw/news/index.php?i=15033&a=12307

Ngai, K.M., 2012, '2011/2012 Budget Speech to National Legislative Assembly, presented by Hon. Kosti Manibe Ngai, Minister of Finance & Economic Planning March 2012', Ministry of Finance and Economic Planning, Government of Southern Sudan, Juba.

Olaloye, A. O. and Ikhide, S. I., 1995, 'Economic Sustainability and the Role of Fiscal and Monetary Policies in A Depressed Economy: The Case Study of Nigeria', *Sustainable Development*, Vol. 3, 89-100.

Poole, W., 1970, 'Optimal Choice of Monetary Policy Instruments in a Simple Stochastic Macro Model', *The Quarterly Journal of Economics*, MIT Press, Vol. 84(2), . 197-216, May.

RT, 2012, 'Chinese Money to "Settle" Sudanese Oil Divorce? RT, 23 April 2012', Retrieved on June 15, 2012 from http://www.rt.com

Simwaka, Kisu, 2010, 'Choice of exchange rate regimes for African countries: Fixed or Flexible Exchange rate regimes?',Munich Personal RePEc Archive, 15 March.

South Sudan Information. Com, 2012, 'Economy of South Sudan', Retrieved on 13 May 2012 from http://www.southsudaninfo.com/Economy_of_South_Sudan

South Sudan Bureau of Standards, Southern Sudan, 2010, 'Release of first Gross Domestic Product (GDP) and Gross National Income (GNI) figures for South Sudan by the NBS', Retrieved on May 23, 2012 from http://ssnbs.org/storage/GDP%20Press%20release_11.08.11.pdf

South Sudan Bureau of Standards, Southern Sudan, 2010, 'Key indicators', Retrieved on June 11, 2012 fromhttp://ssnbs.org/storage/key-indicators-for-southern-sudan/Key%20Indicators_A5_final.pdf

Sudan Tribune, 2012, 'Sudan Asks China for Help in Resolving Oil Dispute with South Sudan', 28 February 2012, Retrieved on 18 June, 2012 from http://www.sudantribune.com

Sudan Tribune, 2012, 'Exclusive – South Sudan Economy on the Verge of Collapse, World Bank Warns', 6 May, Retrieved on June 18, 2012 from http://www.sudantribune.com

Tutor2u, 2012, 'Fixed and floating exchange rates', Retrieved on 11 May 2012 from http://tutor2u.net/economics/content/topics/exchangerates/fixed_floating.htm

The New Sudan Vision, 2011, 'Investor info Southern Sudan: Where forth with the new currency?' Issue#1, Retrieved on 9 May 2012 from http://www.newsudanvision.com/index.php?option=com_content&view=article&id=2339:investor-info-southern-sudan-where-forth-with-the-new-currency-i&catid=5:columns&Itemid=14

Vencatachellum, 2007, 'The Impact of High Oil Prices on African Economies', Economic Research Working Paper No 93 (December 2007), Development Research Department African Development Bank, Tunis Belvedere, Tunisia.

Williamson, John, 1998, 'Crawling Bands or Monitoring Bands: How to Manage Exchange Rates in a World of Capital Mobility',*International Finance*. Blackwell Publishing, Vol. 1(1), 59-79.

Woolf, N., 2012, 'South Sudan Refuses to be Held Ransom by the North',*The Guardian*, 17 May, Retrieved on 18 June 2012 from http://www.guardian.co.uk

Conclusion

Al-Tayib Zain Al-Abdin

The Council for the Development of Social Sciences Research in Africa (CODESRIA) did well to organise a well-attended conference in Nairobi from 28 February to 1 March 2011 under the theme: 'Post-Referendum Sudan Conference 2011'. That was not its first function on the problem of southern Sudan; previously the Council organised a workshop in Juba on 17-18 May 2010 on the subject of 'Political Process in the Sudan', so that the participants could discuss in depth the options of unity and separation in Sudan. It is logical that research centres like CODESRIA should be engaged in applied research which guides decision-makers to take an enlightened view about the problems of their country. This is a normal process in advanced countries but not so in most African states. However, African scholars should continue to do their part of the job persuading politicians and senior government officials to make use of their labour, and the time will come when they would listen. The political problem chosen by CODESRIA for the workshop and the conference, is extremely vital and serious not only for the Sudan and the region but for the whole of Africa. The African fathers chose, during the independence period after the Second World War, to maintain the artificial borders left by the western colonial powers as they are, because any attempt to change them would trigger conflicts and spread havoc among the population of the continent. There is almost no country in Africa which does not share ethnic groups or resources with its neighbours across their borders.

A number of attempts were made by some disgruntled minorities to secede from their mother country for one reason or another. Only Eritrea (1991) and South Sudan (2011) managed to achieve that goal after long and bloody conflicts which lasted for decades. Some people rightly argue that these two examples are special and should not be repeated in other cases; the majority of African elites still do believe in the inviolability of African borders. The specialty of Eritrea is that it was not part of Ethiopia since the eighth century; the British who took it from the Italians in the Second World War and administered it as UN Trust Territory. The UN decided in1950 that Eritrea be made independent as a federated part of Ethiopia which decided in 1962 to end the federal status of the region and absorb it within its territory. The UN kept silent but the Eritreans who opposed the union started their sporadic guerrilla warfare, which never ceased till they achieved their independence in 1991. The war between Ethiopia and Eritrea on the borderline, after the independence of the latter showed that secession does not mean the end of conflict between the predecessor and the successor states. Will the same happen in the case of the Sudan?

The fate of southern Sudan was actually decideda long time ago by the British who occupied the country after defeating the Mahdist state in 1898. They intentionally kept the two parts of the country separated, no citizen could go from one part to the other without permission from the government, and the South was left undeveloped in all aspects of life. The senior British administrators of the three southern provinces used to meet regularly with their counterparts in East Africa and not with those in northern Sudan; education and medical care in the South was handed to Christian missions while the education and health departments in Khartoum were responsible of administering education and health in the North. It was not strange that in the Juba conference of 1947, southern leaders preferred that southern Sudan, because of its unequal development compared with the North, should remain under British colonial administration for some time or linked to East Africa. It was the British officials in charge of the conference who put pressure on southern politicians to accept being part of a united Sudan because it wass the North which was footing the bill for their region.

The first mutiny of the southern corps against the new-born national government took place as early as 18 August 1955, four and a half months before the declaration of independence on 1 January 1956. The British governor-general was the head of the state at the time. Besides, it was only natural for a southern politician to be attracted to the idea of having a sovereign state in the South because of the cultural differences and level of development. At the same time the factor of oil in the South drives politicians to possess all the revenue of oil produced in their regioninstead of sharing it with the North according to the terms of the CPA. It is also true that the Sudanese national governments, since independence, did not do much to bridge the development gap between the two parts of the country or remove the mistrust of southern politicians who felt that they had been marginalised in decision-making for a long time; and that the agreements made with them, by central governments, to give the South a federal status and keep it as a united region, were not fulfilled. The cultural domination of the North over the whole country was opposed by the southern elite who had modern education and international experience. The papers given in the Nairobi conference discussed the various aspects of the serious problem of granting, even for good reasons, the right for self-determination to a minority community in the African continent, and the consequences of separation on the region.

The editors of this book have divided the papers presented in the conference into four parts according to the theme: the first is on the rationale of self-determination in the African context; the second on north-south relations and encompassing issues that may impact the country and the region at large; the third is on the problems of nation-building in the emerging country of South Sudan; and the fourth is on the economic policy recommended for the new state.

In the first part, which has one paper, Mamdani raises serious questions about the significance and validity of self-determination for a minority within an independent African country. How should those committed to Pan-African unity understand the emergence of a new South Sudan? How will we write the history of relations between the North and South; is it a history of one people colonizing another? How did the SPLA, a champion of a united New Sudan, come to demand a separate state? Will the South establish a new viable political order? Will independence lead to peace? He argued that the South managed to win its independence without a military victory due to the external factor of 9/11th which led to the US invasion of Iraq and Afghanistan. On the other side, Nyaba in the foreword defended the right of self-determination on the basis that unity of a country cannot be imposed by force of arms, because the era of imperialism has gone forever. He uses the slogan of the Ethiopian People's Revolutionary Democratic Front when they seized power in Addis Ababa in May 1991, referring to the Eritrean case by saying that: 'Peace is better than unity'. However, the outcome was not exactly peace in Eritrea, and it may well be so for the two Sudans!

The second part comprises of four papers by: al-Abdin, Hawi, Kassahun, and Wassara. All of them acknowledged that there are serious problems and challenges for the country and the region because of the secession of southern Sudan. The first challenge for the Sudan is the future relationship between north and south. Will the two parts maintain peaceful and cooperative relations after secession? Or are they going to end up in endless disputes and conflicts? The two governments have real disagreements about a number of important and delicate issues such as: the residents of Abyei who will decide its future in the referendum, border disputes, fees for oil transportation, sharing the Nile waters, citizenship of residents in the other state, security along the border, border-crossing by pastoralists from north to south and back, support of armed groups in each country against the other etc. These issues are sensitive and serious and they may well lead to conflicts between the two parts of the old Sudan.

If a conflict starts between north and south, it could easily spread to Darfur, southern Kordofan, Blue Nile state, eastern Sudan and it may draw in some neighbouring states. Some of those issues were discussed for many months in Khartoum, Juba and Addis by joint committees from the NCP and SPLM, with the help of the African Union High Level Implementation Panel (AUHIP) led by the resilient Thabo Mbeki, the former president of South Africa, but without success. The two parties could not disagree more on most of the issues. The same quarrelsome attitude which marked the relationship between the two partners all through the Interim Period continued till the referendum time and after. However serious these issues may be, they are not insurmountable if the two governments have a long-term vision for a peaceful and fruitful relationship and have the political will to overcome the difficulties in the way.

The real challenge for the two countries is to leave behind them the mistrust and bitterness of the past and look forward attempting to live side by side as good neighbours in peace, cooperation and harmony. If the two separating states could crossover the difficult hurdles in negotiating their delicate problems, they would facilitate close economic cooperation between the Arab world and African countries for the benefit of all sides. Since things got worse after the attack by the SPLA on Heglig (April 2012), the PSCAU and the UNSC intervened heavily to set a roadmap for the two parties to agree on all their outstanding issues within three months or face international sanctions; the SC even threatened to impose solutions as would be proposed by the AUHIP which facilitates the negotiations between the two parties. The late developments of the negotiations showed some signs of progress, especially after the meeting of the two presidents, al-Bashir and SalvaKiir, in Addis Ababa on 14 July 2012. It is more likely now that the two parties will reach some sort of agreements on many issues, under the internal and external pressures. That may be good enough to stop armed clashes between the two states and allow some form of cooperation on security, oil, Nile water and cross-border trade.

The impact of secession on the North is equally troubling. The diversity of the old Sudan which caused the problem of the South is still there in the regions of Darfur, southern Kordofan, Blue Nile and eastern Sudan. Conflicts started in these regions before concluding the CPA in 2005; Darfur with reduced violence and a number of agreements is still searching for an inclusive settlement, and the two regions of southern Kordofan and Blue Nile which were included in the CPA are not satisfied with their lot, and resumed armed struggle few weeks before the separation of the South. The Sudan government complained to the Security Council that South Sudan is supporting the rebel movement in these two states; that will not resolve the problem which requires a new imaginative approach of managing diversity in the country. The political opposition in the North is not satisfied with the single rule of the NCP which has continued for more than two decades without proper public mandate, democratic institutions or a convincing degree of freedom of expression and association. The two major opposition parties (Umma Party and Democratic Unionist Party) refused to accept the initial invitation of the NCP to join its new government after the separation of the South, unless certain conditions of democratic transformation were realized.

On the economic side, the government lost about 40 per cent of its annual income after the revenue from oil of the South ceased; the loss constitutes more than 80 per cent of foreign currency which is badly needed for basic imports. No wonder the exchange rate for the US dollar has doubled and is likely to increase even further; the prices of commodities has gone up beyond the reach of middle class workers; inflation was about 20 per cent in the last quarter of 2011 and by July 2012 it had reached more than 35 per cent; and unemployment reached alarming figures even among university graduates.

The government has a real battle to manage the economy for the year 2012 without risking a popular uprising like what happened in some other Arab countries. As a matter of fact, that is what happened in June and July 2012. The government was compelled to take off the subsidy from some essential commodities; the decision led to many demonstrations in Khartoum and other major cities. In other words, the consequences of secession for the North are additional problems of security, economy and political stability. Later, we shall deal with the consequences for the South. About the impact on the region, it is clear that the lesson from the experiences of Eritrea and

Sudan is that ethnic and cultural diversity in the African context, unlesswell managed in a fair and equal opportunity for all, will cause dissatisfaction and discord which may lead to conflict. Multiplicity of ethnic groups and cultures are to be found almost in every African countries; in the last few decades when plural democracy has been implemented in a number of African countries, ethnicity has played a significant role in their politics. Thus, the Sudanese example may further trigger secessionist movements in some African states, especially in the Horn of Africa. Conflicts in many African countries like Ethiopia, Nigeria, Uganda, Liberia, Rwanda and Burundi, among others, are mainly explained in terms of ethnic diversities. But is it ethnicity, as such, the cause of conflict? Or is it the political and economic marginalisation of certain groups in society? In most cases marginalisation is exploited by politicised elites who want to enhance their own political career, by capitalising on the misery of their communities. The socioeconomic basis of ethnic hostility should be given due weight in attempting to solve ethnic conflicts. However, the political solutions cannot easily be the separation of a marginalised community from the mother country.

After the independence of African countries in the 1960s, liberal democracy was adopted for a short period before military regimes and the one-party system dominated the scene in most countries. The pretext for authoritarian rule was that multi-party system does not suit the tribal-divided African societies; the autocrat rulers justified their hegemony in the name of building a unified nation instead of fragmenting the society on ethnic lines. They ended up of empowering their own ethnic groups at the expense of marginalising others. During the last decade of the twentieth century, African countries started to go back to some form of democracy in a more steady way. This progress should be encouraged, but its challenges of ethnic diversity should be met in a brave and fair manner.

The third part on the nation-building of southern Sudan included two papers (Zambakari and Bankie). The new state of South Sudan suffers from ethnic clashes in a number of states over land ownership, cattle rustling, blood feuds, water, trespassing boundaries, etc., armed groups fighting against the government, and the unprofessional intrusive attitude of SPLA units. In the year 2009, the result of tribal conflicts was about 2,500 dead and 350 thousand displaced because of military operations in their regions. The problem of managing diversity is not less than that of the old Sudan; there are about 200 ethnic groups in South Sudan, each has its own language, location, customary law and religious beliefs. The government faces a huge socioeconomic problem of the hundreds of thousands of returnees from the North and from other neighbouring countries. Other related factors weaken the ability of the government to face the complex problems of building a viable state: the lack of a minimum infrastructure; the poorly-trained flabby civil service; the weakness of political parties and civil society groups; the hegemony of the SPLA units on public affairs; and the rampant illiteracy rate (85%). The papers in this section recommended that the government of South Sudan should give priority to: the establishment of peace and security among the population; building the government institutions; creation of new conditions for socio-political transformation; making the necessary political compromise in order to carryonboard the different opposition groups; addressing the social cohesiveness and consolidating the rule of law. Bankie's paper is mainly about factors shaping nation-building in southern Sudan, but it dwells much on historical developments of the past while containing less practical policies for the future.

The fourth part on recommending economic policies for the new state included three papers (Yongo-Bure (Chapter 8), Yongo-Bure (Chapter 9) and Ssemwanga). Their recommendations are professional and logical but rather theoretical; the difficulty is to convince politicians to carry out objective economic policies. They caution the government about rising the expectations of people at this early stage; the major part of oil revenue should be utilised on development, namely agriculture and animal services, and in human development of education and health care. The government should do its best to attract investment, create jobs for the people and encourage small-scale industries. Interestingly, two papers recommended separate currency for the South, but the government had already started the process of secretly printing a separate currency before Independence Day. Yongo identifies in his paper a number of quick impact activities and long-term programmes and projects which will lead to sustainable development. However, his advice to involve the population through an open dialogue on decision-making on development may prove to be difficult for politicians to accept. The latest developments have shownwide-scale of corruption in South Sudan to the extent that president Salva Kiir was obliged to write a published letter to a number of senior government officials accusing them of illegally seizing 4 billion US dollars from public money, which they should return. The shutdown of oil in the South (March 2012), because of disagreement with the North on transportation fee, made the economic situation very bleak for the South, according to a World Bank report.

The two questions raised by Wassara, in his paper, are important to the future of the two parties of the old Sudan and to the region as whole: How South Sudan shall co-exist with northern Sudan? How the African Union would contribute to the stabilisation of the region? We keep our fingers crossed waiting for a positive answer for both questions.

Postscript on New Developments

Samson S. Wassara

So many new developments happened after the papers that comprise the chapters in this book were submitted for publication. The very controversial issues raised in the book, especially in the section dealing with consequences of referendum vote for secession, became a nightmare in the relations between the Sudan and South Sudan. The unresolved issues stipulated in the Comprehensive Peace Agreement (CPA) are the very cause of tension and limited war between the Sudan and South Sudan in April 2012. The independence of South Sudan on 9 July 2011 invited a host of complex security relations between the North and the South. The SPLM/A was a national liberation movement, which extended beyond the 1956 boundaries of South Sudan. The CPA was explicit on the southern Sudan alone, but was elusive on Abyei, Blue Nile and the Nuba Mountains. It recommended referendum for the Ngok Dinka and popular consultations as a solution to grievances expressed by the Ingessana and Nuba people. The exercise of popular consultation succeeded in Blue Nile to the disappointment of the NCP regime in Khartoum. Consequently, the process of popular consultations in south Kordofan was marred by irregularities, which resulted in renewed violence. Failure to secure unity of the Sudan compelled the government in Khartoum to declare war on South Kordofan and Blue Nile under the pretext of disarming the SPLA on its territories. This led to the removal of the Governor of Blue Nile using military force. The Sudan went ahead to accuse South Sudan of supporting the SPLA troops in the region. Analysts of north-south relations cannot fail to understand that Khartoum has been attempting to implicate South Sudan in the rebellions in Blue Nile and south Kordofan to justify attacks on oil fields in South Sudan.

Oil production in South Sudan was a security concern for post-referendum Sudan. The bulk of reserves lie in the South Sudan, but the oil is exported in pipelines that run through the territory of Sudan to the oil terminal on the coast of the Red Sea. Several key oil fields lie along the contested north-south border. Another issue of concern is that oil provided as much as 98 per cent of the revenue accruing to the government in Juba. Despite this fact, South Sudan went ahead to close production of oil on its territory. The border areas where oil fields are located remain dangerously militarised to the extent that oil dispute raises stakes for drawing borders between the two countries. Oil has become a notable impediment for establishing normal relations between the Sudan and South Sudan. The dispute over oil has threatened the implementation of other pending issues such as citizenship, trade and border demarcation among others.

The Sudan and South Sudan are virtually in the state of war with one another. This assumption is substantiated by the closure of the common air and land borders. Free movement of people and goods between the Sudan and South Sudan is severely restricted; if not absolutely forbidden. Returning IDPs to South Sudan were caught in the middle of the inter-state dispute. Thousands of people were stranded at the water port of Kosti for months while hundreds of others are unable to leave Khartoum and many other cities in the Sudan. It is only after concerted efforts of the UN agencies that the Organisation of Migration was able to airlift the stranded families from Khartoum to Juba.

The independence of South Sudan and the ensuing conflicts with the Sudan over the many unresolved post-independent issues seem to be drawing countries of the Greater Horn of Africa and China into uncomfortable diplomatic realities. The strained relations between the Sudan and South Sudan affect some countries such as Djibouti, Ethiopia and Kenya. The international community, China and the African Union (AU) are already drawn into the oil dispute between the new neighbours. The launching of an alternative pipeline project intended to run from South Sudan to Lamu in Kenya or to Djibouti increased tension in the region. This development further complicates security, border, citizenship disputes in which oil is used as a weapon of revenge. The dispute led to a shutdown of the oil sector in early 2012, which has triggered a brief border war in April. Most remaining oil wells are now in the South, but the infrastructure such as pipelines; refinery and the export terminal are in the Sudan.

Amid tension and cross-border military confrontations, the President of South Sudan paid an official visit to China in April 2012 to seek economic and diplomatic support. China's role in oil exploitation in South Sudan and in Sudan makes her a potential broker of peace between the two countries. China is well positioned to exert influence in the conflict, given its deep trade ties to the resource-rich south and decades-long diplomatic ties with the Sudan.

During talks held with South Sudanese President, the Chinese President urged the two sides to remain calm and refrain from escalating the current tensions and properly resolve their differences through negotiation. China is making multiple efforts to promote dialogue, mitigate conflicts and maintain regional stability. Chinese ambassadors to Sudan and South Sudan, as well as China's permanent mission to the United Nations, have been mediating between the two sides through multi-track diplomacy. Both South Sudan and the Sudan are under serious economic pressure that could not only make their governments unpopular, but could lead to either of them losing control over the state.

Hence this book offers interesting reading about how scholars identified intractable issues that were expected to derail peace not only in the Sudan and South Sudan, but also complicate relations in the Horn of Africa and East Africa. Disputes between the two countries remained a low-key conflict until it flared into border violence on 10 April 2012. The AU and the UN are actively trying to put an end to the instability.

www.ingramcontent.com/pod-product-compliance
Lightning Source LLC
Chambersburg PA
CBHW051356290426
44108CB00015B/2037